Classroom Companion: Business

The Classroom Companion series in Business features undergraduate and advanced undergraduate books aimed at introducing students to the core concepts, fundamental methods, theories and tools of the subject. The books offer a firm foundation for students preparing to move towards advanced learning. Each book follows a clear didactic structure and presents easy adoption opportunities for lecturers.

More information about this series at http://www.springer.com/series/16374

Alexander Redlein
Editor

Modern Facility and Workplace Management

Processes, Implementation and Digitalisation

Springer

Editor
Alexander Redlein
TU Wien
Vienna, Austria

ISSN 2662-2866 ISSN 2662-2874 (electronic)
Classroom Companion: Business
ISBN 978-3-030-35313-1 ISBN 978-3-030-35314-8 (eBook)
https://doi.org/10.1007/978-3-030-35314-8

This Springer imprint is published by the registered company Springer Nature Switzerland AG
The registered company address is: Gewerbestrasse 11, 6330 Cham, Switzerland

Preface

Real estate (RE) and facility management (FM) are two industries that are very much underestimated. Many students associate facility management with "the new housekeeper with a tie" or the "cleaner with an academic degree". Over the last years, this association started to change especially as the area of workplace management has gained more and more importance. This new domain is an integrator and brings RE and FM to the next level. Its goal is to empower the employees and through this empowerment ensuring the company's goals are reached. Especially in times of a shortage of specialists and knowledge workers, this area becomes the focus of top management. As a group at the Vienna University of Technology that has been engaged in workplace management research for almost 10 years and in the management perspective of RE and FM in general for more than 20 years, we have tried to change this image based on well-founded scientific publications. We have published articles in journals in the area of business administration, management, business optimisation, operation research, risk management and corporate social responsibility to disseminate our findings and better reach other researchers and the C-level management of companies.

Together with other colleagues, practitioners and associations like IFMA and IWFM, former BIFM, we have fostered this change of image. Additionally, we have stressed the importance of FM as a management strategy and the management tasks within RE and FM to reach this goal. But there is another side to this challenge. Being a professor for real estate and facility management teaching internationally on several programs, we have put much effort in the last few years into looking to find good textbooks that support us in teaching this approach and which cover all different management perspectives of real estate and facility management. As this topic has many different perspectives such as organisation and process optimisation, ICT support, financial and cost accounting, it was really difficult to find one book that covers all these areas. And we heard the same demand from numerous colleagues around the world.

When we were asked by the publishing company Springer to write a textbook about FM in 2018, we felt very honoured and saw this as an opportunity to gather our existing lectures and presentations into one book for students as well as for practitioners who want to expand their knowledge. During the discussions with the publisher, friends and colleagues, we decided against a "traditional" textbook but instead include upcoming topics like digitalisation and workplace management because these topics change the requirements for RE and FM as well as the skillset of managers in this industry. This book covers the following areas:

- Macro- and micro-economic impact of RE and FM
- Definition of corporate real estate, asset, property and facility management
- Change management and process optimisation in the area of RE and FM

- IT support, application integration and data warehouses
- Benchmarking
- Digitalisation and its impact on RE/FM/FS
- Workplace management

Fortunately, we have many international friends and could convince them to become coauthors to help cover these different topics at a top and up-to-date level. Moreover, our various industry projects helped to make the book not only a theory textbook but also a practical guide.

This is one of the main points we wanted to achieve with this book. We did not only want to write a textbook covering definitions and standards but to link this theory directly to practice. To reach this goal, we asked several practitioners to be coauthors. In addition, we added many examples from our case studies and consulting projects in order to show the readers how the theory fits into their day-to-day work and how it can be used as solid background for their daily tasks.

Finally, we wish you will gain numberless new inputs and knowledge but also have fun reading it!

Alexander Redlein
Vienna, Austria

Acknowledgements

First, I would like to thank my coauthors, Susanne Hofer, Claudia Höhenberger, Karin Schaad, Eva Stopajnik and Pat Turnbull, for their constant and intense support. I also thank Nancy Sanquist and Wilfried Hauffen who gave me valuable ideas despite not being able to take part in this project as authors. Especially, the discussions with Wilfried provided a great amount of inputs for this book. The dear friendship and extensive exchange with Carolin Bahr, Diane Coles-Levine, Mariantonietta Lisena, Andras Bajai, Sandro Friedrich, Wolfgang Gleissner, Geza-Richard Horn, Klaus Homann, Horst Pichlmüller, Rainer Rohrhofer, Cristian Vasiliu, Peter Ankerstjerne and Wolfgang Wahlmüller not only enabled me to put together the traditional knowledge about RE and FM but also provided many practical examples, showing how definitions and methods are used in practice. Thanks are also due to all my other friends who gave input and supported me. I truly value the friendship, support and input they gave me.

I thank my scientific coaches, Christoph Achammer, Wolfgang Janko and Alfred Taudes, and my university – the Vienna University of Technology – for giving me the possibility to develop my knowledge and expertise in this totally new field.

I also thank my team, mainly Larissa Locsmandy, who did a perfect job turning the different chapters into a comprehensive book with respect to layout, spelling and all the administrative tasks. Thanks to Constanze Schindler for proofreading, optimising our wording and becoming an expert in the areas of RE and FM and to Clemens Baretschneider for his inputs and ICT support.

Special thanks to my family who enabled me to spend a lot of time thinking, making concepts, writing, rewriting, tasking the different inputs and turning them into one book and for their input by questioning my stories and examples and for asking so many questions. They also provided me with many new insights, experiences and perspectives. They are a main source of inspiration to me. And I promise to have more time, Babsi, Caroline and David, now that the book is finished.

I also want to thank my parents who supported and taught me the importance of friendship and ethics. This has made me into the person I am, with a loving family and valuable friendships, which have made this book possible.

Contents

Editors and Contributors

Editors and Authors

Alexander Redlein
is a university professor of Real Estate and Facility Management at the Vienna University of Technology, president of the REUG and past president of the IFMA Austria. Since completing his interdisciplinary studies at the Vienna University of Technology and the Vienna University of Economics and Business Administration, he has been researching, educating and consulting in the area of facility management for more than 20 years. He is head of the research group "Real Estate and Facility Management", competence center for Real Estate and Facility Management, Vienna University of Technology, which consists of 15 researchers. Along with his research activities, he acts as a strategic advisor, setting up FM concepts for international companies and municipalities. Furthermore, he optimises their FM processes ICT and workplace management. As a researcher, he conducted international studies on the macro- and micro-economic impact of FM. His workplace research focuses on how the workplace influences the productivity and well-being of the employees. He also analyses the impact of digitalisation and automation on workplace management, FM and facility services. In addition, he heads the MBA for FM program at the Vienna University of Technology, as well as several FM certification courses in CEE and India.

Affiliation: Competence Center for Real Estate and Facility Management (IFM), Vienna University of Technology, E: redlein@tuwien.ac.at; W: ▶ www.ifm.tuwien.ac.at

Eva Stopajnik
joined the IFM Real Estate and Facility Management of Vienna University of Technology in 2015 as a research assistant.

At the IFM, she is responsible for studies on the demand side of facility management (FM), which does not comprise service providers but companies operating in various industries that need services for their buildings. There she examines trends in the organisation of FM, cost savings, outsourcing and IT support. Her other main research fields are macroeconomic studies. The focus lies mainly on analysing the facility services industry and its size in terms of structural factors such as employment, value added and their relationships. Furthermore, she assesses the impact of digitalisation on the whole industry. She also teaches SAP PM and is involved in other projects, e.g. data structuring projects.

She received her education at the Vienna University of Economics and Business. There she studied International Business Administration, majoring in Tourism Analysis. Before returning to the university, she gained several years of work experience in marketing research in tourism. There she was able to expand her analytical skills by doing extrapolations for all the Austrian skiing areas, calculations of value added and other projects. Furthermore, those experiences allowed her to develop an understanding of hospitality and the typical characteristics of service industries.

Claudia Höhenberger
studied architecture at TU Graz, Austria, and RGU Aberdeen, Scotland. In her studies, she concentrated on urban planning and green spaces, doing research on how these spaces improve people's lives and change the cities they are in. After graduating, she gained valuable experience working in landscape architecture in Zürich, Switzerland. She has been working as a research assistant at IFM Real Estate and Facility Management, TU Vienna, since early 2019. Her work there focuses on digitalisation of facility services and workplace management. This research is once again directed at how spaces affect people's lives. Digitalisation fundamentally changes not only the way we work but also the kind of work we do. Our work processes along with our workspaces will adapt to the technological advances and change themselves. Her work is about all aspects of workspaces, from their design to how they will be used and serviced.

Karin Schaad
has completed her training as a business economist (now BSc) in Facility Management in 1988. She worked in various functions at the University Hospital of Zürich for several years, first as a sector manager, then as a deputy head of Cleaning Services and later as a project manager for various projects in laundry processing and internal logistics.

To complement her FM training, she completed her Master of Science in FM at the ZHAW in Wädenswil. As part of her thesis, she dealt intensively with the topic of automation of FM processes in the hospital and with the use of robotics and sensors in the healthcare sector. She has since repeatedly presented her insights in the form of specialist lectures and was asked to act as a consultant in various hospitals in Switzerland.

After a couple of years as a senior business consultant and segment sales manager in healthcare with the FM Provider ISS Facility Services, she is now back at the University Hospital in Zürich in the role of head of Facility Services.

Pat Turnbull
is president of Workplace IQX LLC, a consulting practice that focuses on strategic, organisational and workplace design to help businesses link vision, strategy, brand and space in order to create exception user experiences (UX) and deliver enhanced business results. She earned her master's degree in Business from the University of California, Los Angeles (UCLA), and is a LEED AP (USGBC Leadership in Energy and Environmental Design Accredited Professional). Additionally, she has been honoured as an IFMA fellow and by CoreNet as Service Provider of the Year.

Currently, she is Global co-chair of IFMA's Workplace Evolutionaries (WE) and also serves on the Board of Advisors for the Stuart School of Business at Illinois Tech. Previously, she served on IFMA's (International Facility Management Association) Global Board of Directors and as chairman of the IFMA Foundation.

She coauthored two international award-winning books *Work on the Move: Driving Strategy and Change in Workplaces* and *Work on the Move 2: How Social, Leadership and Technology Innovations Are Transforming the Workplace in the Digital Economy*. She is an adjunct professor at the Vienna University of Technology (TU WIEN), Competence Center for Real Estate and Facility Management (IFM), Austria, and is a highly rated industry speaker. She resides in Chicago, Illinois, and her passions include sailing, skiing, fine/performing arts and travelling.

Susanne Hofer
has a full professorship in Hospitality Management at the Zürich University for Applied Sciences (ZHAW), Institute for Facility Management, Zürich, Switzerland.

Her research focus is on facility management (FM) in the healthcare context. With her team, they work on a wide range of projects from operational to strategic issues related to health institutions. Furthermore, research results are repeatedly presented to the academic community and to business partners.

She started her carrier with studying Hotel Management and worked a couple of years as hotel manager in different countries. To complete her career, she further studied International Master of Business Administration from the Rochester University, New York, USA, and completed her doctoral dissertation facility management in Hospitals at the Charles Sturt University, Bathurst, Australia.

Besides her lectures activities and research projects, she is also member of the board of directors in healthcare institutions.

Contributors

Susanne Hofer
The ZHAW Zurich University of Applied Sciences
Zurich, Switzerland
susanne.hofer@zhaw.ch

Claudia Höhenberger
Vienna University of Technology
Vienna, Austria
claudia.hoehenberger@tuwien.ac.at

Alexander Redlein
Vienna University of Technology
Vienna, Austria
alexander.redlein@tuwien.ac.at

Karin Schaad
University Hospital Zurich
Zurich, Switzerland
karin.schaad@usz.ch

Eva Stopajnik
Vienna University of Technology
Vienna, Austria
eva.stopajnik@tuwien.ac.at

Pat Turnbull
Workplace IQX LLC
Chicago
IL, USA
Pat.Turnbull@patturnbull.com

Abbreviations

ADA	Americans with Disabilities Act
AI	Artificial Intelligence
API	Application Programming Interfaces
AVG	Automated Guided Vehicle
BA	Building Automation
BD	Bidding and Negotiations
BYOD	Bring Your Own Device
BYOT	Bring Your Own Technology
CA	Construction Administration
CAAD	Computer-Aided Architectural Design
CAD	Computer-Aided Design
CD	Construction Documentation
CAFM	Computer-Aided Facility Management
CRE	Corporate Real Estate
CREM	Corporate Real Estate Management
CSR	Corporate Social Responsibility
DD	Design Development
DLR	Digital Land Register
DRG	Diagnosis-Related Group
DWG	Drawing
DXF	Drawing Exchange Format
EAI	Enterprise Application Integration
ECC	Education Competence Center
EPC	Event-Driven Process Chains
ERP	Enterprise Resource Planning
ER	Entity Relationship
FM	Facility Management
FS	Facility Service
FTE	Full-Time Equivalent
GDPR	General Data Protection Regulation
GIS	Geographical Information Systems
HR	Human Resources
HSSE	Health, Safety, Security and Environment
HVA	Heating, Ventilation and Air-Conditioning
ICT	Information and Communication Technology
IFR	International Federation of Robotics
IoT	Internet of Things
KPI	Key Performance Indicators
MBA	Master of Business Administration
MD	Managing Director
MEP	Mechanical, Electrical and Plumbing
MIS	Management Information System
ML	Machine Learning
OECD	Organisation for Economic Co-operation and Development
OLTP	Online Transaction Processing
RE	Real Estate
REIM	Real Estate Investment Management
ROI	Return on Investment
SAP	System Applications and Products in Data Processing
SaaS	Software as a Service
SD	Schematic Design
SLA	Service-Level Agreement
SL	Service Level
SMS	Short Message Services
SQL	Structured Query Language
TfL	Transport for London
VDMA	Verband Deutscher Maschinen- und Anlagenbau
VPN	Virtual Private Network
WPS	Workplace Strategy
XI	Exchange Infrastructure
XML	Extensible Markup Language

Facility Management: An Important Industry Sector

Alexander Redlein and Eva Stopajnik

A. Redlein (ed.), *Modern Facility and Workplace Management*,
Classroom Companion: Business, https://doi.org/10.1007/978-3-030-35314-8_1

Learning Objectives

The students should know the following:

- How large this industry is in Europe and the United States
- The roles within the Real Estate industry and their representatives
- The terms Real Estate, Asset Property and Facility Management and to differentiate between their diverse goals
- The terms and goals of FM according to the EN 15221 and the ISO 41011 (2018) in detail and to apply them in practice
- Understand how leading companies set up their internal FM and act in the area of outsourcing

1.1 Introduction

If I asked you what Facility Management (FM) was, I guess you would give the answer "cleaning" or another Facility Service (FS). This is what most of my students do. However, this is a total misunderstanding. Facility Management is more. It is a management strategy

- To define the demand for infrastructure and services of the core business
- To source the service provision
- To control the service delivery
- To update the whole management loop, if the core business changes (EN15221-4 2018)

Why is this management strategy "Facility Management" and why are these Facility Services so important?

We, as human beings, spend more than 90% of our time in buildings during work, meetings, living and sleeping. FM has to manage these buildings, its infrastructure and the services necessary to keep these buildings up and running and to support the users with food, safety and security. Facility Management influences our well-being, our motivation and our performance by providing a healthy environment.

Furthermore, as a matter of fact, this industry has a huge *macro-* and *microeconomic* impact.

1.2 Macro-economic Impact

The operational Facility Services together are a key industry worldwide. They are not shown as an item on its own in most of the statistics.

The EN 15221–4:2011 provides a taxative list of Facility Services. This list can be used to identify the relevant services and industries in the statistical classification of economic activities in the EU (called NACE). Data for all those economic activities is presented in the official annual detailed enterprise statistics by Eurostat. Eurostat is the statistical office

	EU28	DE	UK	FR	IT	AT	RO	HU
Manufacturing	27%	34%	16%	23%	32%	29%	28%	38%
Wholesale and retail trade; repair of motor vehicles and motorcycles	19%	18%	17%	19%	19%	19%	23%	17%
Professional, scientific and technical activities	10%	10%	16%	10%	8%	8%	6%	7%
Information and communication	8%	7%	11%	9%	7%	5%	9%	7%
Transportation and storage	8%	6%	7%	9%	9%	8%	8%	9%
Administrative and support service activities	8%	7%	11%	8%	5%	6%	5%	5%
Construction	8%	6%	9%	9%	7%	9%	7%	5%
FS in total	**7%**	**8%**	**7%**	**8%**	**7%**	**7%**	**6%**	**6%**
Real estate activities	4%	5%	3%	4%	3%	5%	2%	3%
Accommodation and food service activities	4%	3%	4%	4%	4%	5%	2%	2%
Electricity, gas, steam and air conditioning supply	3%	2%	2%	3%	3%	3%	5%	4%
Water supply; sewerage, waste management and remediation activities	2%	1%	2%	1%	2%	1%	2%	2%
Mining and quarrying	1%	0%	1%	0%	0%	0%	3%	0%
Repair of computers and personal and household goods	0%	0%	0%	0%	0%	0%	0%	0%

Fig. 1.1 Value added at factor cost in percentage of total value added at factor cost for non-financial business economy (NACE B-N, S95, excl. K) for 2016. Only countries included that did not show more than two missing values. Own calculation on the base of annual detailed enterprise statistics (Eurostat, last modified 2019), sorted according to the size in EU

of the EU. The value added at factor costs of these services stated in the enterprises statistics is shown in Fig. 1.1 "Value added at factor cost in percentage of total value added at factor cost for non-financial business economy" (Eurostat last modified 2013). The following figures are setting the results in relation to the total value added at factor cost/number of employees for the NACE sectors B-N and S95 excluding K for 2016.

The Facility Service industry is the eighth largest in the EU28 and the fourth largest in Germany. It generates 7% of the value added at factor costs in the EU.

The same method was used to derive the number of employees working in this industry. As Fig. 1.2 shows, according to the number of employees, this industry is even more important. In the whole EU it is 4th. In Germany, Italy, Romania and Hungary it is even 3rd. Around 10% of the employees within the EU and in the European countries work in this industry (Fig. 1.3).

The picture is similar in the United States. There are also around 10% of employees working in this industry.

1

	EU28	DE	FR	IT	AT	RO	HU
Wholesale and retail trade; repair of motor vehicles and motorcycles	23%	22%	22%	23%	24%	23%	21%
Manufacturing	21%	25%	19%	25%	23%	30%	28%
Administrative and support service activities	11%	12%	13%	8%	8%	8%	9%
FS in total	**10%**	**13%**	**9%**	**10%**	**9%**	**10%**	**10%**
Professional, scientific and technical activities	10%	9%	9%	9%	9%	5%	9%
Construction	9%	8%	11%	9%	11%	9%	8%
Accommondation and food service activities	8%	8%	7%	9%	11%	4%	5%
Transportation and storage	8%	8%	9%	8%	7%	9%	9%
Information and communication	5%	4%	6%	4%	4%	4%	5%
Real estate activities	2%	2%	2%	2%	2%	1%	3%
Water supply; sewerage, waste management and remediation activities	1%	1%	1%	1%	1%	2%	2%
Electricity, gas, steam and air conditioning supply	1%	1%	1%	1%	1%	2%	1%
Mining and quarrying	0%	0%	0%	0%	0%	1%	0%
Repair of computers and personal and household goods	0%	0%	0%	0%	0%	0%	0%

Fig. 1.2 Number of employees as a percentage of all employees in non-financial business economy (NACE B-N, S95, excl. K) for 2016. Only countries included that did not show more than two missing values. Own calculation on the base of annual detailed enterprise statistics (Eurostat, last modified 2019), sorted according to the size in EU

When we compare Figs. 1.1 and 1.2, we see that the value-added position is lower than the position according to the number of employees. What does this mean? There are two main answers. The wages paid in this industry are lower and there are more part-time employees. When we consider the very low wages, which is also an expression of the collective treaty, we have to assume the employees within this industry are not always very well-educated. Especially in industries like cleaning and security, employees can have very different levels of education (Redlein and Stopajnik 2019b).

Example

There are people with higher education from foreign countries that work in this industry because their education is not recognised in the country they live in or for other reasons. At the same time, there are people in this industry with almost no education that are not really capable of proper reading and writing. Training people with almost no education is quite hard.

When we later talk about digitalisation and the demand for new skills, we come back to this situation.

The FS industry also "behaves" differently than the rest of the economy as the buildings are more "resilient". As soon as they are constructed, they need services. These

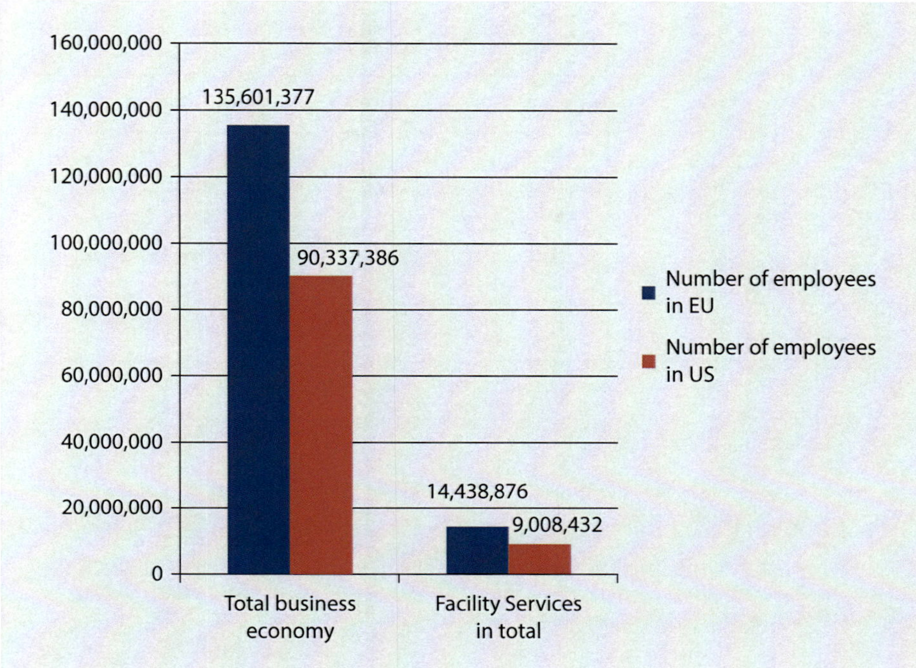

Fig. 1.3 Comparison between the numbers of employees for business economy and for the FS sector in the United States and the European Union, from 2014 (Birca 2017), own calculation on the basis of data collected from the US Census Bureau NAICS website (United States Census Bureau 2016) and IFM study (Redlein and Stopajnik 2017)

services have to be carried out locally and cannot be offshored. Therefore, this industry is more resilient towards economic crises. This can be seen in Fig. 1.4. During and after the economic crisis of 2009, most of the economies shrunk, but this was not the case for the Facility Service industry. It was steady. In the recovery phase, it even grew faster than the other industries.

1.3 Micro-economic Impact

On the micro-economic level – the level of a company – Facility Management is also very often underestimated. According to several studies like IFMA, between 10% and 18% of the total expenditure is related to Real Estate and Facility Services. The German professor for Real Estate economics Karl-Werner Schulte stated in his books that between 25% and 50% of the assets of companies consist of Real Estate and the equipment and assets related with their buildings (Schulte and Hupach, 1998). But even if a company does not own its buildings, they mostly own specific equipment and the furniture that is built in or needed to run the core business. This represents a large portion of their assets in their balance sheet and leads to quite high costs in the form of depreciation.

1

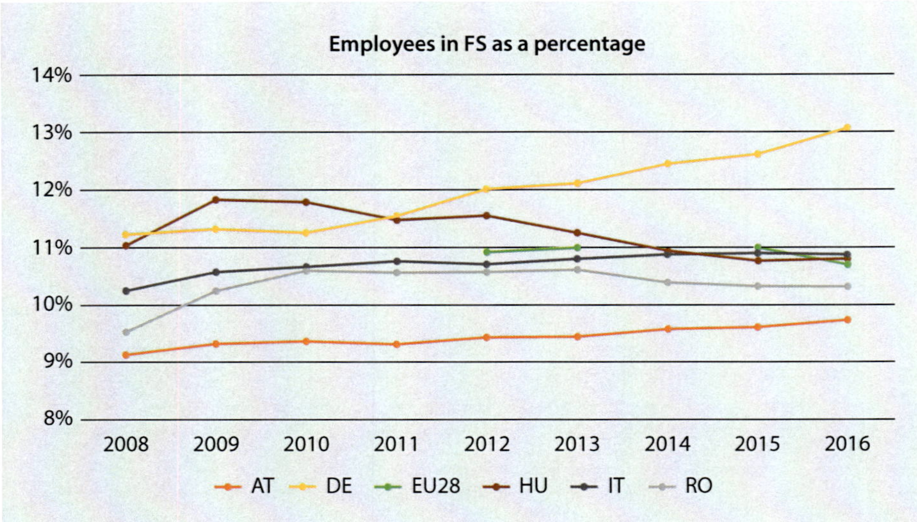

Fig. 1.4 Number of employees as a percentage of non-financial business economy (NACE B-N, S95, excl. K). Own calculation on the base of annual detailed enterprise statistics (Eurostat, last modified 2019; Redlein and Stopajnik 2019a)

Example

A worldwide known example is Walmart.

In 2018 Walmart used 5537 buildings in the United States and 6548 outside the United States, a total of 12,085 buildings, of which they owned 6869.

Of their total capital expenditures of 10 million dollars, they spent almost 3 million on new shops or remodelling.

Property and equipment had a value of $185.1 million in total and $107.7 million as net value (minus the already done depreciation). The total value of the assets according to the balance sheet is $204.5 million. That means that in the case of Walmart around 50% of its assets consists of land ($25 million) and property plus equipment. This figure is totally in line with the statement of Schulte. It is even a little bit more than he reported.

Non-cancellable operational lease of $15.4 million plus the depreciation of $77.5 million leads to almost $93 million dollar of costs. The rest of the costs of running Real Estate and facilities like energy, hard and soft services are not identifiable. But when we set these two items in relation to the total revenues of $500.3 million, this leads to more than 18%. Therefore, the study of IFMA for the relation of expenses to revenues is true for Walmart, too (Fig. 1.5).

Example

Another example is my university TU Wien. Our asset value, according to the balance sheet of 2017, is almost 157 million Euro. The value of the buildings and other infrastructure like furniture is around 22%. Regarding the total value, we have to take into consideration that my university owns no buildings but leases almost 100%. In our profit and

Walmart Inc. Consolidated balance sheets				
	As of January 31,			
(Amounts in millions)		2018		2017
Assets				
Current assets:				
Cash and cash equivalents	$	6,756	$	6,867
Receivables, net		5,614		5,835
Inventories		43,783		43,046
Prepaid expenses and other		3,511		1,941
Total current assets		59,664		57,689
Property and equipment:				
Property and equipment		185,154		179,492
Less accumulated depreciation		(77,479)		(71,782)
Property and equipment, net		107,675		107,710
Property under capital lease and financing obligations:				
Property under capital lease and financing obligations		12,703		11,637
Less accumulated amortization		(5,560)		(5,169)
Property under capital lease and financing obligations, net		7,143		6,468
Goodwill		18,242		17,037
Other assets and deferred charges		11,798		9,921
Total assets	$	204,522	$	198,825
Liabilities and equity				
Current liabilities:				
Short-term borrowings	$	5,257	$	1,099
Accounts payable		46,092		41,433

Fig. 1.5 Balance sheet of Walmart 2018. (Walmart Inc. 2018, p. 57)

loss statement the leasing costs alone make up 56,4 million Euro. This means, with a total turnover of 351 million Euro, the leasing costs alone for our building are 16% of the total revenues. (TU Wien 2017)

Consequently, you could argue that these high costs are only true for the service and whole selling industry. But having analysed the current trends in manufacturing, we see that this sector is becoming more and more sophisticated.

Example

One example is the Carl Zeiss AG. They mainly produce lenses and optics. Their main raw material is quartz sand. The production itself takes place in high-class clean rooms. One of the projects of Geza-Richard Horn, in charge of the Facility Management at Carl Zeiss, was to construct and run a high-class clean room of 26.000 m^2. This infrastructure ranked second to personnel cost. Therefore, we can state that also modern manufacturing is asking for high-level production facilities leading to high operational costs and extraordinary asset values in the balance sheet.

Now why is Facility Management so important for companies? When we take the example of my university, we can state easily that without the management of the costs of €56 million only for the leases, the expenses would be easily increased by 5–10%. That would lead to a growth of cost of more than €3 to 6 million per year, which means that the total profit of my university, now €12 million, would be lowered by 33% or even by 50%. Now consider how many professors and assistants my university can hire for this amount of money.

So proper Facility Management is very important to companies as the total volume of cost is very high and the proper management of the asset value is important to receive loans more easily from banks or shareholder investments.

1.4 Roles Within Real Estate Industry and Representatives

If we look at publications, many stakeholders call themselves Facility Manager. FM is quite often mixed up with single service provision. For clarification, we will analyse the different roles in Real Estate and Facility Management, their goals and representatives.

There are three roles within Real Estate and Facility Management:

1. The user/tenant
2. The owner/investor
3. The service providers (◘ Fig. 1.6)

These roles have different goals. Let us consider that we are tenants of a flat. What would we like to have if our wishes came true? A penthouse in the middle of Vienna, plenty of space with a big terrace and a perfect view. When it comes to cost, we would like to spend very little on this, so to say, maybe 100–200 Euro per month. I know that this is not possible, but let us just have this dream. Or even more, that we get paid for using this flat. If my name were not Alex Redlein but rather Justin Bieber or Robbie Williams, that would maybe become real.

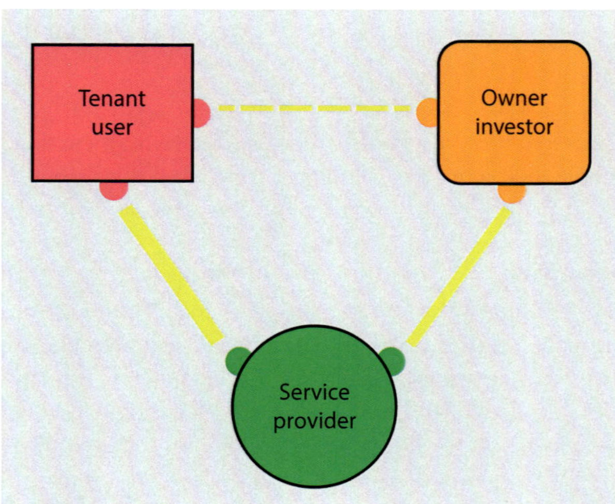

◘ **Fig. 1.6** Roles within the Real Estate industry. (Author's own figure)

But there are also other business cases. Let us look, for instance, at the start-up scene. There, large companies offer office space to start-ups at almost no costs. What is the purpose of this business model? The start-ups have to go through a detailed evaluation process so that the sponsoring companies know exactly the value added of the innovation provided by the start-up. In return, the start-up grants the holder of the space the right to presell their company. As mentioned above, there are also various other business models. We will give more examples in ▶ Chap. 6.

Let us now analyse the goals of the owner. The owner is in most cases also the investor. The owning/investing company is mainly looking for an optimal return on its investment. The company would like to get the rental fee of the above-mentioned penthouse for a small apartment in the basement. Therefore, the tenant is to pay his return on the owner's primary investment. The market mechanism provides a balance between the interests of the owner and those of the tenant.

The last role is the service provider. This type of company provides the services to keep the building and its surrounding infrastructure up and running. Their goal is to provide as many services as possible for a fair price and therefore earn a decent revenue. Most of them have their contractual agreement with the owners, as they service the building themselves. Thus, the owners make the decision which party they ask for the services. In most cases, the service fees are then charged to the tenants as operation costs of the buildings. The owner only pays for repairs, replacements and improvements directly.

What we can learn from the description of the roles and their goals:

The owner places the initial investment and decides on the operation of his building.

The tenant is the only one who pays all costs and the return on the owner's investment. Without him, there would be no return on investment and no income for the owner. In addition, the service charges would have to be taken over by the owner reducing his ROI (return on investment).

The Corporate Real Estate Triangle, which is very prominent in the Anglo-Saxon world, concentrates mainly on the investor/owner. In contrast to this statement, we realise that without the tenant there would be no investments as there would be no ROI. So all players on the market have to concentrate more on the requirements and demands of the tenant/users.

But who is the user?

The user is not a single role. It comprises several interest groups:

1. The top management – the C-level
2. The employees
3. The clients of the company

What are their individual requirements and goals?

The owners of the companies have their focus on low costs. However, in the last 5 years a new trend has come up: the focus on the satisfaction of the employees, their well-being and commitment to the company. The C-level now has to balance the cost reduction efforts with the requirements of their employees.

The employees love to have their own, large offices. It is very well known that the environment you work in represents your status in the company. When you start as a youngster, you mainly work in a very efficient open office environment, in the United States sometimes even together with 100 people. In Europe there would be maybe 20–30 people sharing the same office. Team office is the correct term. Once you have climbed the management ladder, you will share your office with about four people, and when you have reached higher C-level, you will get your own office. It shows that you have forged ahead.

The last type of office requires most of the space, which stands in contrast to low cost. In addition, this type of office reduces communication and therefore innovation. Thus, at present, there are attempts to abolish this pattern of showing hierarchy. New ways of working are being utilised more often. But still, there is a trade-off between the employees' requirements and the goals of the C-level regarding efficiency.

Why should we now consider the clients' demands?

Example

Let me give you a personal, practical example. I went for a family trip to a seminar hotel in the Alps. We had already been driving for 5 hours and my kids had constantly been asking when we would arrive. Finally, we reached the village, where the hotel is located. I was looking for a signpost of the hotel. Nothing to be found. Because I was too much concentrated on the search for the signs, I overlooked a speeding camera. I was not angry but I was not relaxed anymore. At the end of the village, luckily there was a sign. It led me further out of the village. Then there it was and there was even a garage. As it was snowing, I tried my luck. I rang the bell of the garage. The voice was not very pleasant. What do you want? I said that I had a reservation and would like to drive into the garage directly so that my children would not have to get out in the heavy snow. "No this is not possible!" was the answer. You have to show up at the entrance where we will help you to unload. After 10 minutes of discussion, I was permitted to the garage and then I learned why they wanted me to come to the entrance first. No signposts again. As a pathfinder myself, I assumed that the entrance was where most of the cars parked. I was right. When my son stepped out his first discovery was a broken bottle just beside my car. Quite a danger to him, to step on it. After 20 minutes of unloading and getting to the elevator, we were standing in front of the reception. Nobody was there, as we were not fast enough. My family and I were irritated. We did not really want to stay at this unfriendly hotel although we have not really got to know it and its "hotel" services. Therefore, what can we learn from this story? The Facility Services, like pathfinding, receptionist, etc., that we as clients faced as the first impression of this hotel did not really foster our willingness to do business with them.

Therefore, Facility Services can influence the degree to which a client is willing to place a contract to a high degree. Let us consider a typical office setting.

When I have to look for a parking lot for half an hour before I can get to the office of a future business partner, and if the receptionist tells me the person I am looking for does not exist, or he/she cannot find the place where the meeting shall take place, then I will not be in a proper mood to work with this company in the future. Therefore, the Facility Services like parking lots, reception, and meeting rooms influence to a high degree my willingness to do business and to stay in business with a company.

Therefore, it is very important to take into consideration all the diverse requirements of the different user types to fulfil their needs in a proper way.

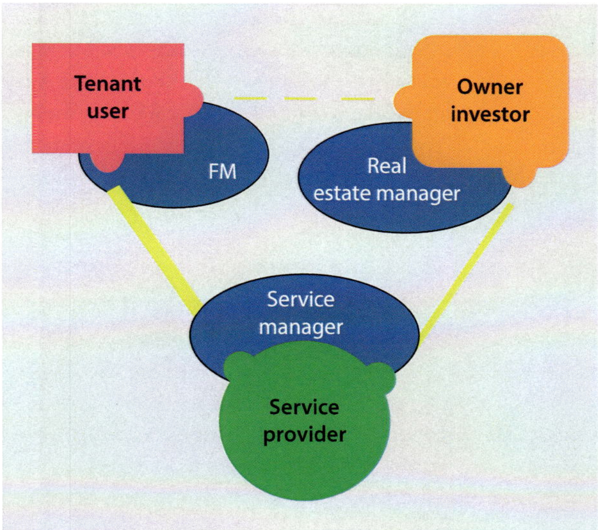

Fig. 1.7 Roles and their representatives in the Real Estate industry. (Author's own figure)

When we now come back to the overview of the roles, I would like to add the respective representatives to each role type:

- In the daily business, the owner is represented by the Real Estate Agent and the Asset and Property Management.
- The service provider has service managers in place as a point of contact to the owners and tenants.
- The Facility Manager represents the tenant/user (Fig. 1.7).

All of these representatives have the knowledge on how to manage facilities. In industry practice, many of the companies also claim to do the Facility Management. I personally prefer to give the job title Facility Manager to the tenant's representative. To illustrate why I will give you an example.

Example

My team supported an international wholesaler in their bidding for a new Facility Service provider. We analysed the demand, put together the requirements and asked service providers for offers. After having selected the best offers, the companies were invited to give a presentation in front of a panel at the client. The panel consisted of the CEO of the company, the Facility Manager and a representative of the purchase department. The company ranked best before the hearing did a perfect presentation and gave good answers to all the questions. At the end, when they asked why we should select them, the representative of the company said: "because we can also do your Facility Management". When they left the room, we could "see" two virtual speech bubbles above the CEO and the Facility Manager. The CEO was comparing his internal Facility Manager with the representative of the company and the cost he could save by firing the employee. The Facility Manager recognised that this company was going for her job. Therefore, in the evaluation afterwards she found many weaknesses in the offering and the company did not win.

1

So, what can we learn from the given example: All the representatives of the roles and their companies know how to manage facilities, but especially if we focus on the tenant and his outsourcing, we should give this representative the job title Facility Manager.

Before giving the definition of Facility Management, I will first introduce the definition of Asset Management and Property Management and why these concepts are missing the tenant/user orientation, which is perfectly covered by Facility Management.

1.5 Corporate Real Estate, Asset and Property Management

There are many management terms around Real Estate, but quite often, a common understanding is missing. In order to differentiate between those terms a schema was developed with an overview and explanations of the different management disciplines. The explanations include definitions, aims and tasks (Teichmann 2007, p. 5).

Corporate Real Estate Management (CREM) is an umbrella term and comprises Portfolio, Property, Asset, Facility and Building Management (Teichmann 2007, p. 5).

Definition

CREM is often defined as "value and success-oriented acquisition, handling and disposal of properties under use or possession of corporations". (Glatte 2013 p. 1)

The aim of CREM is the identification and use of Real Estate "as a success factor and to increase the competitiveness of the core business" (Teichmann 2007, p. 13).

Real Estate Portfolio Management includes the planning, monitoring, realisation and controlling of sets of Real Estate assets (Teichmann 2007, p. 10). A portfolio manager's role is to "create value through a unique [investor-specific] design of the portfolio" (Kämpf-Dern 2009, p. 11).

The duties of the manager are mainly strategic planning and risk assessment, cash flow management, reporting requirements and sales, purchases and refinancing activities. Furthermore, the manager supervises the Asset Management Company and is responsible for professionals at portfolio level (Kämpf-Dern 2009, p. 11, based on Rondeau et al. 2006) (◘ Fig. 1.8).

Definition

Asset Management is defined in the international norm ISO 55000 as the "coordinated activity of an organisation to realize value from assets". "Realisation of value will normally involve a balancing of costs, risks, opportunities and performance benefits". (ISO 55000 2014, p. 37)

The aim of Asset Management is the development and realisation of a value-oriented Real Estate strategy (Teichmann 2007, p. 17). The role of the Asset Manager is to "ensure that the operations of an asset are focused on achieving the ultimate goal of the owner and of the investment" (Kämpf-Dern 2009, p. 11).

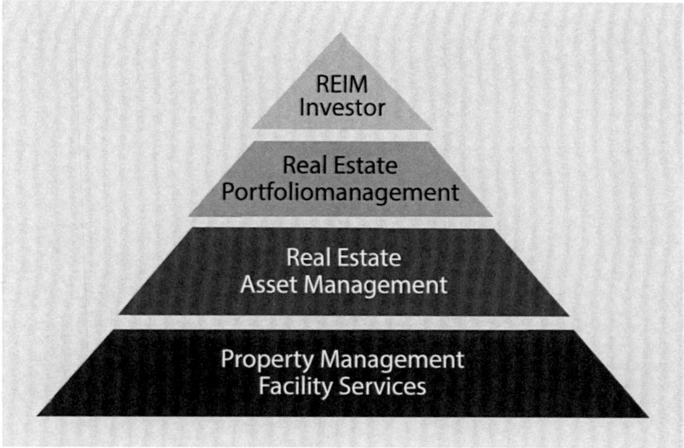

Fig. 1.8 CREM triangle. (Based on Teichmann 2007)

Portfolio and Asset Management means the controlling/steering of an asset portfolio according to risk and return aspects. It includes the preparation and implementation of decisions in respect to financial assets of third parties (Bundesverband Investment und Asset Management e.V. (BVI) n.d.).

It is the process of value increase of a building portfolio lasting from acquisition until sales according to goals of an investor (Dubben and Sayce 1991). The goal is to achieve return according to the risk appetite of the owner/investor. It is mainly orientated on the ROI of the investor. It provides strategic guidelines regarding the tenant mix but does not intervene in the selection and retrieval process.

The Asset Manager supervises the Property Management Company.

Property Management represents the holistic approach of active, result-oriented, strategic and operative financial management of a single Real Estate or Real Estate portfolios according to the goals of investors/owners.

In practice, the commercial services are mostly done internally by the company itself. The infrastructural and technical services are commonly subcontracted. Property Management controls these services and its provision. The mainly commercial-oriented Property Management takes over the tasks for the owner on a trust basis. It is the single point of contact for the service providers taking care of the common areas and equipment and the tenants of the serviced properties (Teichmann 2007, p. 19).

1.6 Lacks of CREM Triangle

The whole CREM triangle and the underlying management roles concentrate on the investor and its ROI. The other roles (tenants/user and service providers) are only included in the focus of Portfolio, Asset and Property Management to the extent as they contribute to this ROI. The user orientation and the definition of the user demand are only included to develop and refurbish proper assets to gain the demanded ROI. The European norm EN 15221–1:2006 defines Facility Management as the “integration of processes within an organisation to maintain and develop the agreed services which support and improve the effectiveness of its primary activities” (EN 15221-1 2006). On

1

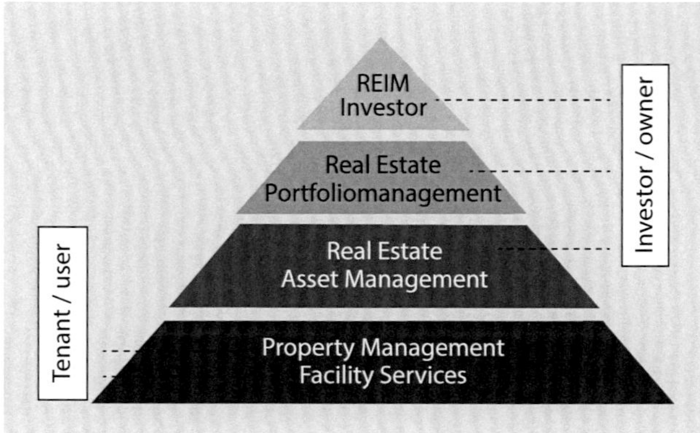

Fig. 1.9 New CREM triangle including tenant. (Based on Teichmann 2007)

the operational level Facility Management should create the required environment for the end user (EN 15221-1 2006, p. 10).

So Facility Management is the only discipline that includes the user's perspective. All other disciplines of CREM are owner- and investor-oriented. Therefore, there is a shortcoming considering the users' needs, especially on the strategic level. While Portfolio Management and Asset Management operate on the strategic level, the operative management is taken care of by the Property and Facility Management.

The developed schema of CREM by Teichmann was developed further to include the perspectives of the involved parties. We have not changed the wording of Facility Management in the bottom of the CREM triangle, although it should be considered "only" as the knowledge on how to manage a facility and not the job title FM. From this perspective the term Facility Service would be better (Fig. 1.9).

Definition of FM (EN/ISO)

European countries and the United States defined FM differently in the past. The reason is that various interest groups developed FM, based on different historical and cultural background and conditions. In the UK mainly architects, like Keith Alexander, for instance, supported the subject. In the United States, furniture manufacturers first discovered FM. Later, the investment aspect and the management focus became more important in the Anglo-Saxon countries.

The Netherlands have always been very service oriented. Even the buildings – providing different types of space – are seen as a service since companies do not ask for buildings but for the serviced workplace for a team, e.g. a meeting room. The German-speaking countries are more technically oriented. Building automation, IT support and maintenance are in their key focus.

Facility Management is an important part of the strategic management of an entity. As described above, it includes the human-centric approach and concentrates on the users and their demands.

One of the first recognised definitions for FM was set up by IFMA as one of the world's largest and widely recognised international association for Facility Management professionals, supporting 24,000 members in more than 100 countries.

Definition

"Facility Management (FM) is a profession that encompasses multiple disciplines to ensure functionality, comfort, safety and efficiency of the built environment by integrating people, place, process and technology". (IFMA 2019)

FM has to safeguard functionality, comfort and safety of buildings but the focus is on the human being and the user's orientation. FM is to bring together the "3 P's": place, people and process.

The standard EN 15221 defines Facility Management as follows:

Definition

"In general, all organisations, whether public or private, use buildings, assets and services (Facility Services) to support their primary activities. By coordinating these assets and services, using management skills and handling many changes in the organisation's environment, Facility Management influences its ability to act proactively and meet all its requirements. This is also done to optimise the costs and performance of assets and services". (EN 15221-1 2006, p. 4)

According to EN 15221 FM is the "Integration of processes within an organisation to maintain and develop the agreed services which support and improve the effectiveness of its primary activities (EN 15221-1 2006, p. 5).

We can recognise that this definition concentrates on the management perspective. "By using management skills and handling many changes in the organisation's environment" (EN 15221-1 2006), this management discipline has the aim to enable the core business for necessary changes and to create value. Especially the perspective of enabling necessary changes is very important today, as digitalisation is dramatically changing the way companies do business. Therefore, an enablement of this change is crucial for the survival of the companies.

The most recently established definition of ISO 41011 (2018) on FM also includes the management as well as the user focus. It defines FM as:

Definition

"Organisational function which integrates people, place and process within the built environment with the purpose of improving the quality of life of people and the productivity of the core business". (ISO 41011 (2018))

This most recent definition also brings into focus the quality of life of people and the productivity of the core business. We can see the link to workplace management focusing on the well-being of people and their productivity by providing optimal workplace environment. It also focuses on the enabling or in other words the adding of value to the core business.

1

Neither EN 15221 nor ISO 41011 (2018) concentrate on the value of the assets and the ROI of the owner, but on the value generation for the core business by healthy productive employees who can concentrate on their work in order to reach the goals of the core business supported by perfectly fitting infrastructure and services.

We can derive a more precious picture what FM means from the Facility Management model according to EN 15221 annex A shown in ◘ Fig. 1.10.

The following texts are taken from the EN 15221–1, which was prepared by the Technical Committee CEN/TC 348 "Facility Management".

> "An organisation relies on its primary processes in order to achieve its strategic objectives. Changing market forces and developments coming from legislation, technology, mergers, etc. influence these processes constantly. These changes must be managed and structured in strategic, tactical and operational levels, in order to remain viable and compliant.
>
> The support processes – like FM -, which can be a part of the organisation or be delivered by external service providers, have a direct impact on the efficiency and effectiveness of the primary activities. The distinction between the primary activities and support services is decided by each organisation individually; this distinction has to be continuously updated". (EN 15221-1 2006)

The organisation is made up of three levels:
- Client (corporate level)
- Customer (business unit level)
- End users (persons receiving Facility Services in a permanent or temporary way)

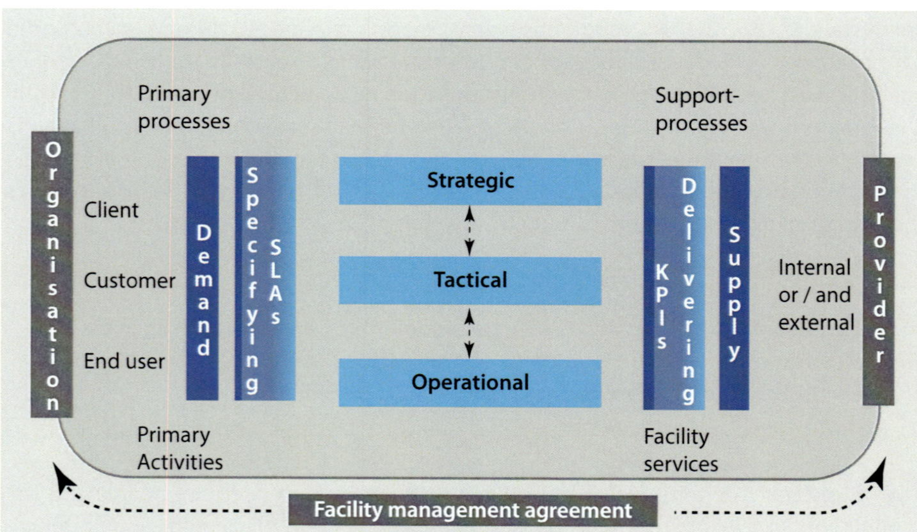

◘ **Fig. 1.10** Facility Management model according to EN 15221 annex A. (EN 15221–4 2011, p. 7)

» "It's the responsibility of the client to procure the required Facility Services, whereas the customer specifies and orders the delivery of these services within the conditions of a Facility Management agreement. On an operational level, the end users receive these support services where appropriate". (EN 15221-1 2006)

The Facility Manager has five main management tasks:
- To specify the demand at the three levels (strategic, tactical and operational)
- To source the required services to proper internal or external supply
- To control the service provision
- To analyse if the demand defined in the first task is really efficient and effective for the core business or if they have to be adapted
- To adapt the demand specification if the core business changes (EN 15221-1 2006)

The demand on the strategic level acts as a framework for the rest of the definitions of the demand. The strategic level aims to achieve the objectives of the organisation in the long term through:

» - "Defining the Facility Management strategy in compliance with the organisation's strategy (e.g. ownership versus leasing, strategic guidelines on out- and insourcing)
- Policymaking, elaborating guidelines for space, assets, processes and services (e.g. size and quality definitions for workplace types per person)
- Active input and response
- Initiating risk analysis and providing the direction to adapt changes in the organisation (e.g. risk analysis and policies in respect of number of service providers)
- Initiating Service Level Agreements (SLAs) and monitoring Key Performance Indicators (KPI's) (e.g. availability of equipment and services)
- Managing the impact of facilities on the primary activities, external environment and community
- Maintaining relations with authorities, leasers and tenants, strategic partners, associations etc.
- Supervision of the Facility Management organisation" (EN 15221-1 2007)

The strategic level can only be defined together with the board of directors to make sure that the long-term goals of the company as well as upcoming strategic changes are properly included in the specification.

The tactical level has to secure the fulfilment of the strategic level and specifies more short-term details. It is more oriented on the demands of the core processes of departments like sales, production and financial accounting.

» "Tactical level is to implement the strategic objectives in the medium term through:
- Implementing and monitoring guidelines for strategies;
- Developing business plans and budgets;
- Translating Facility Management objectives into operational level requirements;
- Defining SLAs and interpreting KPIs (performance, quality, risk and value);

1

- Monitoring compliance to laws and regulations;
- Managing projects, processes and agreements;
- Managing the Facility Management team;
- Optimising the use of resources;
- Adapting to and reporting on changes;
- Communicating with internal or external service providers on a tactical level". (EN 15221-1 2007)

The operational level has to secure the fulfilment of the strategic and tactical level. It directly targets the end users, which means all employees and clients of the company. The operative service provision is connected with or even equals the operational level. Operational level is "to create the needed environment to the end users on a day-to-day basis through:

- Delivering soft services like cleaning, landscaping, safety and security and hard services like maintenance, repair in accordance with the SLA;
- Monitoring and checking the service delivery processes;
- Monitoring the service providers (internally and externally);
- Receiving requests for service, e.g. via help desk or service line;
- Collecting data for performance evaluations, feedback and demands from end users;
- Reporting to tactical level;
- Communicating with internal or external service providers on an operational level". (EN 15221-1 2007)

It is important to understand that an external service provider can provide the external services and support the internal Facility Management department. According to EN 15221, the isolated provision of one or more services is not to be considered as FM. Therefore, it is not possible to outsource the complete function of Facility Management. The internal Facility Manager has access to all internal information and knows the strategic goals and developments. Consequently, this person in charge can better understand the demands of the customer, being part of it. The internal Facility Manager is on the one hand the ambassador of the employees and their demands, the representative of the customer (the management board), and on the other hand the internal consulter of the management board, supported by the external consultants, lawyers and Facility Services providers with all their experience from other projects.

To sum up, the strategic level can only be performed internally, but an external partner can advise and support the internal Facility Manager. The tactical level can be for the most part outsourced. The operational level can be fully outsourced.

The internal Facility Manager (this can also be a person, holding the function Facility Management in addition to other responsibilities) and the external Facility Services Manager should not be seen as competitors. It can be more of a win-win situation. The internal FM can define the demand more properly and convince the board easier of its necessity as there is a deep trust relationship. The external service provider can help to leverage the efficiency and effectiveness of the service provision easier as it is his core business.

How can we use the definition of Appendix A of the EN 15221 in practice? Let us take the example of my university again.

Example

My university is now more than 200 years old. Several years before this anniversary the management of the university had a look at the buildings and the related infrastructure and came to the conclusion that the current situation is not appropriate for our anniversary. Together with our property owner, strategic scenarios were drafted. One was to set up a totally new campus outside Vienna in a development area of the town with brand new buildings and infrastructure covering the existing and new demand in a very promising way, or to stay in the current place and "just" refurbish and optimise the usage of the existing buildings.

As you can imagine both scenarios were supported by different groups. Some people loved the idea of a campus like MIT and Stanford. Others were in favour of the optimisation, as the full funding of the new campus seemed to be quite challenging. To find a solution we applied Appendix A. First, we defined the strategic goals of the university. We identified two main ones:

1. To attract students, as our funding by the state depends on the number of students
2. To acquire and retain the top researchers for our university, maybe to even get a Nobel Prize winner

When we focused on the first goal, we asked which criteria was most influential for the student's choice of a university. My students always answered that the reputation of the university and the faculty come first. Nevertheless, when I questioned further, they came up with preferences such as enjoying life in pubs and clubs and so on, the amenities of good public transportation and the bon viveur in general. So, when we compared the two scenarios, we found out that on the one hand the new part of the town would give many possibilities and much space to develop further, but on the other hand would also have several disadvantages:

- Public transportation was only available by one bus line
- The housing situation had to be developed to provide affordable living for the students
- No restaurants or pubs were around. We would have to construct them or invite them over to our place

The current location is in the middle of the city of Vienna with more than 150 pubs nearby, several hypermarkets, food stores and other possibilities to buy goods. As it is downtown, there is a developed housing scene. So all in all, the infrastructure is much better in the current location, but the possibilities to grow were considered limited.

Hence, in a further step we analysed the current utilisation and then the possibilities to grow. We set up guidelines for space. We differentiated according to the different roles like dean, professor, assistant, and student. Then we also considered the different requirements of the faculties, as some only do desk research, whereas others needed different types of laboratories to carry out teaching and research. This led us to space guidelines including size and quality definitions for workplace types per type of person per faculty. Multiplying the square meters per person with the current number of employees and students gave us a first insight in the demand. Then we made a forecast of the number of people that we have to support in the future. By comparing this with the space rented

1

and the space available (or that can be further developed), we concluded that the current location would also fit in this perspective.

So we decided to stay, to optimise the space utilisation and to activate hidden space reserves.

In the next step, each department was analysed. The given space and service specifications were put in relation to the current usage. In my case, we have two main parts. The FM research and the Academic Competence Centre providing ERP (Enterprise Resource Planning System) training materials, but also hosting these systems and supporting teachers from secondary schools and universities in their daily teaching and research in the area of ERP systems. The FM research and the set-up of training materials and systems are quite comparable. They need team offices but also focus rooms for concentrated working. The system provision itself is different, as it requires accessibility 24/7 and asks for specific rooms to be provided. It needs server rooms with high availability of power, cooling and Internet. The call centre itself also has specific demands on noise reduction, etc. However, the workspaces there are much smaller than those for the teams doing research and setting up teaching materials and systems. Therefore, we used the space saved at the call centre for more convenient team offices and a lounge area to sit down, relax and exchange ideas with others from the team. We also run an executive MBA (Master of Business Administration). The students use the meeting room for a long weekend each month. This course also asks for specific services. Access has to be granted during the weekends and cleaning is also needed; otherwise, the washrooms and the kitchen would not be useable after Saturday midday. This was included in the operational service demand as normally universities are not really "operational" during weekends.

This all together shall give you some examples of our demand definition on the strategic level (location), the tactical level of my department and the operational level of the required services. Based on this requirements' specification, the internal FM department of my university sourced the services. The location requirements including refurbishments and activation of hidden space reserves are covered by the new rental agreement with our landlord. The operational services were put to a bidding to find proper Facility Service Companies. As we could not find one company capable to provide us with all the services, we split the contracts into two, one for the soft services like cleaning and security and one for the hard services like maintenance.

As our university and my department are facing changes, we also keep the demand definition up to date. For example, as I had won a rather large research proposal, we had to enlarge the workspace covering the demand of the new team and to add specific services in the area of room climate.

The FM department controls the service provision so that the service companies provide the specified services properly.

As we now know what Facility Management is according to the ISO and EN standard, let us compare this with the current situation in companies. Have the companies already incorporated the suggestions and definition of the EN and the ISO standards? Let us have a look at the current situation of FM within the large European countries and at current trends within FM to give an answer.

1.7 Status Quo of FM Within European Companies

Since 2005, the Vienna University of Technology has carried out surveys in several European countries. In these countries, the largest companies (according to their turnover) were interrogated on how they organise their FM. In the past 3 years, the survey was conducted in Germany, Austria and Switzerland – also called the D-A-CH-region – and in southern European countries like Spain, Turkey, Bulgaria and Romania. This was done to cover the mature markets of the D-A-CH region and to compare them with the developing markets of southern and eastern Europe. The following subsections will give an overview about the internal organisation and outsourcing of Facility Services. It must be stated that the situation in medium- and small-sized enterprises is different, but it can be assumed that "best practice" from large companies will be adapted by medium- and small-sized businesses after a short period of time.

1.7.1 Internal Organisation of FM Within Large Companies

According to the survey, the number of companies with an own FM department has increased since 2005. In the southern countries, internal FM departments were less common around 2005 but they have been catching up rapidly. In the meantime, in the D-A-CH region as well as in the southern countries, more than 70% of companies have an internal FM department or employees clearly responsible for the Facility Management tasks mentioned above. Only in Turkey the number of internal FM departments is still lower (◘ Fig. 1.11).

The FM departments focus on different strategic objectives. Companies in the D-A-CH region, which are considered to be the mature FM markets, no longer emphasise cost reduction and cost transparency. Other aims such as sustainability, quality,

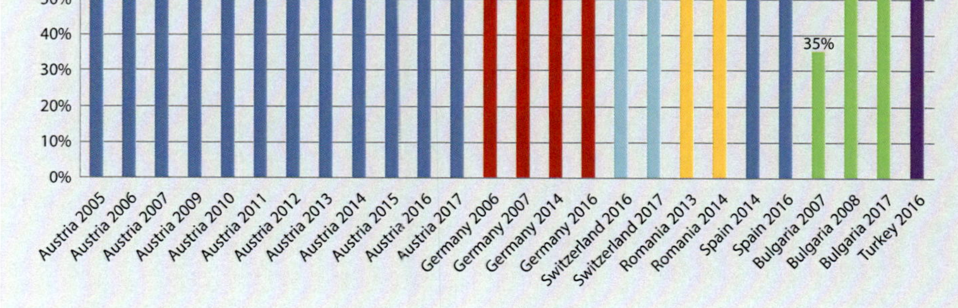

◘ **Fig. 1.11** Companies with their own FM department. (Author's own figure)

1

value retention, service and flexibility are as important. In Switzerland and Austria, sustainability is ranked most important. German companies have flexibility as their highest mentioned strategic goal. This is not the case in southern European countries, whose markets are considered to be the developing ones. In Spain and Bulgaria, the most important objectives still are cost reduction, cost transparency and outsourcing. So we see that the mature markets like UK and the D-A-CH region are concentrating more on the value added of FM and less on the cost-saving side, whereas the emerging and developing markets like the southern European countries are collecting the low-hanging fruits and therefore concentrate on cost reduction. We believe that will change as soon as they become more mature (◘ Fig. 1.12).

In the beginning, Facility Management was positioned quite often as a line function. This was necessary as these departments did not only perform the strategic tasks described in the standard EN 15221 (like Definition of Demand), but also carried out a lot of the Facility Services on their own. As companies started to outsource services and to concentrate on the management function, FM became more and more a strategic function and was therefore implemented as a staff function. This trend has reversed slowly since 2011. Due to economic challenges, many companies moved people, for example, from doing maintenance of the production lines into internal Facility Service provisioning. The goal was not to lose highly specialised employees, as most of the companies are facing shortages in these sectors. Enormous differences can be observed between the D-A-CH region, Bulgaria and Spain. In the D-A-CH region, between 15% and 25% of FM departments are staff functions now, while in Bulgaria and Spain almost 70% are staff functions (◘ Fig. 1.13).

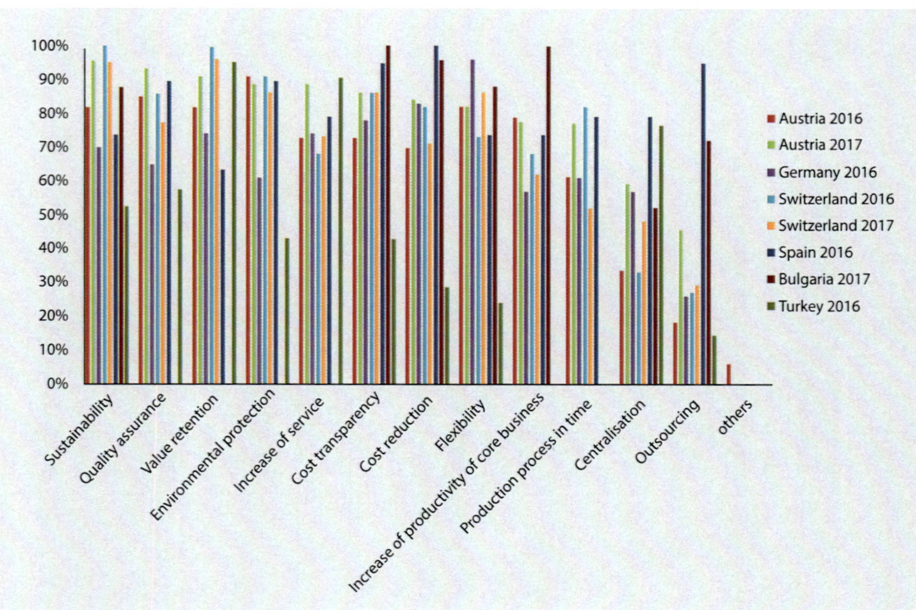

◘ **Fig. 1.12** Strategy of the FM department. (Redlein and Stopajnik 2018)

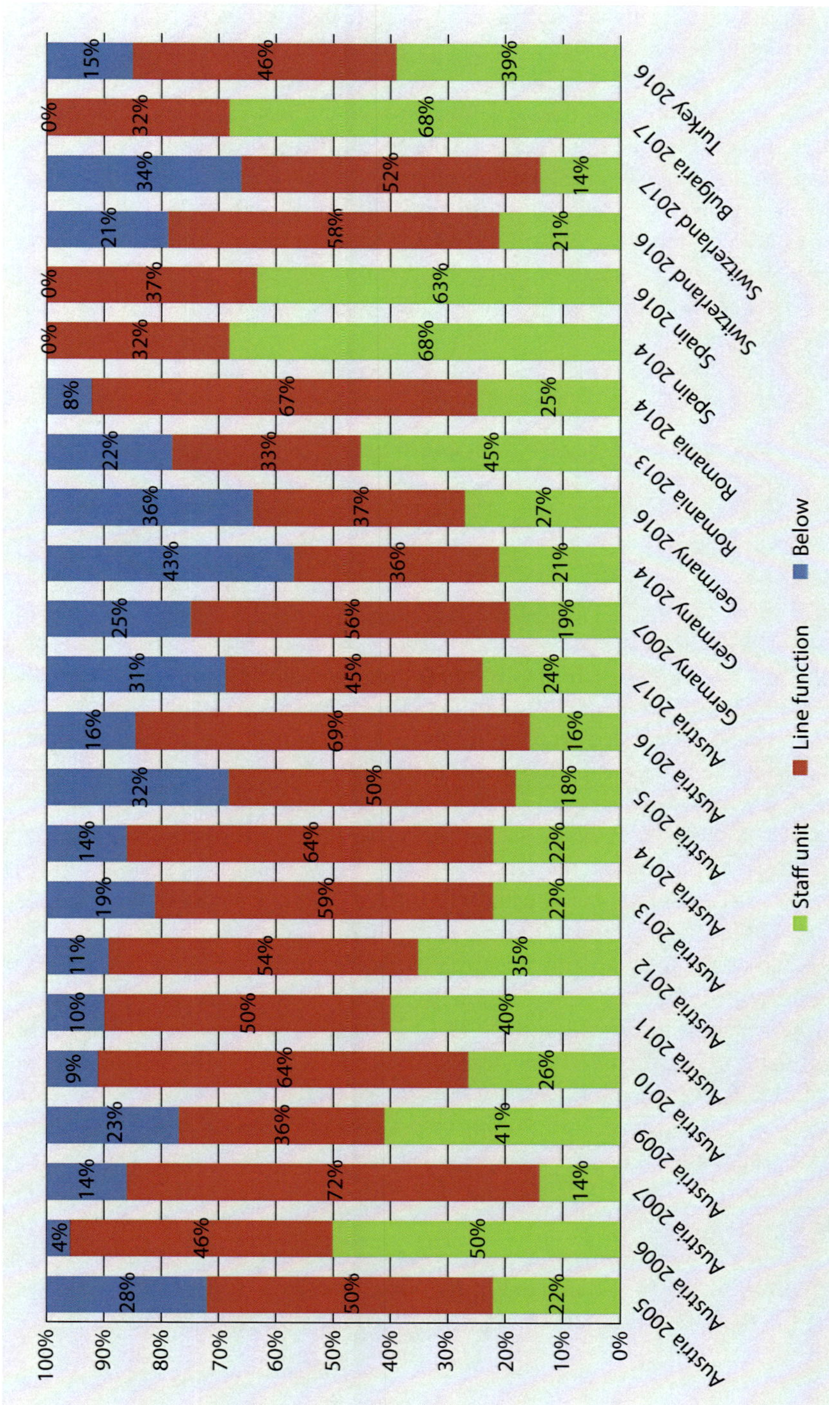

Fig. 1.13 Organisation of FM. (Author's own figure)

Over the years, the number of companies with only one or two managers taking care of the strategic and tactical Facility Management tasks has increased. Only Germany behaves differently, as its companies are larger than those in the other countries analysed. In Romania and Turkey, even half of the surveyed companies only employ one or two employees to carry out management tasks. These companies have outsourced the whole service provision. Examples are large automotive companies that have two people taking care of the management tasks. These employees cannot execute any maintenance tasks for a company with more than 10.000 employees. These services are outsourced to Facility Service providers. On the other hand, the other extreme is also visible sometimes. A small proportion of companies still employs their own FM workforce with more than 50 or 100 people and also execute the service provision in parts (◘ Fig. 1.14).

1.7.2 Outsourcing of Service Provision

The top outsourced services during the past 10 years were "cleaning", "winter services", "waste disposal", "electricity", "maintenance", "catering", "security" and "fire protection".

According to the eighth EU directive, companies of public importance have to implement an internal control system. This system is to safeguard the accuracy of the financial statement as well as to secure the compliance of the company with all relevant laws and regulations. Facility Management, especially in the area of "winter services", "security" and "fire protection" and "maintenance", has to safeguard many laws (like safety and fire protection regulations). Therefore, "winter service", "maintenance" and "inspection" are currently quite often outsourced, not only to reduce costs but also to transfer risks to the service providers. To transfer the entire risks, the contract has to be drafted in a proper way. The highest courts of several European countries have a consensus, namely, that the bidding and the contract have to include quality service-level agreements (SLAs). Additionally, the corresponding key performance indicators have to lead to penalty payments for the service company in the case of a breach of the contractual stipulations. Only if the customer addresses that issue in the outsourcing process, the risk of operation is transferred. The more of these stipulations are included, the less is the control effort, the customer has to carry out during the duration of the contract. However, that does not absolve the customer from the responsibility to inform the service company should they recognise failure or danger.

Example

To give an example, if the owner of a building recognises that the snow is not removed properly, he has to inform and admonish the service company to fulfil the contract as agreed and, in the case of life-threatening danger, action has to be taken immediately.

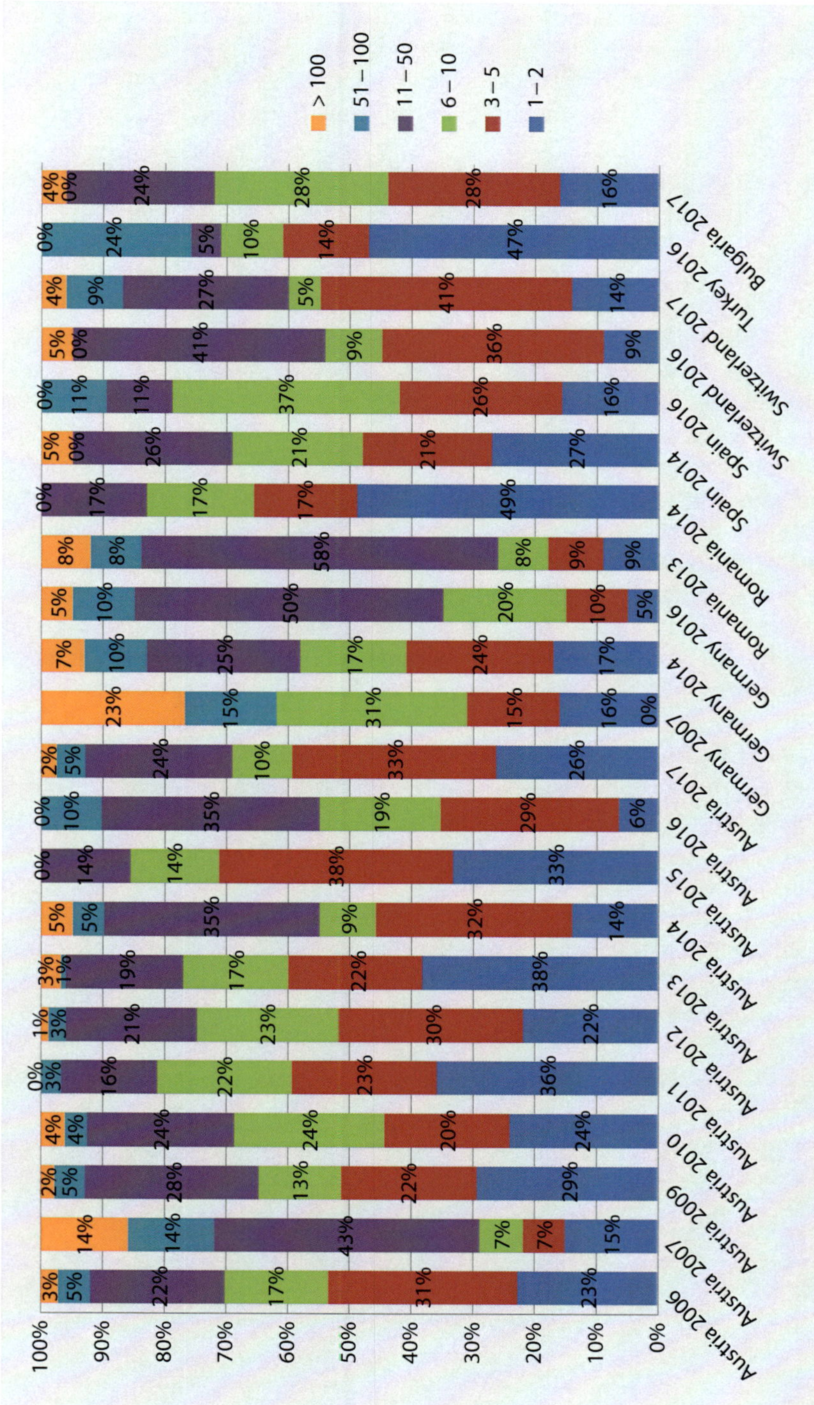

Fig. 1.14 Number of employees in internal FM departments. (Author's own figure)

Large companies still rely on a great number of service providers. The number has decreased over the years, but still, 20% of the large companies have more than 10 service providers for their Facility Service provision. This requires much internal coordination and effort. On the other hand, to concentrate only on one or two providers bears also risks. If the company goes bankrupt, the full-service provision is at risk. Even if the single service provider has just been taken over by another company, the strategic goals of the new owner and the quality of the services will possibly change which also may have a negative impact on the core business of the customer.

Another aspect is that most of the service providers have their origin either in the soft or the hard service sector. The companies with a hard service provisioning background subcontract the soft services very often and ask for a management fee to handle these services. Now the customer's company has to analyse if it can do the management for the same fee or even at lower cost taking into consideration the internal efforts. The companies that have developed from the soft service sector try to cover as many services as possible with their soft service employees, who are not technicians by education. As almost 80% of the inspection tasks can be carried out by people without formal certification, being "just" trained on the job (Pichlmüller 2008), quality issues can arise in some cases. This is another reason for engaging more than one company. The last important reason is that if a customer has subsidiaries in more than one country and, for example, is spread over the whole of Europe, it is hard to find one service provider based in all relevant countries. This is the case in most of the analysed companies on the demand side as they are the largest companies in Europe. The top 500 companies are almost the same in the countries analysed (◘ Figs. 1.15 and 1.16).

The decision-making process about selecting a service company depends mainly on the strategy of the internal FM department. It is not surprising that the most important selection criteria for external service providers go hand in hand with the strategic objectives of the internal FM departments: The most important selection criteria are competence, quality, flexibility and engagement in the mature markets. In southern Europe – emerging and developing markets – the price and the price-performance ratio are more important. This goes fully in line with the strategic goals of the different countries mentioned above (◘ Fig. 1.17).

Considering the duration of the contract, there are two trends:

1. There are a large numbers of long-term contracts, especially in the area of technical maintenance.
2. The number of longer-lasting contracts instead of one-year contracts is growing.

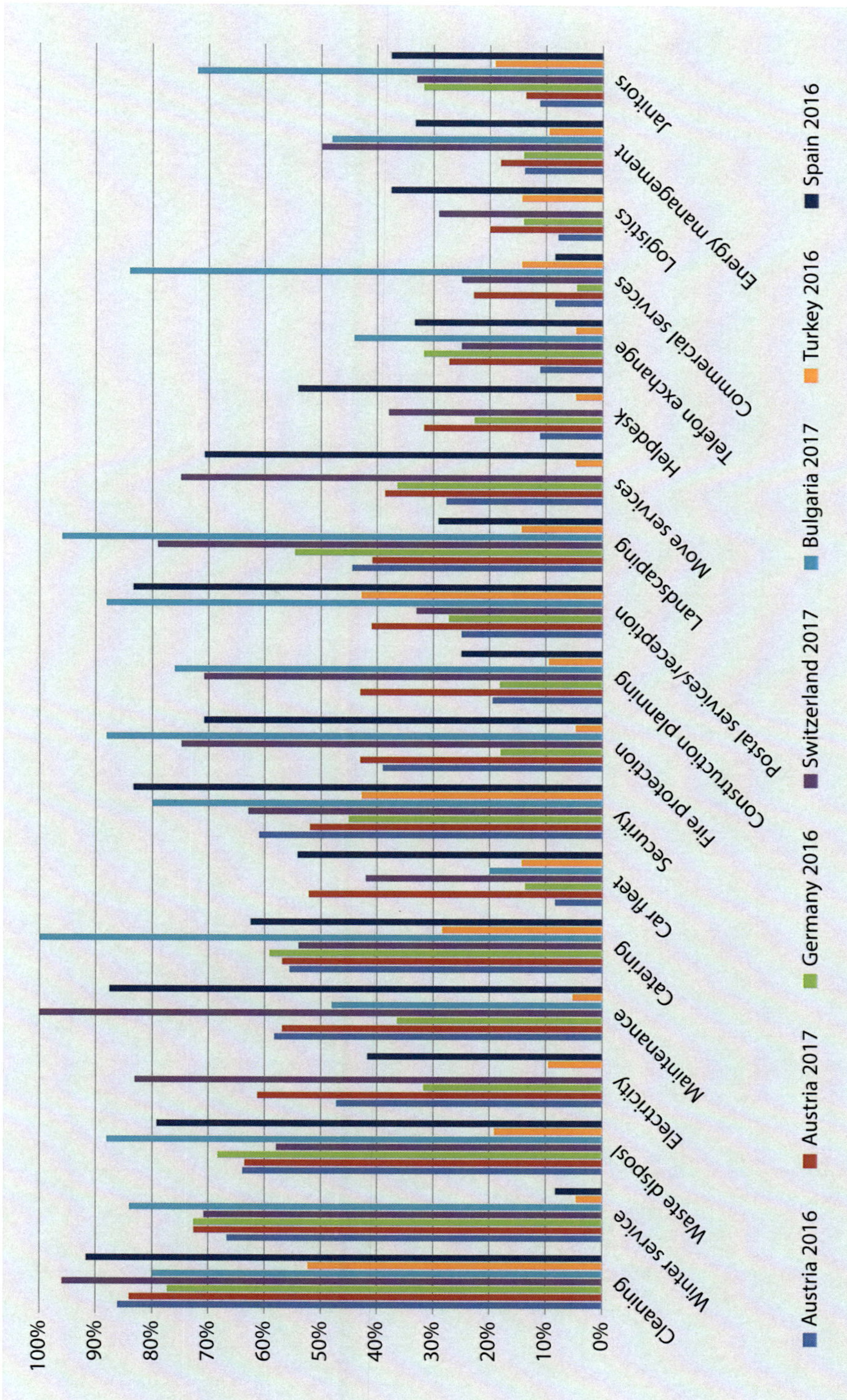

Fig. 1.15 Areas of outsourcing. (Author's own figure)

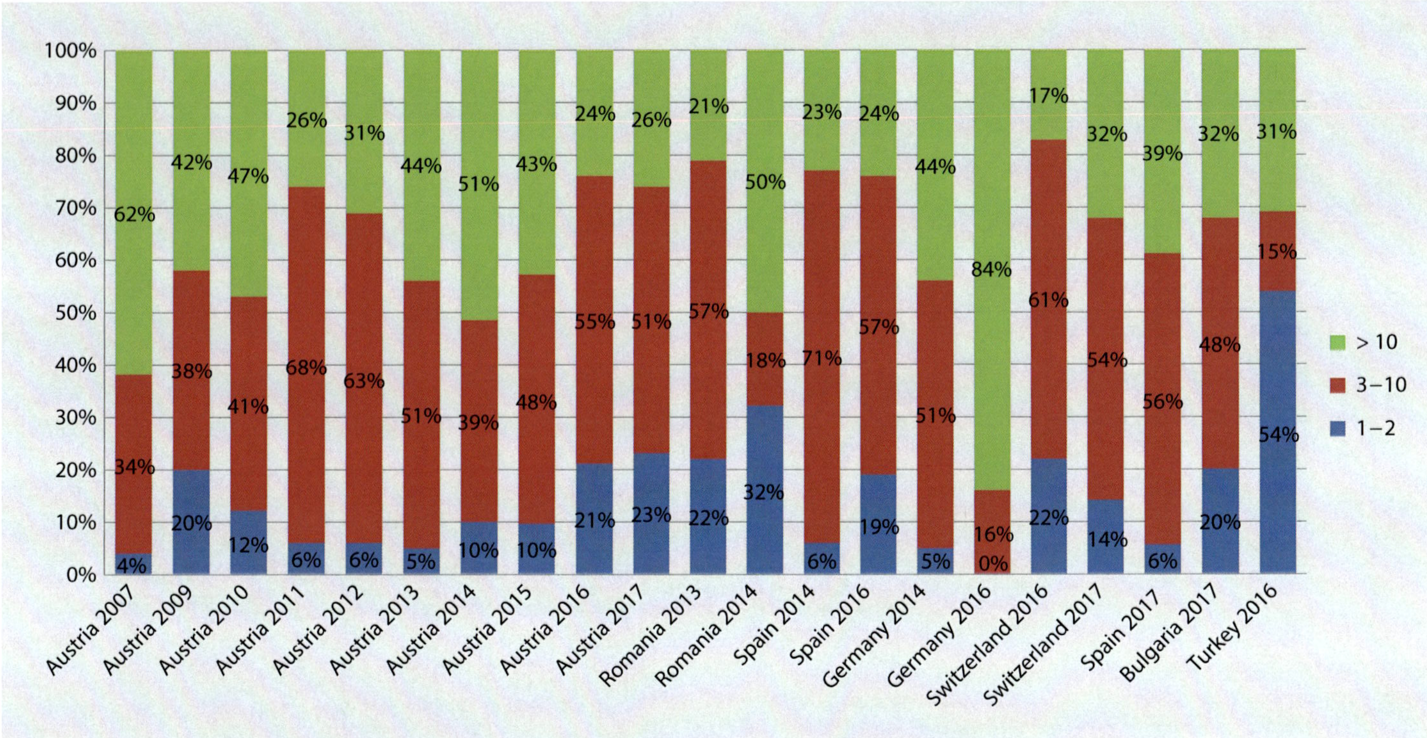

Fig. 1.16 Number of contractors. (Author's own figure)

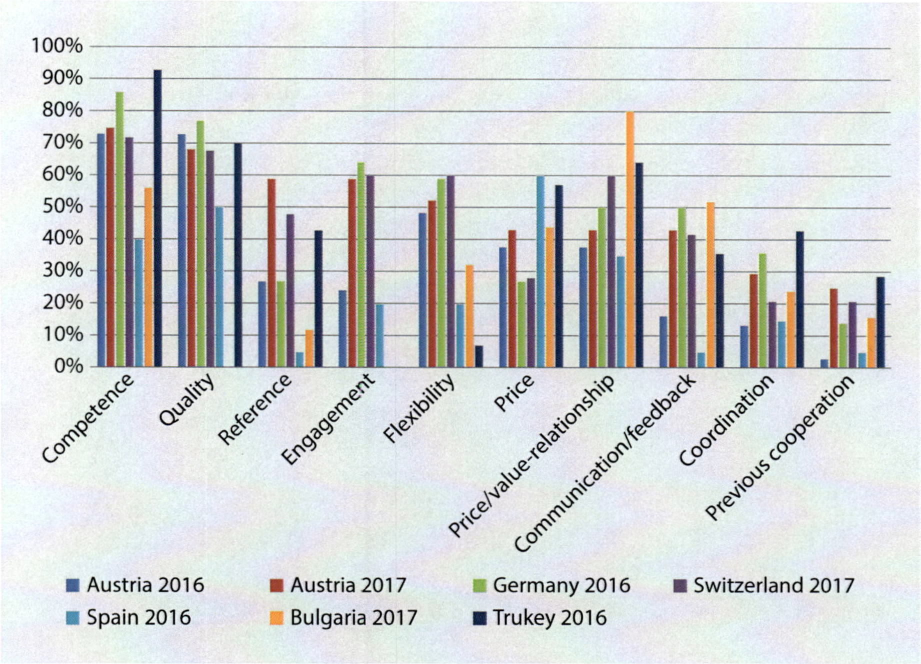

Fig. 1.17 Selection criteria for external service providers. (Author's own figure)

Companies have noticed that much effort is needed to request new biddings every year and that the internal costs rather exceed the possible savings due to new contracts. Likewise, it is not guaranteed that tendering lowers costs. Transition costs and start-up costs can create additional costs. Long-lasting partnerships help to perform better over time. This is evident especially in the area of technical contracts, since the training of a new contractor, e.g. to instruct the employees about the location of all equipment and their proper operation, binds many resources for both the demand and supply side (Fig. 1.18).

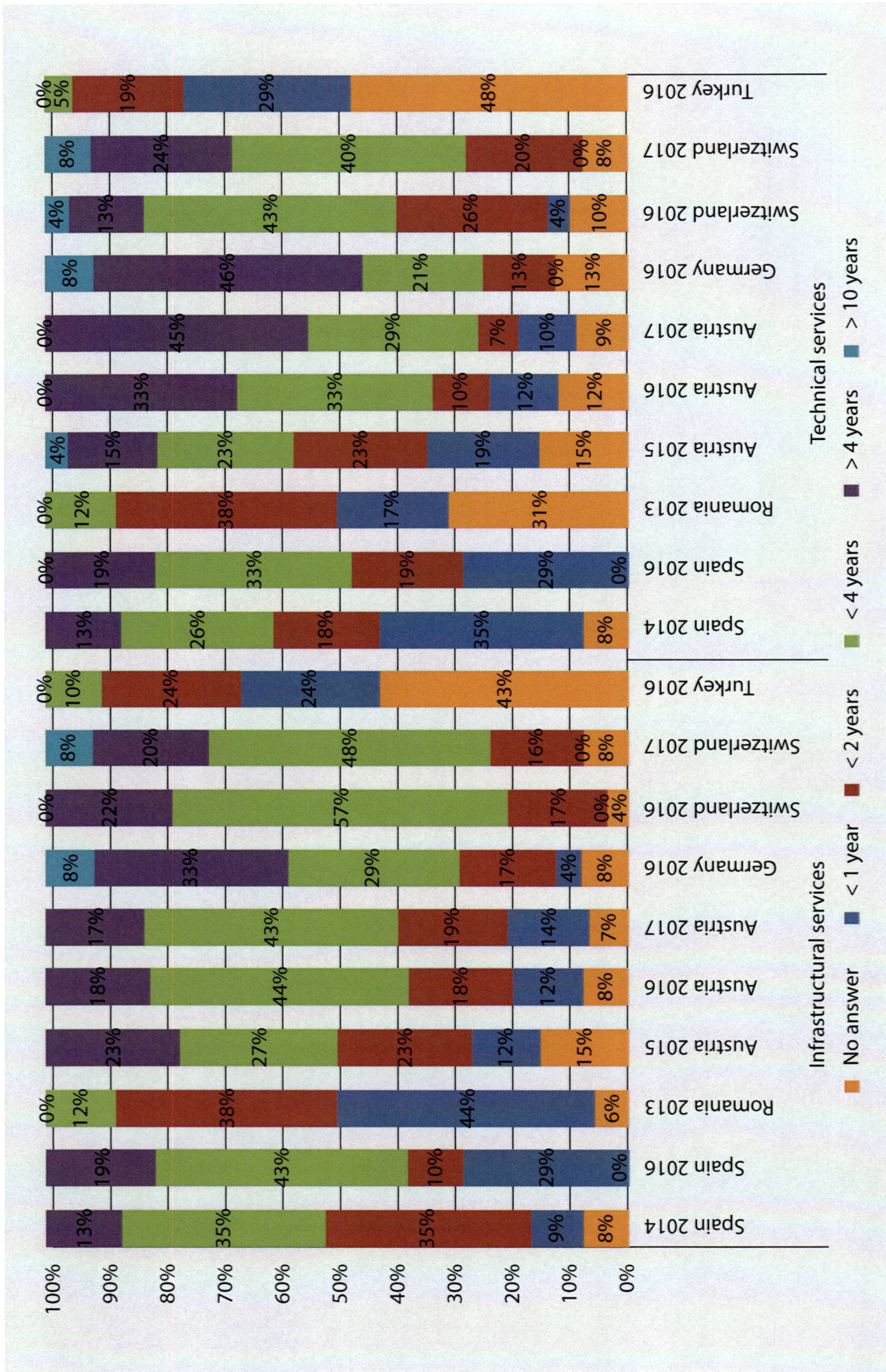

Fig. 1.18 Duration of contracts with external service providers. (Author's own figure)

1.8 Conclusion

As we can see, most of the analysed companies in the EU have introduced their own FM department carrying out the demand definition, the sourcing and the controlling of the service provision. Most of the operational services are outsourced to service providers. Above all, the soft services are handed over, along with the major hard services like maintenance. The strategic goals vary. The companies in the developed or mature markets look more for sustainability and focus already on subjects like workplace management. The developing markets still focus on cost reduction. They are searching for the low-hanging fruits.

Let us investigate the mentioned hierarchy in detail in the following chapters of the book. The next three chapters concentrate on the basics:

- Optimisation of Facility Management itself by process optimisation due to business process reengineering and IT support
- Measuring results by reporting SLAs and KPIs.

Based on these topics we will then cover the trends of the more mature markets like sustainability and workplace management.

Review Questions

1. How large is the size of the outsourced Facility Service industry according to its value added and the number of employees working around buildings in Europe?
2. Why are the positions according to value added and number of employees different?
3. What are the roles in the Real Estate industry and their representatives?
4. Define Corporate Real Estate, Asset, Property and Facility Management and name the goals of the different management strategies?
5. Describe the scheme of Appendix A of the EN15221 and what management tasks of FM can be derived of this scheme?
6. How is the organisation of FM set up in the large companies around Europe?
7. What is the difference in the behaviour of the large companies in the mature versus the developing markets?
8. How do large companies deal with the service provision? How high are the outsourcing rates of the operational FS?

References

Birca, S. (2017). *Market Size regarding Facility Service Industry in terms of employees int the US.*
Bundesverband Investment und Asset Management e.V. (BVI). Accessed Aug, 2019.
Dubben, N., & Sayce, S. (1991). *Property portfolio management: An introduction*. London: Routledge.
EN 15221-1. (2006). Facility management. Terms and definition, Austrian Standards.
EN 15221-1. (2007). *Facility management – Part 1: Terms and definitions, European Committee for Standardization*. London: British Standards Institution.
EN 15221-4. (2018). *Facility management – Part 4: Taxonomy, classification and structures in facility management*. Austrian Standards, Accessed 01 Dec, 2018.

1

Eurostat. (last modified 2013). Glossary:Value added at factor cost", in *Statistics explained*. Available at http://ec.europa.eu/eurostat/statistics-explained/index.php/Glossary:Value_added_at_factor_cost. Accessed 4 Aug, 2016.

Eurostat. (last modified 2019). *Detaillierte jährliche Unternehmensstatistiken für das Baugewerbe (NACE Rev. 2, F), Detaillierte jährliche Unternehmensstatistik für den Handel (NACE Rev. 2, G), Detaillierte jährliche Unternehmensstatistik für Dienstleistungen (NACE Rev. 2, H-N und S95), Detaillierte jährliche Unternehmensstatistiken für die Industrie (NACE Rev. 2, B-E)*, in *Structural business statistics (sbs)*. Available at: http://ec.europa.eu/eurostat/search?p_auth=vsrRef94&p_p_id=estatsearchportlet_WAR_estatsearchportlet&p_p_lifecycle=1&p_p_state=maximized&p_p_mode=view&_estatsearchportlet_WAR_estatsearchportlet_action=search&text=Detaillierte+j%C3%A4hrliche+Unternehmensstatistik. Accessed 17 Jan, 2019.

Glatte, T. (2013). *The importance of corporate real estate management in overall corporate strategies*. Germany: CoreNet Global whitepaper.

IFMA. (2019). *What is facility management*. Houston: International Facility Management Association. Online: https://www.ifma.org/about/what-is-facility-management. Accessed 26 Feb, 2019.

ISO 41011 (2018). Facility management – Vocabulary, Austrian Standards.

ISO 55000 (2014). Asset management – Overview, principles and terminology. https://www.iso.org/standard/55088.html. Accessed Aug, 2019.

Kämpf-Dern, A. (2009). *Immobilienwirtschaftliche Managementebenen und –aufgaben. Definitions- und Leistungskatalog des Immobilienmanagements*.

Pichlmüller, H. (2008). *Integrated facility services – Synergien im Bereich der operativen services*. Wien, Austria: TU Wien.

Redlein, A., & Stopajnik, E. (2017). *Current labour market situation and upcoming trends in the European facility service industry. Journal of Facility Management Education and Research*. Vienna, Austria: Research group for Facility Management/TU.

Redlein, A., & Stopajnik, E. (2018). The Organization of Facility Management in Europe in 2016 and 2017; Hauptvortrag: 26th EBES Conference, Prag (eingeladen); 24.10.2018 – 26.10.2018; in: "26th EBES Conference - Prague", ISBN: 978-605-67622-5-3; S. 58–59.

Redlein, A., & Stopajnik, E. (2019a). The Facility service industry as a driver of the economy, ARES Conference 2019, Phoenix (invited): 9.4.2019 – 13.4.2019; in "Thirty-Fifth Annual Meeting", p. 65.

Redlein, A., & Stopajnik, E. (2019b). Facility Services: A Solid Industry during Recession, ASFM Conference 2019, Phoenix (invited): 15.10.2019 – 18.10.2019 ASFM Fall 2019 Colloquium and IFMA World Workplace.

Rondeau, E. P., Brown R. K., Lapides, P. D. (2006). Facility management. 2. Auflage. New York: Wiley, ISBN: 0471700592.

Schulte, K.-W., & Hupach, I. (1998). Bedeutung der Immobilienwirtschaft. In K.-W. Schulte (Ed.), *Immobilienökonomie. Band 1 Betriebswirtschaftliche Grundlagen*. Munich-Vienna: Oldenbourg.

Teichmann, S. A. (2007). Bestimmung und Abgrenzung von Managementdisziplinen im Kontext des Immobilien- und Facility Managements. In *ZIÖ – German Journal of Property Reasearch"2/2007*, p. 5–37, published in Schulte K.W., Institut für Immobilienwirtschaft.

TU Wien. (2017). *Die TU Wien in Zahlen*. Wien. Online: https://www.tuwien.ac.at/wir_ueber_uns/zahlen_und_fakten/#c45588. Accessed 26 Feb,2019.

United States Census Bureau. (2016, 12). 2014 SUSB *"Annual Data Tables by Establishment Industry"*. Retrieved 15 May, 2017 from United States Census Bureau: https://www.census.gov/data/tables/2014/econ/susb/2014-susb-annual.html

Walmart Inc. (2018). *Walmart 2018 annual report*. Arkansas USA. Online: https://s2.q4cdn.com/056532643/files/doc_financials/2018/annual/WMT-2018_Annual-Report.pdf. Accessed 26.02.2019.

Optimisation of FM/RE Management

Alexander Redlein

A. Redlein (ed.), *Modern Facility and Workplace Management*,
Classroom Companion: Business, https://doi.org/10.1007/978-3-030-35314-8_2

Learning Objectives
The students should:
- Know of which parts an organisation consist
- Know how to apply a methodology like business process reengineering to optimise the RE/FM organisation
- Know the steps to model processes

2.1 Introduction

The organisation of a company is the way people and resources are organised to accomplish the goals of the company. An organisation consists of two main parts:
- The company organisation structure (like functional, divisional, matrix)
- The process-oriented organisation or structuring of operation

Definition

The organisation structure defines organisational units like departments, staff unit and divisions and their responsibilities, goals and duties, but also the hierarchy of the organisation and therefore the relationship between the units. In addition, it determines the information flow between the different levels and parts of management.

The optimal structure depends on the organisation's goals and strategy. There are two fundamental ways to set up the structural organisation (Business Dictionary n.d.):
1. The centralised structure: the top layer of management has most of the decision-making power and controls tightly the underlying departments and divisions.
2. The decentralised structure: the decision-making power is distributed and the departments and divisions have different degrees of independence. They have to be in line with their strategic goals but within these borders they can make their own decisions.

The organisational chart illustrates the organisational structure. The top of the structure is the executive board. In the following we can find line functions and staff units:
1. The line functions are departments which generate revenue (sales, production, etc.), and their managers are responsible for achieving the organisation's main objectives by executing the key functions.
2. The staff units are responsible for activities that support line functions. In most cases staff units directly report to the executive board or the head of a line function. In the example of controlling, this department sets up goals and controls the execution, but does not carry out the execution. In cases of deviations, it contacts the relevant organisational units and sets actions together with them. They also report periodically to the board and the departments and divisions (Business Dictionary n.d.).

2

Below you can find an organisation chart of a typically profit-oriented company.

According to EN15221, all management tasks have to be carried out by one organisational unit, either a staff unit or a line function. As we mentioned above most of the units not only carry out the management tasks, but also provide Facility Services. Therefore, the companies running FM like that set up the FM department as line function. If the full-service provision is outsourced and the unit concentrates "only" on the management tasks, the unit is very often set up as a staff unit (◘ Figs. 2.1 and 2.2).

Another often-used structure is the matrix management. In this structure, an individual or team reports to more than one person/organisational unit (◘ Fig. 2.3).

This structure is quite often used in the Facility Service industry. The teams running buildings are on one hand organised, e.g. in a geographical or client-orientated structure and on the other hand get training and knowledge updates from product-specific knowledge centres. In full-service provision companies like ISS and Atalian, these knowledge centres equal the different products like cleaning, security, heating, ventilation, and air-conditioning. In this way, the geographical or client-orientated structure secures the satisfaction and growth in an area or with a client. The knowledge-orientated structure secures the up-to-date service provision of the local teams.

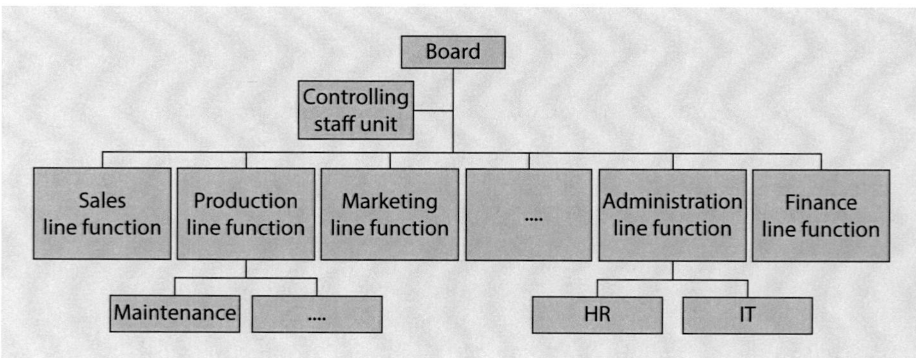

◘ **Fig. 2.1** Organisation chart of a profit-oriented company. (Author's own figure)

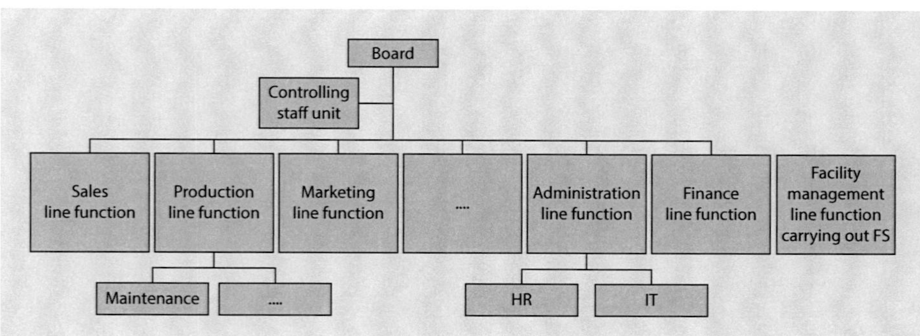

◘ **Fig. 2.2** Organisation chart of a profit-oriented company with Facility Management. (Author's own figure)

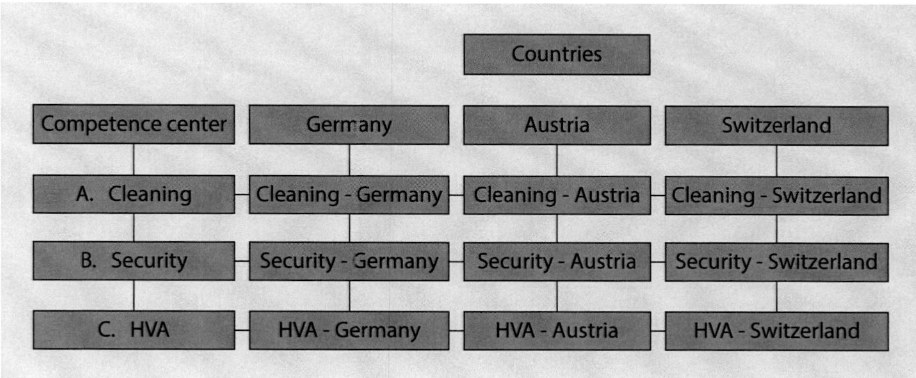

Fig. 2.3 Matrix management. (Author's own figure)

These structures follow Frederick Taylor, who developed management the first time from a scientific viewpoint. His breakthrough insight optimised labour productivity using the scientific methods; it opened an era of effectiveness and efficiency. Taylor's ideas prefigured modern quality control, total quality management. But Taylor looked on persons like machines with tasks he optimised (Gareth 1986). For several years, companies are facing new challenges (Wouter et al. 2018):

- **Quickly evolving environment.** All stakeholders' demand patterns are evolving rapidly: with the demand to adapt to fast-changing priorities.
- **Constant introduction of disruptive technology.** Established businesses and industries are being commoditised or replaced through digitisation.
- **Accelerating digitisation and democratisation of information.** The increased volume, transparency and distribution of information require organisations to rapidly engage in multidirectional communication
- **The new war for talent.** As creative knowledge- and learning-based tasks become more important, organisations need a distinctive value proposition to acquire – and retain – the best talent.

According to the research of Mc Kinsey (Arnowitz et al. 2015), with 1900 executives, they are adapting their strategy (and their organisational structure) with greater frequency than in the past where 82% of them went through a redesign in the last 3 years. The trends described above are dramatically changing how organisations and employees work. The new paradigm is to run organisations as living organisms. Agile organisations are both stable and dynamic at the same time. They include stable backbone elements that evolve slowly and support dynamic capabilities that can adapt quickly to new challenges and opportunities.

In the article, McKinsey describes the transition in the following way (Fig. 2.4).

> "According to current publications only a few companies have fully transformed themselves into agile organisations, but more and more companies are considering implementing this type of organisation for at least some parts of their operation" (Arnowitz et al. 2015).

2

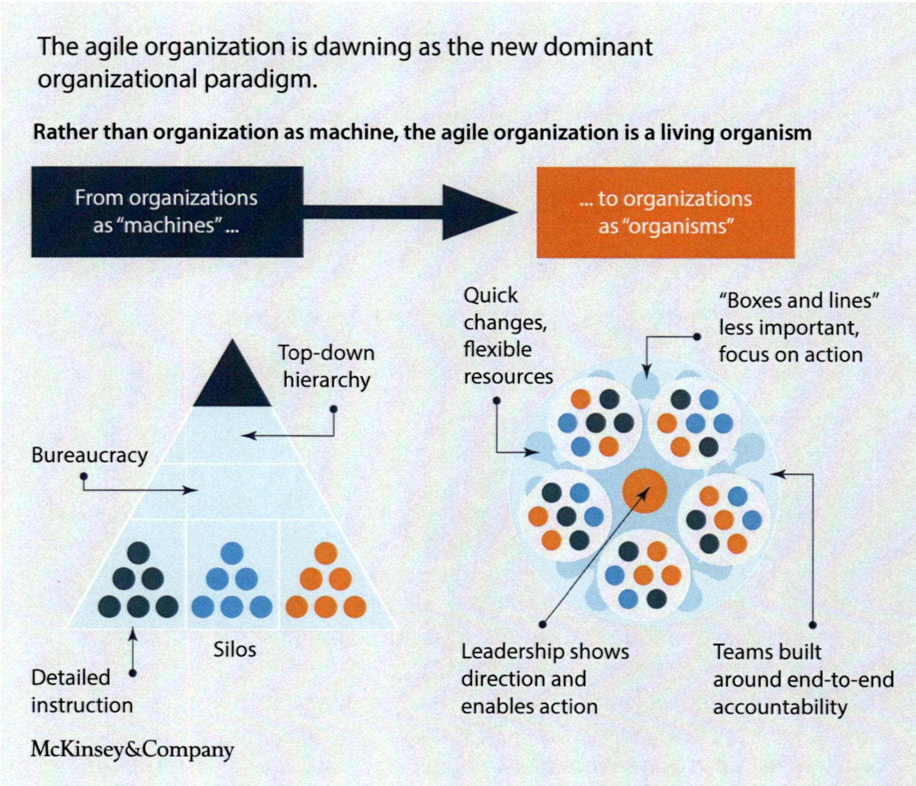

Fig. 2.4 Exhibit from "The five trademarks of agile organizations", January 2018, McKinsey & Company, ▶ www.mckinsey.com.

But let us concentrate now on the second part: the process-oriented organisation, as this is also the main focus of the EN1521–5. In his book "Competitive Strategy", Porter describes the value chain of companies. His work changed the focus from single departments and the attempt to optimise them to the processes. Porter's value chain emphasizes the view on the whole system and how inputs are changed into the outputs applying processes. Porter defined processes as a chain of activities common to all businesses. He divided them into primary and support activities, as shown below. The primary activities represent the value chain, generating the income for the company.

Example

Manufacturing companies create value by acquiring raw materials and using production lines to convert the raw materials into products that give more value to their customer than only the raw materials. Retailers select either special products or even a broader selection of products and present them to customers. Since the customer now finds interesting goods that he may not have known about, this brings value to him. All industries need supporting activities. Within the support activities, Porter points out the activities providing the firm's infrastructure. These activities provide, for example, the buildings in which production lines are located, showrooms with fitting rooms and catering, etc.

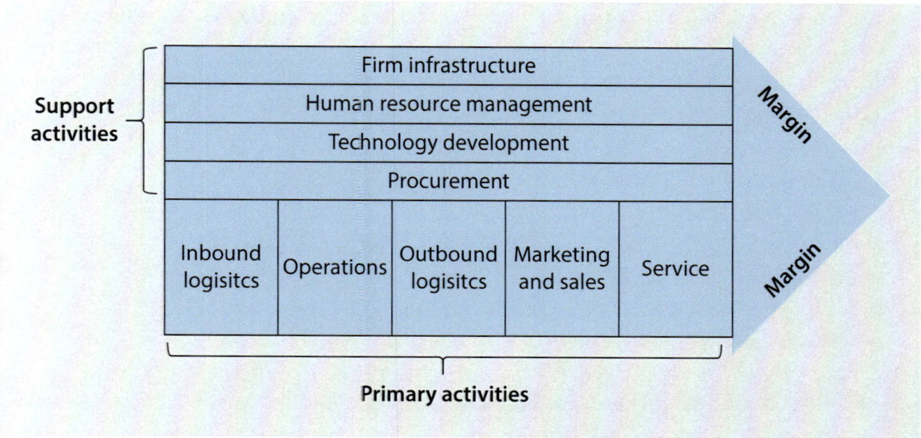

Fig. 2.5 The value chain. (Based on Porter 1985)

The underlying processes are the Facility Management processes. This approach is taken up by EN15221–5 (Fig. 2.5).

2.2 Processes

Definition

The EN 15221-1 defines FM as the "integration of processes within an organisation to maintain and develop the agreed services which support and improve the effectiveness of primary activities" (EN 15221-1 2006).

Therefore, FM processes have great importance for the delivery of FM and its services in an enhanced way. How can we now optimise processes in FM? The aim of the EN 15221–5 "is to provide guidance to Facility Management (FM) organisations on the development and improvement of their FM processes to support the primary activities" (EN 15221-5 2018). With the help of this standard, organisations should be able to understand the importance of Facility Management processes to their effectiveness and understand the need to assess the maturity of their existing processes. This will provide a basis for developing and improving the facility management processes through a consistent, process-based management approach. Effective process management enables external changes in legislation, directives, codes and regulatory issues to be quickly embedded at all levels of the organisation and to assess the impact of these changes on FM Agreements and FM Process Auditing. It enables external changes in economic development, to be embedded at all levels of the organisation and on providing audit trails for transparency and governance requirements.

The scope and structure of the FM processes are dependent on the specific needs of each industry (healthcare, automotive, insurance, public); therefore, the importance of certain FM processes differ from one organisation to the other. For example, a FM process in a large hospital organisation will have a different importance than the same process in an organisation with mainly common and uniform office workplaces.

"Effective and efficient use of resources will be achieved by:

(a) clear responsibilities of the process owner;
(b) accurate documented workflows;
(c) adequate flow of accurate data;
(d) precise descriptions of the requirements as a result of the analysis of the demand of the primary process (output);
(e) process activities are fulfilled by competent personal;
(f) outputs are professionally monitored" (EN 15221-5 2011, p. 16)

EN15221–5 states that "The guidance provided in this standard established the need for the FM processes to start with analysing and having a clear picture of the client organisation and its primary processes as a basis for the development of the FM strategy" (EN 15221-5 2018, p. 5). Nevertheless, the standard itself does not include a methodology or "blueprint" for the steps necessary to carry out the definition or optimisation of the process organisation. As the standard is lacking to provide a methodology for this step, the authors suggest the methodology of business process reengineering as a general methodology. It was used in several case studies providing excellent results. The methodology presented in the next chapter is based on this management methodology but is also enlarged to cover the demands of Facility and Real Estate Management and the Facility Service industry.

2.3 Business Process Reengineering

A few years ago, most companies were organised according to Taylor's guidelines. Work was split up into small tasks, which were carried out by specialists. Between these specialists, there was a lack of communication or even communication barriers. It was almost impossible to reach goals with respect to time, cost, quality and innovation leadership. Therefore, a change took place within most of the organisation.

The baseline for all these changes is the needs and expectations of the customers. By changing the organisation (processes and company organisation structure), the company should be able to provide a better service to the customer according to his needs and should be easily capable of adapting to changes in the customer's requirements.

Companies began to define their customers' needs and their core competencies to fulfil the demands. The core competencies of a company are the specific abilities, which differentiate a company from others. Based on this, business process reengineering was used to "optimise" the core processes. Business process reengineering leads to a fundamental rethinking of the processes within a company. The goal of this rethinking is not only to fulfil customer demand but also to save time and lower costs. This leads to a new conception of how work/tasks have to be done.

Instead of Taylorism, which is characterised by the division of the work into small tasks carried out by different specialists, business process reengineering combines tasks that belong together into larger process steps. These larger steps have to be carried out by one person instead of many (Kiechel 1993, p. 38–52). The main goal of business process reengineering is to define simple processes with few interfaces through creative reintegration and redesign of the core processes (Servatius 1994, p. 5 and p. 49). This also entails a change of the organisation. The current horizontal organisation is changed into a vertical organisation characterised by teamwork.

In order to be able to carry out these changes, the general management has to support these activities. According to business process reengineering, the change process consists of the following parts (Servatius 1994, p. 42):

2.3.1 Renewing

In this step the needs of the customers are analysed and new business areas are defined (Watermann 1987; Servatius 1988, p. 34ff; Prahalad and Hamel 1991). Especially the younger generations have different demands: for them, use is more valuable than ownership. Whereas in former days, people wanted to own a car, now it is important to have access to mobility when and where it is needed. Classical sale of cars is going down, whereas service offerings for car sharing are dramatically increasing. The automotive industry has to face this and change its business model. But not only "Generation Z" is driving this change. The older generation is also changing; never before in history were there so many older people living on this planet. In many cases, they are also wealthier and enjoy greater comfort. Offerings for comfort, cosiness and wellness are becoming more and more important and people are willing to spend more in these areas. Not to be forgotten the platform economy that changes the way offerings can be made to potential customers and the transparency the platforms offer them. The ease of information access and the possibility to compare offers also has dramatic influence on the customer expectations and experience. That is also the reason customers are not looking only for fulfilment of their demands, but also for the "wow" effect, which is provided by special, unique services customised especially for them. This step is to recognise all these changes to deliver a proper perspective of the current and future customers and their demand.

2.3.2 Relocating

In the next step, changes of the location and production methodology are to be defined (Servatius 1985, p. 286ff; Kröger 1994): This area refers to the emerging technologies such as the Internet of things (IoT), big data, artificial intelligence (AI) and machine learning (ML), but also augmented and virtual reality and robotics. These new technologies have become affordable in the last few years and therefore more use scenarios are now technically and economically feasible. These technologies are not only making automation possible, but also providing user-centric products and services for the cost of mass products. This enables the disruptive change of the production techniques and the offerings to customers. The production process sometimes even includes the customer as the "designer" of his "product". An example are clothes that can be designed by the customers.

Example
For example, the back of a jacket can have a slogan on it that is designed by the final customer. This unique jacket brings more "value" to the owner than just a designer jacket, as it is "unique". Nevertheless, the cost of production is the same, as the production process is fully automated.

2.3.3 Reengineering

The next step represents the core of business process reengineering, which includes the redesign of the core processes and the change of the company's organisational structure (Hammer and Champy 1993; Davenport 1993; Peters 1993): This subject will be addressed in detail in the following pages. It mainly concentrates on recombining single tasks into larger actions and the engagement of better-trained people who can solve problems or act on demands immediately.

2.3.4 Revitalising

The next step is to develop the knowledge of the employees (Argyris and Schon 1978; Servatius 1994, p. 251ff; Senge 1990; Argyris 1990): Especially when the use of new technology is planned, then the employees have to be trained in their use. Not all IT tools are so easy to use that there is no need for training. This step often receives less attention, since the budget is overdone in the former steps and the go live is approaching fast. But untrained people cannot use the systems properly and their acceptance of the new tools will be low. Also the results for the customers will be influenced by the proper training of the people.

2.3.5 Reframing

The last step is to realise the mental change by changing the subjective behaviour (Watzlawick et al. 1967/1974; Watzlawick et al. 1974/1988, p. 116 ff): When new services are offered and especially to create the "wow" effect, people have to leave their comfort zone, go new ways, use new tools and behave differently. All these changes of the mindset have to be supported by training in order to change consumers' perspectives properly. Only if this reframing of the perspective is done properly will this whole change be successful.

Example
An example is a training I did. We tried to teach the students the emerging technologies and how they can be used to generate client-specific products. At the final thesis describing how they will use this in their daily practice, a student stated that as a Real Estate Agent he cannot provide the "wow" effect and personalised services as this is connected with too much effort and does not pay off. This is not true. Ten minutes of social media research would have enabled the Real Estate Agent to address his potential client in a much more specific, targeted and purposeful way, by using information about his family situation, desires and "likes".

2.3.6 Steps of Business Process Reengineering

Business process reengineering itself consists of the following steps (Servatius 1994, p. 50):

1. Communication of the necessary changes
   The communication of the goals and areas of changes has to be done by the board of directors. In this step, the teams and the process owners have to be defined for each process. This step should give confidence to the middle management, trade union and employees. Change can often lead to fears about employment, which leads to opposition to change.
2. Identification of the core processes
   The core processes, which are important for the success of the company, have to be defined. The basis for the estimation of which core processes are important for success is the description of these processes at a high level of abstraction.
3. Selection of the core processes
   Core processes that have the highest need for change (not working properly, causing problems, not fulfilling customer needs, possibility to change processes): This step also includes the definition of more detailed goals for the selected processes regarding time, cost and quality.
4. Analysis to understand processes
   This step is based on workshops, interviews and observations. It is quite often supported by external consultants as they might bring in new ideas.
5. Collect ideas for redesign and optimisation
   This step is carried out together with the process team and internal/external process specialists to find new ways of carrying out processes.
6. Development of concept
   Based on the gathered knowledge and ideas, a concept for the optimisation of the core processes is defined. This concept includes the process steps, the organisation and the ICT support. In this step, the following principles have to be taken into account:
   - Relocation of decisions to working level
   - Definition of tasks per organisational unit in a way to reduce interfaces
   - Reduction of controls
   - Combination of organisational units
7. Coaching of process owner
   The last step is the coaching and training of the process owner and his team, so that they are capable of taking over the new tasks and responsibilities.
   All these steps should follow the core principles (Hammer and Champy 1993):
   - Follow the natural sequence of process steps
   - Definition of process variants (e.g. simple/difficult task)
   - Redesign of customer contacts
   - Introduction of a responsible person for all customer contacts to coordinate all tasks carried out for each customer
   - ICT to enable new solutions

The change process, based on the results of the business process reengineering, can be carried out in two different ways: either by a radical change of a few core processes (American attempt) (Hammer and Champy 1993; Johansson et al. 1993; Morris and Brandon 1994) or through a continuous improvement within the current structures following the example of Kaizen (Imai 1986) (Japanese attempt). The model exemplified by the American attempt leads to a lot of challenges with the employees who often oppose the changes. It also causes problems with the trade unions, as they fear that the changes cause the loss of jobs. The Japanese way often cannot reach the goals as changes happen very slowly and the final target can only be reached after a long period of time. Combining these two extremes leads to the European method of change management through business process reengineering. The European method makes changes step by step and in this way the whole company is changed and not only a few core processes. It also includes tasks to change the habits and the qualification of the employees (Frei et al. 1993). This European method of change management is also called evolutionary change management.

For process optimisation and change management in the area of core business, the methodology of business process reengineering is known and accepted. Business process reengineering provides a methodology for managing the change process. It can be used for every project within every industry reaching from production processes to office automation. Consultants and managers are well trained in this methodology. Therefore, internal or external support can be found easily. In business management, literature best practise examples can be found for several processes within different industries.

As defined above the methodology described here was mainly used to optimise the core processes. The last years and several use cases proved that the methodology can also be used for optimising Facility and Real Estate Management and service processes. To cover the specifics of this industry for several steps, the use of specific tools is suggested and even some steps were added.

The methodology of business process reengineering carries the risk to model the as-is status in strong detail. This procedure takes a long time. As the team members have to carry out their "normal work" beside the project, they become tired. As a result, when the as-is analysis is finished, they are not willing to support the next steps. As a solution to this problem, the research team combined the steps "Analysis to understand processes" and "Collect ideas for redesign and optimisation". This was done in an easy way. The process steps not being carried out properly or being missing at all were included in the as-is analysis, but they were marked with a red colour. This means that the starting points for improvement were already included in the as-is analysis. This change in methodology led to more encouragement of the team members as they could already see in the as-is analysis where changes and optimisation should take place. In some cases, the should-be structure was already developed.

This change in methodology made it easier to carry out the next step, "Development of concept". In this step the should-be situation has to be defined. As the process steps that were missing or not properly carried out are already included and marked "red" within the process charts, the starting point for the optimisation is already defined. As such, the time and effort needed to define the should-be situation are reduced dramatically.

The experience of the application of the methodology in RE/FM led to a new methodology consisting of the following steps:

2.4 Enlarged Business Process Reengineering Methodology

2.4.1 Define Strategy for FM and Goals of the Project; Prepare Project

The first step is a definition of the strategy of FM and the goals of the project based on the general strategy of the company. The value analysis is an efficient methodology to support this step. The value analysis can be used to optimise products and immaterial objects like processes and concepts. It was developed by General Electric at the end of the 1940s as a tool for cost reduction. Since 1962, it has also been used in Europe, with the goal of analysing and optimising the structures of functions under the aspect of value increase. Based on this idea, value analysis soon developed into a more powerful tool than a simple method for cost reduction. In this new form, it could be applied not only to the quick and effective generation of new concepts, but also to the improvement of existing ones (Lechner et al. 2001, p. 371 and especially Coenenberg 1997), 479 f). The first basic step of the value analysis, according to DIN 69910 and ÖNORM A 6750–6757, helps to carry out the preparation of the business reengineering project (◘ Table 2.1):

As mentioned in the standard the results of Step 1 make it possible to check the result of the project at the project end. Especially in the area of RE/FM, this step is very important, as the projects are long lasting. A new construction or refurbishment takes several years. In the meantime, the strategic goals of the company may change and the new construction may not be necessary any more. Therefore, a proper definition of not only the current situation but also the longer-lasting goals is important. As the core business is under permanent change and digitalisation speeds up the required adaptations, the necessary flexibility has to be included in the goals to ensure a proper result of the change project. To make sure the long-lasting developments are included, this step

◘ Table 2.1 Steps of the value analysis (table compiled by author)

Basic steps	Intermediate steps	Goals
Step 1 Prepare for value analysis	Intermediate step 1 Set up goals in rough outlines	The first step is a definition of the goals. This makes it possible to check the result of the project later. The details can be added later in the project. In the case of the FM projects, this step has to be carried out together with the Facility Manager and the board of directors.
	Intermediate step 2 Plan value analysis work	The next step is the creation of a project schedule (people, tasks, time, etc.). The required persons must be selected and teams must be formed. They must be informed about the personal resources they have to spend and the work they have to deliver for the project. This step is headed by the Facility Manager.

2

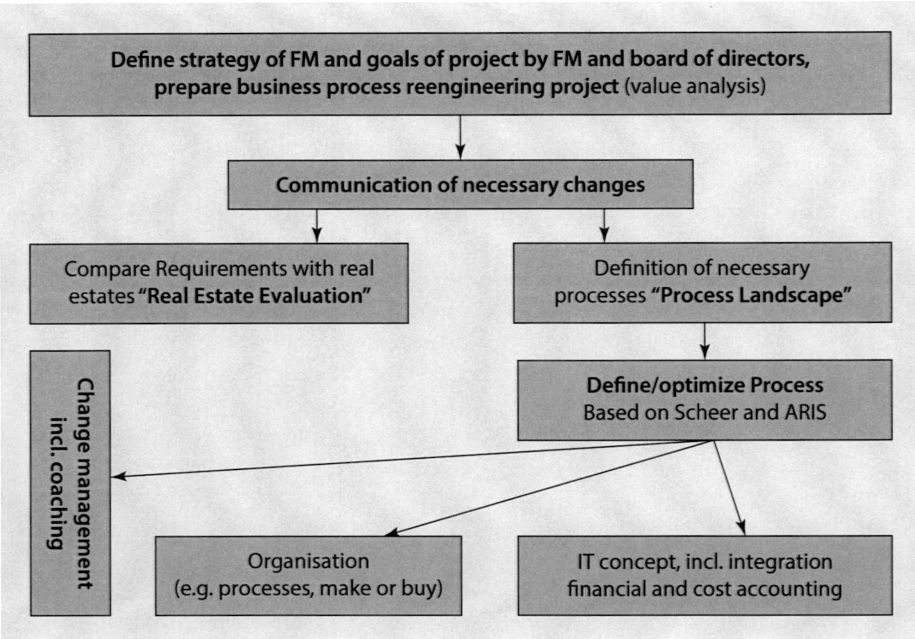

Fig. 2.6 Enlarged methodology of business process reengineering for optimising RE/FM. (Author's own figure)

has to be carried out together with the Facility Manager and the board of directors. In this step, the teams and the process owners also have to be defined. It also helps to prepare the next step, "communication", as all relevant persons are identified and the project schedule is defined (Fig. 2.6).

2.4.2 Communication of the Necessary Changes

The communication of the goals and area of changes has to be done by the board of directors. This step should give confidence to the middle management, trade union and the employees, who often oppose change due to their fears about employment. If this step is not carried out properly, there is the danger of rumours that may make the successful realisation of the project impossible.

Example

An example was a project where a new enterprise resource planning software was implemented. The consultant supporting the implementation had not done business in the FM industry but had perfect knowledge of the functionality of the ERP system. The company knew their processes in detail, but had no familiarity about the possibilities of the IT tool and how to map their demands to the tools. In addition to the aforementioned steps, the project should involve an optimisation of the current processes that should take place in the project. As the consultant did not know the specifics of the industry, he could not give input. The company itself was also not well-informed about the possibilities, for example, in the area of automation. So the managing director (MD) invited me to join in and provide advice regarding the best practise. However, he did not inform the other team members about my role in the project. So my first day was rather tough. None of the team members wanted to exchange with me. In the evening, I asked them to join me for a beer and asked them about their apparent retention. The project manager of the company started with very open words. "You are here to take over my job!" "No" was my answer. "I am a professor at the university and I want to stay there". Then the project manager of the consultant company said: "Then you're going for my job!" Again I stated that I represent a university which is not carrying out this type of job. I told them that I was just there to give some best practise examples of optimisation of FM processes with this ERP software and to provide several feasible implementation scenarios that we had studied beforehand. Luckily, because of the open words we only lost 1 day. In the other project, it was impossible to reach the desired goal as rumours of the goal of the project influenced respondents' answers in such a manner that a successful project was no longer possible.

2.4.3 Real Estate Evaluation to Compare Requirements with Existing Real Estate

The current strategic requirements ask for more than space. New ways of working require an inter-coordinated mix of room climate, noise reduction, flexible furniture settings, etc. and several concerted service offerings. Not all current buildings can provide this. So the existing real estate portfolio has to be analysed to determine if it can fulfil the requirements and accordingly refurbished, updated or even exchanged.

Example

An example was the strategic goal of a hospital association to established hospitals with special focus instead of general hospitals. They decided to have one focused on accidents and sport injuries. As the association wanted a good coverage, they decided on several spots in large cities as well as some in the countryside. One existing hospital in the countryside was selected. The plan was to refurbish it so that it could cover the new services. But this type of clinic needs special equipment like magnetic resonance tomography and computer tomography. This equipment requires approximately as much energy as a medium-sized village. But the existing hospital only had a "normal" power supply and the utility provider was not prepared to supply the required capacity. In addition, this type of equipment is also very heavy. Therefore, it has specific requirements concerning bearing capacity to the floor it is put on. Also these requirements were not supported by the existing hospital and lead to enormous additional costs. If these requirements were already considered in the selection of the place, the costs could have been reduced dramatically.

2.4.4 Definition of the Necessary Processes/Process Landscape

In this step, the necessary FM processes have to be defined. Therefore, the goals have to be analysed to derive the processes. The landscape has to safeguard that all aspects of the strategic goals of the company relating to Real Estate and Facility Management are covered. Therefore, in the landscape all relevant processes have to exist.

Example

To give a practical example: If a company has the strategic goal of reducing their energy consumption by 10% in the next year, there has to be a process to make sure that the FM department knows who is using how much energy and where. The landscape also has to make sure that one or several processes cover the development and implementation of measurements for the reductions and the controlling of the results. In one case, for example, the board of directors had as strategic goal to be 100% compliant with all laws and standards. These compliance goals asked not only for well-designed preventive maintenance and inspection processes, but also for a process of ensuring that all changes in relevant laws and regulations led to an update of the maintenance and inspection routines and scheduling. The basis for this in-depth analysis and optimisation is the definition of more detailed goals for each process regarding time, cost and quality and the descriptions of the processes at a high level of abstraction.

2.4.5 Define Optimised Processes

Based on the gathered knowledge and ideas, a concept for the optimised processes is derived. This step uses workshops, interviews and observations. The internal team is quite often supported by external consultants, as they can bring in new ideas and question existing routines. The ARIS model is a well-known modelling methodology that can be used for this step. It consists of four "views" which describe the following elements (Scheer 1994):

1. **Process view**: This part of the model supports the description of processes. The description can be on a very abstract level using flow charts or on a very detailed level using event-driven process chains (EPC).
2. **Data view**: This part supports the description of the required data structure. The description is mainly done by entity relationship diagrams (ER diagrams) showing the required entities like building, floor and room and the relations between them.
3. **Organisation view**: This part describes the organisational structure. The organisational units and their structure roles are defined. A role represents employees carrying out similar tasks to one another.
4. **Control view**: This view brings together the elements of the views described above, showing the relations between them. That means it describes the flow of process steps, describes which process step is carried out by which organisational unit (role) and defines which step is supported by which ICT (information and communication technology) tool.

The result of this step is the control view that includes the process steps, the roles carrying out the different steps, the new organisation and the ICT support. The outcomes of this concept are also the required changes in organisation (new organisation structure) and ICT (e.g. new tools, change of existing tools, the new ICT landscape and integration of tools). The relevant steps are described in more detail in the following subchapter.

2.4.6 Change Management for Organisation and Coaching of Process Owner

According to the requirements of the concept, the organisation has to be changed. New roles have to be defined and task description have to be set up, the last step is the coaching and training of the process owner and his team, so that they are capable of taking over the new tasks and responsibilities.

2.4.7 ICT Implementation

According to the requirements of the concept, the new ICT landscape must be implemented and integrated. An overview of the existing tools and emerging technologies to support the new processes and the activities is given in the next chapter.

Most of the companies ask at the end of the process if the new concept really pays off – in other words, whether all the changes are delivering the required effects. If one of the goals is cost reduction, activity-based costing is a proper approach to calculate savings.

Definition

Activity-based costing is an approach to solve problems of traditional cost management systems. It allows linking costs to activities. So with the help of activity-based costing, it is possible to allocate costs to products and services. Activity-based costing often identifies cost drivers in a process, thereby finding ways to reduce the costs or to charge more for costly processes (Schumann 1992).

With activity-based costing, it is possible to identify costs of an FM process. First of all, the time needed to carry out each step of the process has to be identified. Then for each step, it is necessary to determine which role (type of employee) carries it out and how often the step is carried out. In the next step, the time of all process steps being carried out by a specific function is summarised. By multiplying the results with the wage per hour of the function, the total cost for each function to support the process can be calculated. Summing up the costs of all functions results in the costs for the process. In addition, all investments for the change management project, the optimisation of existing IT and the cost of new tools and potential outsourcing costs have to be included. By comparing the result of the as-is process with the figure of the should-be process, the decrease of cost can be calculated.

2.5 Practice Example of Business Process Reengineering

In the example described in detail in part 2.6, the process "failure handling" is described before and after the introduction of Facility Management. By comparing the processes, it is possible to calculate time and cost savings and as a result to make conclusions on the profitability of the optimisation. According to the new methodology, the following steps were carried out:

Example

Several interviews with the Facility Manager and the board of directors were conducted in order to define the Facility Management strategy as well as the goals of the project. The main goals in the project were to reduce costs by 10% and to increase customer satisfaction rating by 0.5 grades (satisfaction was evaluated on a scale from 1 through 5, and at the moment it is graded as 2.3). In the second step, the necessary changes were announced by the management. After this the process, the landscape was defined. It included the process "customer order and trouble treatment". Next, the existing documentation was analysed. The main problem of the existing version was that several different departments and persons were responsible for customer orders and trouble treatment. There was no common help desk collecting all of the customer orders and problems. Steps which often caused problems were then marked with a red-coloured shadow.

Then all optimised FM processes were defined in workshops with the FM team and external consultants. Not only the management, but also the employees carrying out the operational work were included. The goal of this step was to gain detailed information and include the people who do the job and therefore know it thebest. In addition, by including them, the acceptance of the designed solution increases, since it is a result derived together with the team. To identify the activities of the different roles, each process step was marked with the colour of the responsible role. The same colours were also used in the below figure (time and cost savings) to identify the roles there. This leads to the optimised process shown in the diagram "should-be". In contrast to the as-is status, there is one customer centre and an IT-based ticket system. In this way, the allocation of problem to responsible personnel can be handled more easily. In addition, the work of the internal service team is now done by an external company based on a value contract.

Based on this first optimisation concept, the time and cost savings were modelled in a diagram to show the advantages of the new process within Facility Management (see figure below). The time calculation is placed in the right bottom corner of each step in the process modelling. This calculation is based on how many days per year and how many times per day the process takes place. This figure is multiplied with the time in

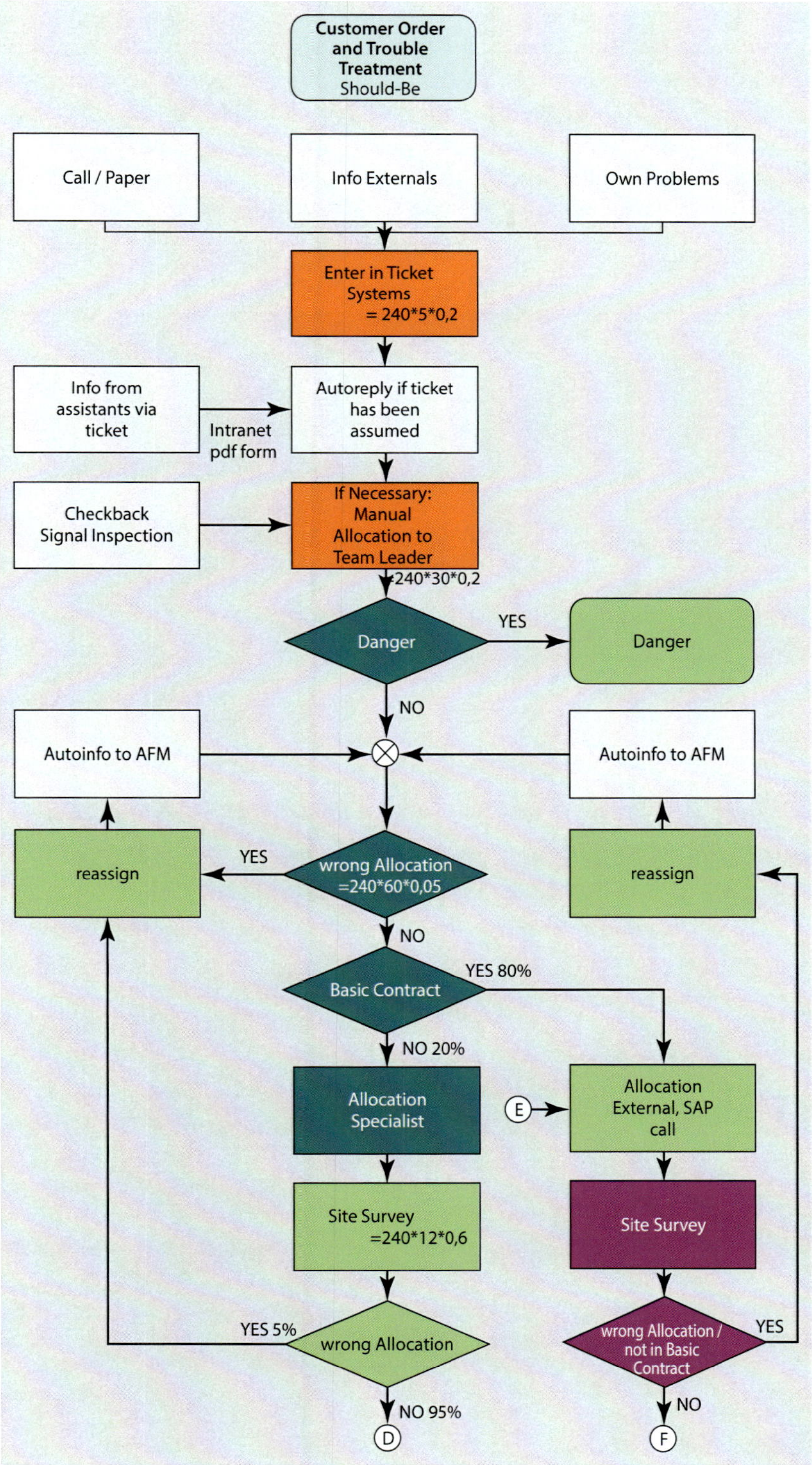
Customer Order and Trouble Treatment Should-Be
Call / Paper
Info Externals
Own Problems
Enter in Ticket Systems = 240*5*0,2
Info from assistants via ticket
Intranet pdf form
Autoreply if ticket has been assumed
Checkback Signal Inspection
If Necessary: Manual Allocation to Team Leader
240*30*0,2
Danger
YES
Danger
NO
Autoinfo to AFM
Autoinfo to AFM
reassign
YES
wrong Allocation =240*60*0,05
reassign
NO
Basic Contract
YES 80%
NO 20%
Allocation Specialist
E
Allocation External, SAP call
Site Survey =240*12*0,6
Site Survey
YES 5%
wrong Allocation
wrong Allocation / not in Basic Contract
YES
NO 95%
NO
D
F

hours needed to carry out the step. In case of a decision, the value is split proportionally to the defined probability that this branch is carried out. Potential loops within the process flow are already included in the calculation. The values of the multiplication are listed in the above figure. In the next step, the figures are summarised, which are also included in the above figure leading to the time needed for each role to carry out that process. After multiplying the hours with the costs per hour, the total costs per role are shown. Then the values are summed up to the total costs for each of the process scenarios.

	Facility Manager	Manager Cleaning	Manager Technic	Technician	Manager Security	Security	External	Total
Process As-Is								
Inspection	50		1105	2232				
Preventive Maintance	80		2124	2320				
Cleaning	35	850						
Security	80				830	4320		
Catering	60							
Failure Handling	70		1471	1764			180	
Time (hours)	375	850	4700	6316	830	4320	180	**17571**
Vague per hour	100	70	80	50	70	30	30	
Costs (euro)	37500	59500	376000	315800	58100	129600	5400	**981900**
Process Should-Be								
Inspection	35		286	1430				
Maintance	54		367	1370				
Cleaning	23	621						
Security	34				631	2997		
Catering	29							
failure handling	24		194	643			68	
Time (hours)	199	621	847	3443	631	2997	68	**7081**
Vague per hour	100	70	80	50	70	30	30	
Costs (euro)	19900	43470	67760	172150	44170	89910	2040	**439400**

Time and cost savings

As can be seen in the diagram, this optimisation leads to an internal cost reduction from €981.900 (sum of the total costs) to €439.400. This means a saving of € 542.500 or 55%. These savings are the result of a more automated service feedback and less work for the high rated area manager. Additionally, the cost for the internal service man is cancelled. But there was an increase of costs due to the external value contract. This leads by a part of €356,000 for the external service to a total cost reduction of 19%.

Therefore, the decision was made to implement the new process. For this step, change management was applied.

2.5.1 Modelling of Processes

This chapter describes the different steps to define a specific process in detail. But let us start by defining what a process in general is.

Definition

EN15221–5 gives the following definition: "a process is a set of interrelated or interacting activities, which transforms inputs into outputs" (EN ISSO 9000 2015). That means, processes are sets of activities, with a specific order of these activities (workflow), a starting point and endpoint and clearly defined inputs and required outputs.

They always convert the same inputs into the same outputs. A second characteristic is that they are executed frequently. It makes almost no sense to define a process when it is carried out once a year or even less frequently, unless this process is something like disaster management. Processes have to be set up for the specific circumstances and requirements of an organisation. All processes together define the process landscape.

The processes itself consists of several of the following two elements:

» 1. "Activities: the tasks that are needed to complete deliverables
2. Sub-process: a discrete process operating within the bounds of other broader processes. Sub-processes are parts of a workflow. Sub-processes are used if specific steps are carried out in different processes or to describe steps in more detail. Sub-processes are often used to give a workflow greater transparency". (EN 15221-5 2018)

Example

A common example of a subprocess is the procurement process. The steps necessary to procure items and services are used in several other processes. When a "refurbishment" is carried out, services and items have to be procured, including painting, carpeting and also new furniture. Additionally, the process of "maintenance" requires the procurement either of spare parts like filters or of the maintenance services themselves, if they are carried out by external companies.

The use of subprocesses helps to improve processes in two ways:

1. Several process sequences are used in several areas. As shown in the examples above, the steps of procurement are necessary in the processes of "new construction" and "refurbishment", as well as in the process of "maintenance". Instead of adding to all these processes the different activities "to procure items", a subprocess can be defined and referenced wherever it is needed. This makes the process workflows shorter and easier to be read and understood.
2. A second advantage is that if the subprocess of "procurement" has to be changed, for example, by adding an additional release – only the subprocess has to be adopted, and then all references are updated automatically. This reduces the efforts of changes dramatically and also the possibility of errors (EN 15221-5 2018).

But what do we have to define when we want to describe a process? EN 15221–5 gives the following picture:

(a) Trigger: FM processes are triggered by changes on every level of the organisation (requests for change by end user, customers and clients). In addition, the outputs of processes may also trigger the start of other processes. A process has a specific acknowledged starting point (with inputs) and a definite end point (outputs).

(b) Input/output: A process consists of inputs and process activities and creates outputs. Inputs into the FM processes are tangible assets, resources, data/information and conditions.
The output could be a delivered Facility Service and a standardised facility product, but, for example, also a negotiated contract, a completed invoice or a final decision (which then may be an input for another process). The outcome of a process is the satisfaction of requirements. Therefore, outputs from FM processes are facilities, decisions, proposals, data/information and results.

(c) Process workflow: A process is a set of activities. Therefore, a process is described as the workflow of the activities carried out, checking the quality, supervision of the process (including the response to defaults) and evaluation of the quality of the outputs.

(d) Roles: The activities are carried out in execution of identified responsibilities. A role represents a person with specific competences, knowledge and skills.

(e) FM processes are linked to the demand of the organisation.

(f) Demands may arise at the strategic, tactical and operational level.

(g) The demands that are identified are transformed into FM requirements.

(h) FM processes influence the effectiveness of the primary processes.

(i) Processes should be continuously improved (EN 15221-5 2018).

The following figures give a graphical expression of these different objects (◘ Fig. 2.7):

According to EN15221–5, the following are process differentiation and process types (◘ Fig. 2.8):

> "Processes can be differentiated by levels, runtime, repetition, exceptions, ranges, extent of structuring and parallel working. The structure of the processes is shown in process maps. The process levels are operational, tactical or strategic level and horizontal or vertical levels.

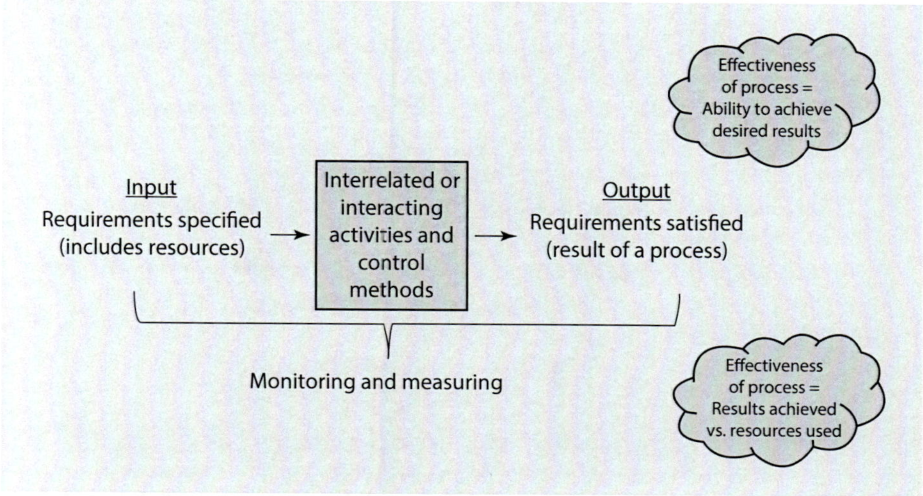

Fig. 2.7 Generic process EN 15221–5. (Based on EN 15221-5 2018, p. 10)

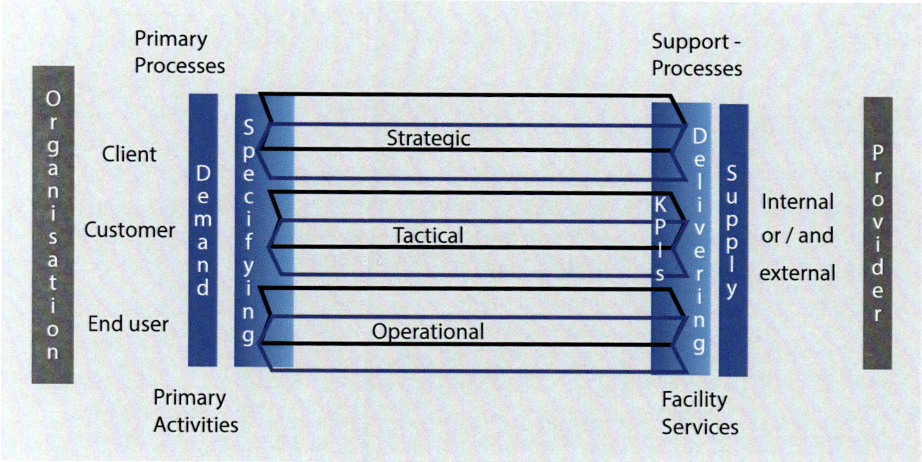

Fig. 2.8 Relationship of FM processes to the Facility Management model. (EN 15221-5 2018, p. 15)

Horizontal processes run in a specific level of FM (operational, tactical and strategic) and therefore can be mapped easily to these levels. These horizontal processes link the demand with the supply side and lead to the fulfilment of the requirements of the primary processes.

Vertical processes run in-between the levels and connect these levels with each other, these vertical processes deal mainly with the changes in the organisation and therefore consist of communication back and forth (decisions, trends and developments) and have to achieve the targets to link the FM organisation with the changes of the primary processes as well as to give feedback to the decision making levels from the FM perspective" (EN 15221-5 2018).

2

> "Process runtimes can be divided into short, medium and long-term processes. Short-term processes are executed within minutes or hours, some within days. Long-term processes are executed within weeks or even months.
>
> Repetitive processes are categorized into highly repetitive processes (e.g. cleaning, security), which are executed daily, or one off processes, which are executed only once during a long period of time (e.g. construction of new buildings).
>
> Process exceptions indicate the level of fulfilment of the set of activities as planned. Exceptional processes cannot be planned accordingly.
>
> Process range describes the extent of the impact of a process, and indicates the influence of the process within an organisation or even beyond it". (EN 15221-5 2018, p. 14)

2.6 Definition/Optimisation of a Process: Practical Example

2.6.1 The Goal

What are now the relevant process characteristics that we have to define when we want to define or optimise a process? The first step is to define the goal of the process and its relation to customer needs. Let us take the example "failure handling". A "goal" can be defined as follows:

Definition

"Goal is the cost optimised correction of the failure according to the SLA agreed with the customer to fulfil his needs. In addition measurements are to be taken to reduce the possibility and impact of the failure in the future to secure the customer satisfaction and requirements."

As there are only few formal criteria to evaluate a process workflow, it is important to define the goal of the process in the first step to ensure that the final process really secures the delivery of this goal. Very often, when I asked my students to draft failure handling processes, my students asked for cost optimisation and fast repair at the same time, which is a trade-off. The faster the problem has to be fixed, the more it costs.

Example

For example, if a central service team were to fix a failure of an elevator, there are several ways to reduce the time until the failure is corrected and the person is released. One could either place several teams across the area of engagement or increase the number of teams. But all these measurements would increase the costs. If the elevator is in a residential building, the legal time limit for the liberation action has to be respected. This is the relevant service level (SL) defined in the service-level agreement (SLA). This SL defines the relevant resources and therefore the cost.

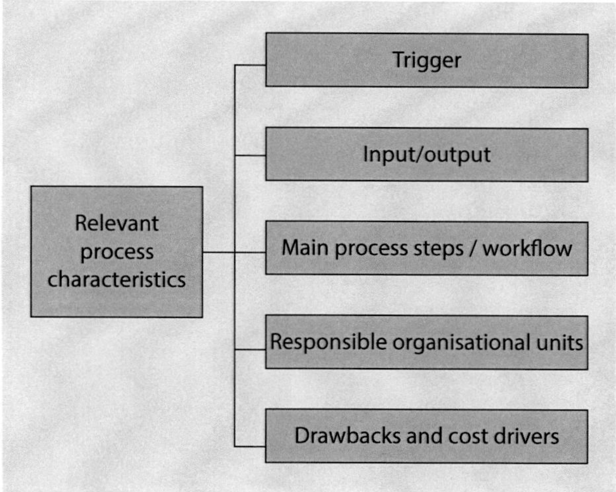

Fig. 2.9 Characteristics of processes. (Author's own figure)

After this step, the other relevant process characteristics defined from the listing of EN15221–5 and listed in Fig. 2.9 have to be specified.

2.6.2 Trigger

The trigger starts the process. The definition of the trigger is very important, as it provides the interface for all stakeholders of the process. What do I mean by this? Let us take the example of a failure handling process. The trigger can be an email, a message from the building automation system or a telephone call. Only if the person recognising the failure knows the proper trigger can he or she can start the process properly.

The trigger has to be selected carefully.

Example

Imagine you are a property management company. Ideally, you would like to have an email or a web formula that sends you a report as trigger. This would work perfectly if your tenants have web access and are used to this technology; however, if this is not the case, these triggers cannot be employed, as your tenants will not be satisfied. The triggers mentioned above would not work at all if you are a web service provider and your Internet access is not working whatsoever. Then your clients cannot send you an email or a report and you will not learn that your services are not available. The other extreme is that your tenants can hand over failure notices to all of your employees, does not matter where and when. This is very convenient for your tenants, but how can you make sure that all notices are delivered to the relevant teams to take care about the failure? In addition, take into consideration that your tenants may deliver some notices to service companies you hired for solving problems. These employees have no information regarding to whom they should deliver the information.

In addition to human reporting problems, a trigger can also be the condition of a piece of equipment or the time it has been used (e.g. hours of employment). In this case, the building automation system or sensors may trigger the process. These examples show that the proper definition of the trigger is essential. By defining the trigger, you determine the channels and interfaces you will use in the future for a proper cooperation.

2.6.3 Inputs

The next important characteristic is the required inputs. In FM these inputs can be "tangible assets (equipment, desks, buildings, etc.), resources (manpower, energy, space and data/information) as well as certain conditions (status of operation, cleanliness etc.)". As an example, the technical equipment of a building is the input for the operations and maintenance processes, the data and even results of former maintenance activities are more inputs to the maintenance process. The required resources are the necessary manpower; the handling materials, which are needed; and the energy for the technical equipment. Conditions can be summarised as the required framework, such as the timeframe in which a maintenance task can be executed, the operating status or age of the equipment, which also impacts the setup of a maintenance plan and its implementation (EN 15221-5 2018).

2.6.4 Outputs

> "Outputs are usable facilities (clean desks, maintained equipment, set up of office devices), final decisions (proposed maintenance strategy) proposals (next steps, triggering of alternative tasks), data (equipment data, materials, consumables), information (reports on energy consumption, KPIs), and results (new set up of desks after relocation) conditions (state of safety and security, operational state of technical equipment) and also supplied facility services and standardised facility products" (EN 15221-5 2018).

2.6.4.1 Process Flow Chart

For the majority of FM and FS process optimisation projects, the processes can be described by using flow diagrams. This method is easy to apply. Other methods like modelling with event-driven process chains (EPC) or even unified modelling language can show more information or even be the basis for automatic generation of program code, but need more training to be applied properly. The flow diagrams consist of five elements shown in the figure below.

Activities, also called process steps, are represented by rectangles. The text in the rectangle describes the activity carried out. As a verb describes best an activity, the text should include a verb. (In the case "analyse the failure", the verb "analyse" best describes this activity.)

Arrows connect the process steps and point out the direction between the steps (■ Fig. 2.10).

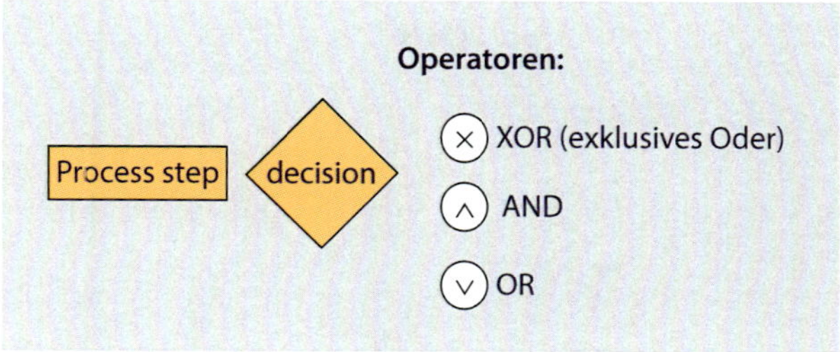

Fig. 2.10 Elements of workflows. (Author's own figure)

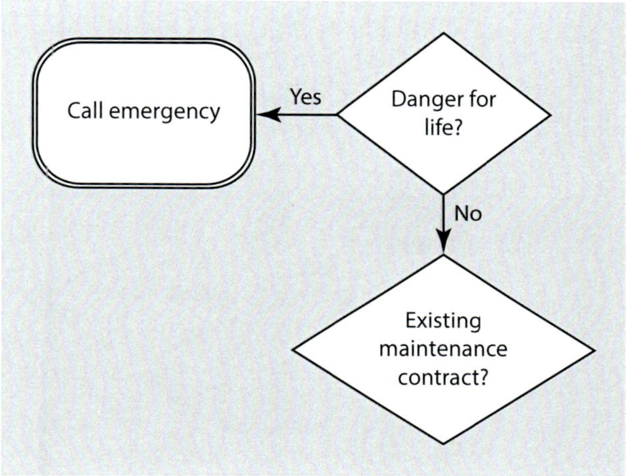

Fig. 2.11 Example for decisions workflow. (Author's own figure)

The next elements are decisions. A rhomb is the symbol for a decision. The decision has at least two outgoing arrows. Above the arrow lines, the condition in which these arrows are selected/used are written. In the example "danger for life", there are two possible conditions: There is danger for life or there is not. In the case that there is a danger for life, the responsible person should make an emergency call. Otherwise, the process goes on with the next step: The decision whether a maintenance contract exists (Fig. 2.11).

The graphic above shows also a subprocess element. The "call emergency" symbol represents a subprocess. It is the rectangle with round corners. The subprocess is defined in an additional flow diagram.

The last elements used to describe workflows are "operators". They start or end a junction. The most important operators are:

1. XOR
   - As starting point: Either one or the other path is used. But only one can be used.
   - As endpoint: One of the path have to be completed that the next step can be carried out.
2. OR
   - As starting point: Either one or the other path is used. In contrast to XOR it is possible for more than one path to be used.
   - As endpoint: One of the paths has to be completed so that the next step can be carried out.

2

3. And
   - As starting point: All paths have to be used.
   - As endpoint: All paths have to be completed that the next step can be carried out.

A typical process flow of a failure handling process is shown in the next figure (◘ Fig. 2.12).

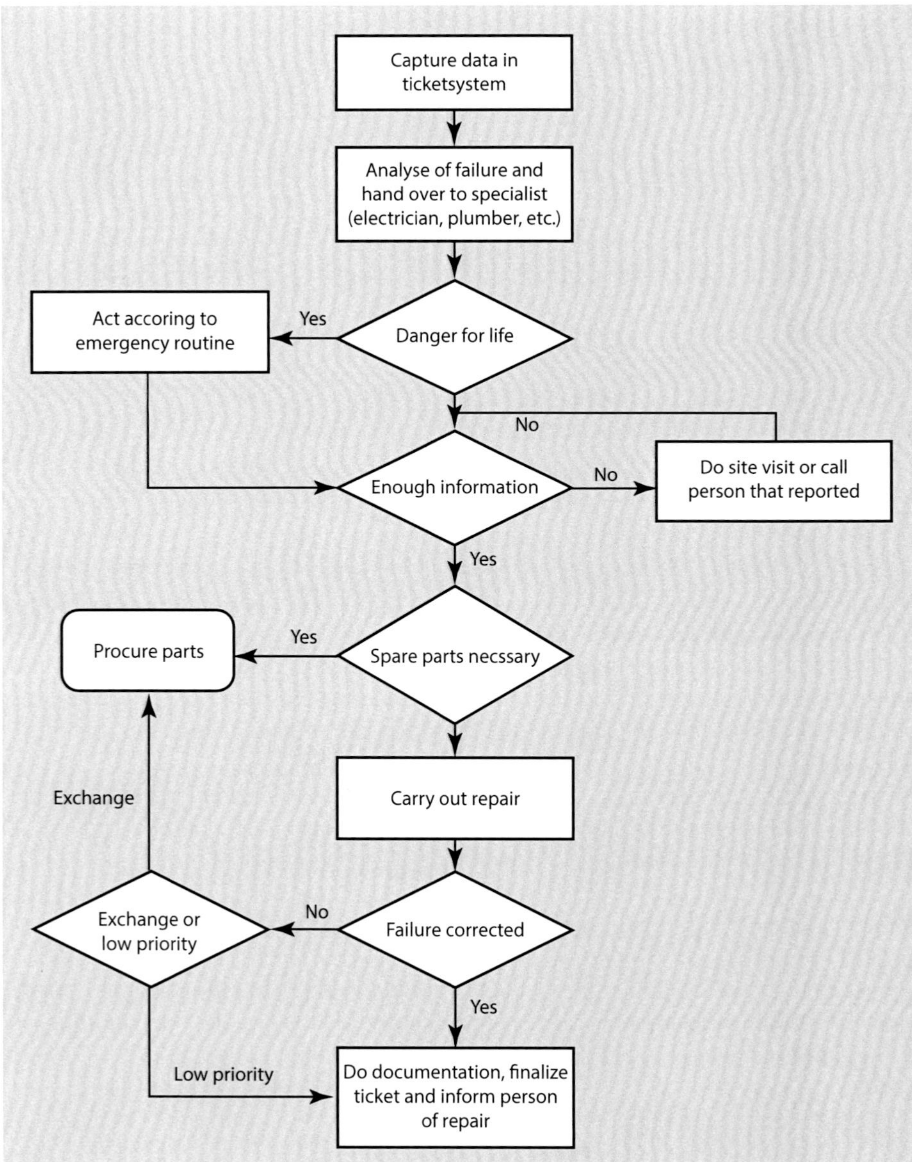

◘ **Fig. 2.12** Failure handling workflow diagram. (Author's own figure)

2.6.5 Role

Definition

"Process activities are actions performed by specific actors, usually persons, in the planned order to reach the target outcome" (EN 15221-5 2011, p. 12).

» These actors are categorised according to roles. A role characterises specific knowledge, competencies, capabilities and responsibilities of persons. Roles can be "call centre agent", "plumber", or "electrician". A person can have the knowledge of one or several roles according to his education and training. "The competency of persons has also a major input on the efficiency and effectiveness of a workflow, e.g. a qualified person may reach the target in terms of the quality level, but only the competent person will do it in an efficient and effective manner.

» In order to start the logical set of activities, the roles of the involved people have to be clear, as well as their capacities and their competences. It is evident, that a person will have to decide in which tasks he/she will be working with which capacity" (EN 15221-5 2011, p. 12).

The relevant roles in our example are:
- Call centre agent
- Scheduler
- Craftsman (like electrician, plumber, carpenter)
- Procurement

Normally the notation of the responsible role for each activity is an ellipse beside the process step. As this makes the diagram rather large, in my daily practise I use colours instead of the ellipse. This means each role is connected with a specific colour that represents this role. In our example, the roles are linked to the colours as listed below:
- Call centre agent: yellow
- Scheduler: green
- Craftsman (like electrician, plumber, carpenter): blue
- Procurement: red

The workflow including the responsible roles is shown in the next figure (◘ Fig. 2.13).

This methodology has proved its usability and efficiency in the many case studies carried out. Nevertheless, the appliance is still very time consuming.

Example

Therefore, the examples in EN15221–5 can be used as more detailed starting point. "The guidance describes Facility Management processes including organisational processes, management and performance review processes and the processes for negotiating service levels and managing performance in service delivery" (EN 15221-5 2011, p. 16). EN15221–5 names several examples of processes clustered into the strategic, tactical and operational level.

2

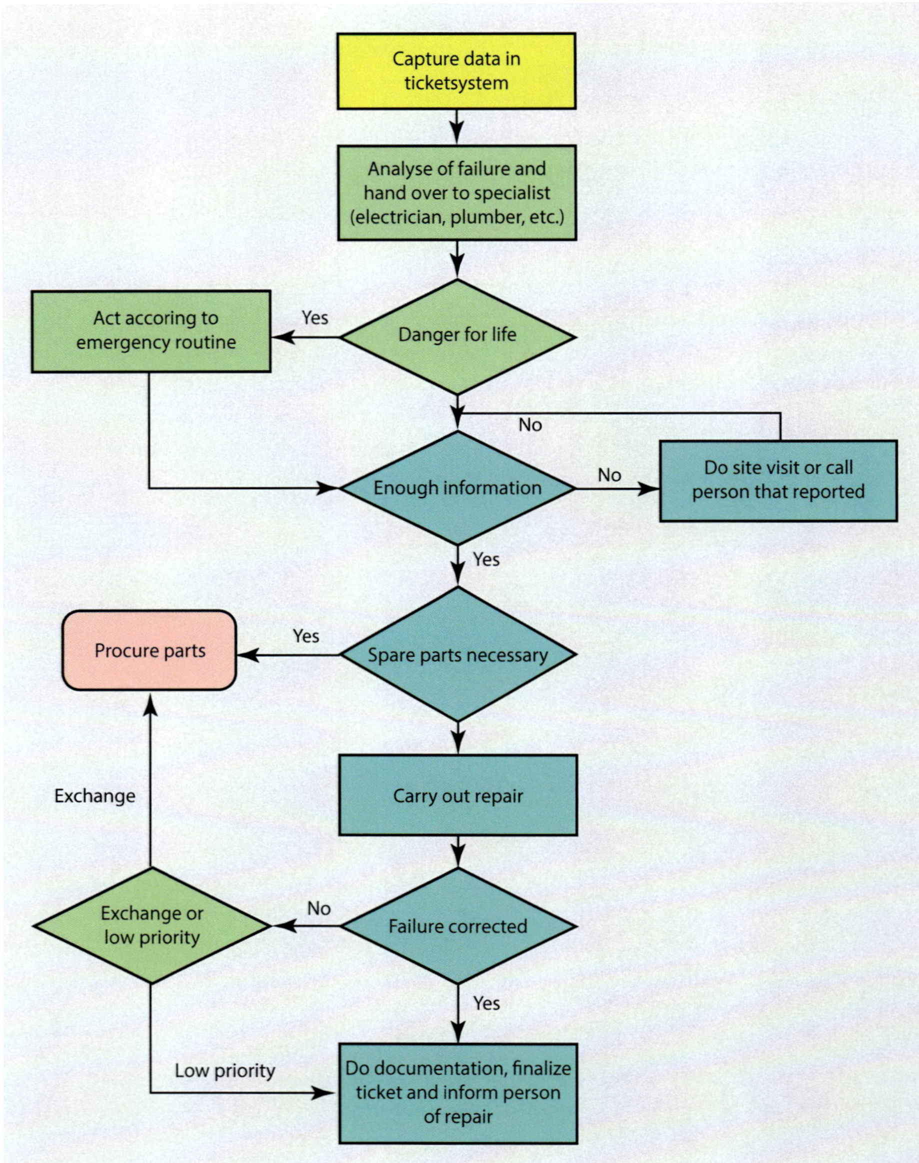

Fig. 2.13 Failure handling workflow diagram incl. roles. (Author's own figure)

Examples of strategic processes are shown in the next graphic (Figs. 2.14 and 2.15).

In addition to the overview of the processes, EN15221–5 also gives more details on some of the processes. Examples of these details are shown in the previous graphic. Tactical and operational processes and further details are also listed there (see Figs. 2.16 and 2.17).

These overviews can be a good starting point for the development of FM processes within your own company.

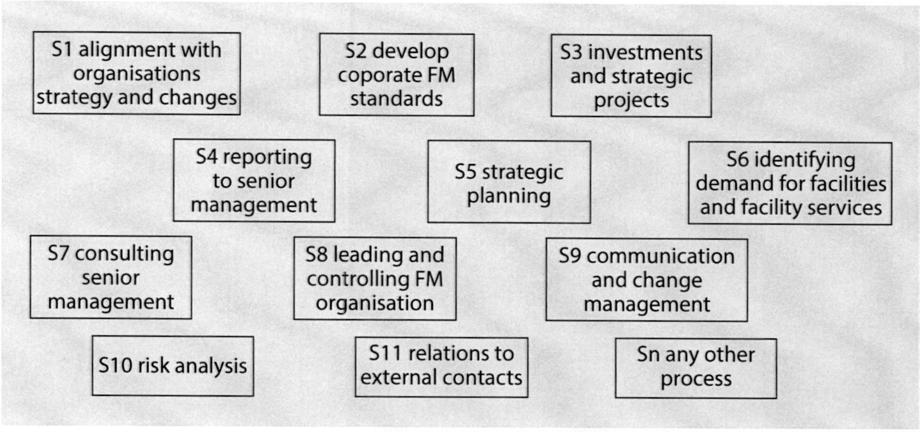

Fig. 2.14 Examples of strategic processes according to EN15221–5. (Based on EN 15221-5 2018, p. 17)

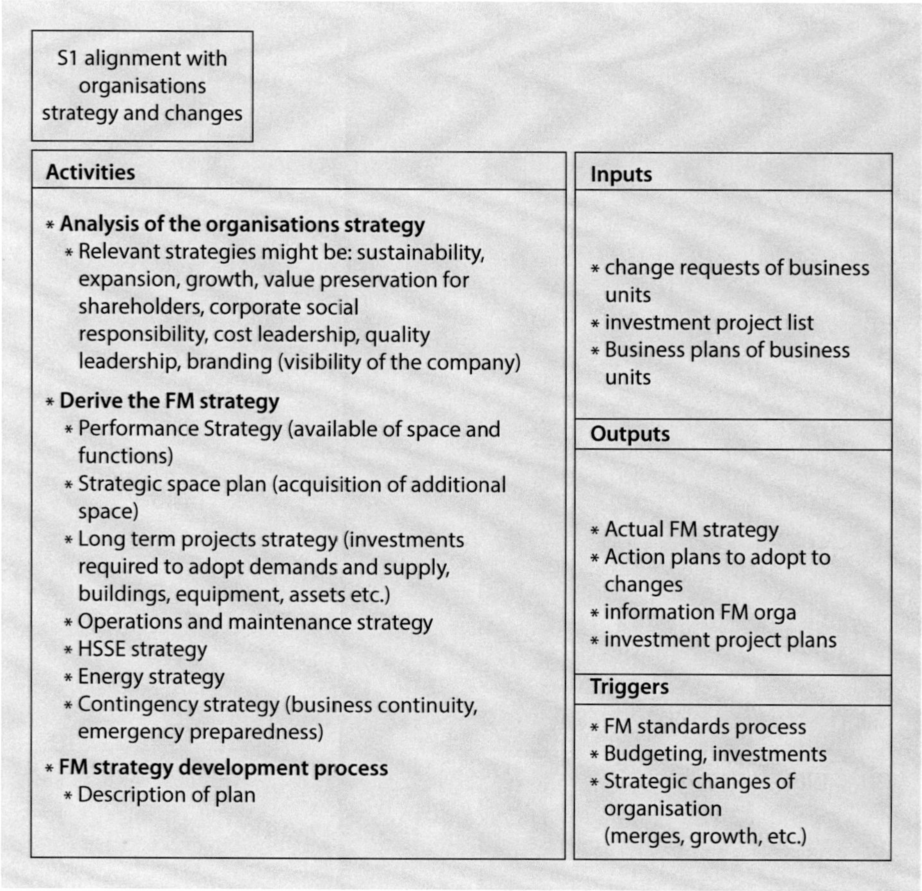

Fig. 2.15 Further details of processes provided by the EN15221–5. (Based on EN 15221-5 2018, p. 17)

2

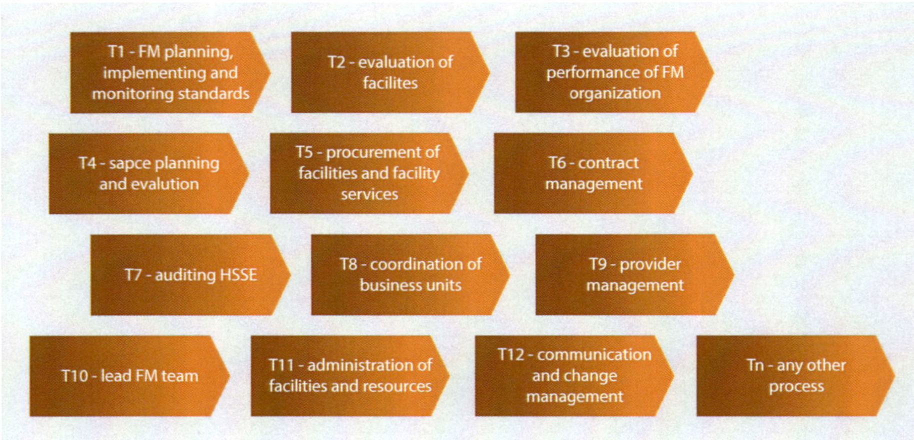

Fig. 2.16 Tactical processes according to EN15221–5. (Based on EN 15221-5 2018, p. 23)

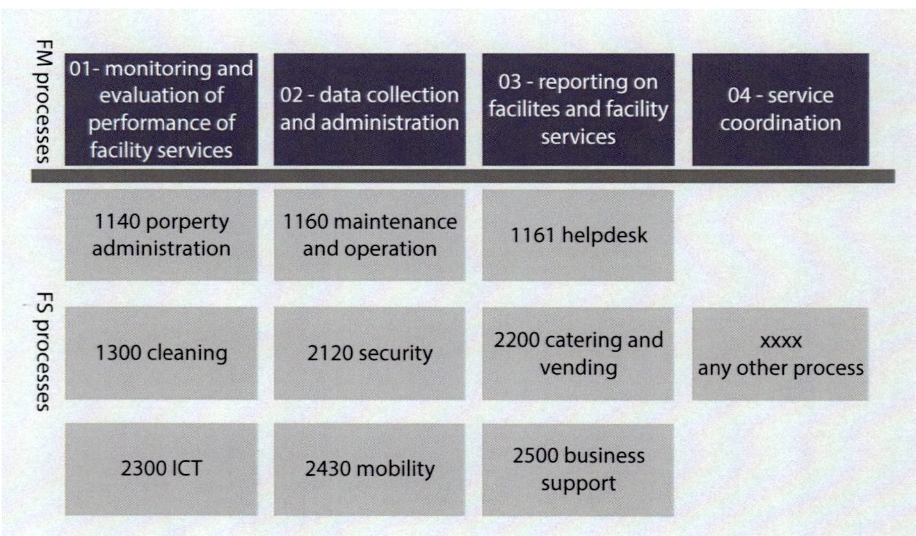

Fig. 2.17 Examples of tactical and operational processes according to EN15221–5. (Based on EN 15221-5 2018, p. 31)

2.7 Conclusion

The chapter gave you three major inputs:

1. What are the different models of an organisation structure that exist and what are the pros and cons of the different models?
2. Which methodology can I use to optimise the FM/RE organisation? What steps do I have to carry out to guarantee a successful change?

3. How is the optimisation of an individual process done? How is this optimisation linked to the roles (type of employees) in carrying out the steps, the organisation structure and the future IT support?

Therefore, this chapter provides you with all the toolsets necessary to optimise the FM organisation and define the required skillset of the employees and the requirements of the needed IT support.

In the next chapter the different IT tools, their general functionality and the pros and cons of their usage are described in more detail.

Review Questions

1. What different models of organisation structure did you learn? What are their pros and cons?
2. Describe the steps of business process reengineering.
3. Describe the possible areas and steps to "reframe" your mindset during the optimisation process.
4. Describe the steps of a process optimisation. What additional data is necessary to define processes properly?

References

Argyris, C. (1990). *Overcoming organizational defenses – Faciliating organizational learning*. Boston: Allyn and Bacon.

Argyris, C., & Schon, D. A. (1978). *Organizational learning – A theory of action perspective*. Reading: Addison-Wesley.

Arnowitz, S., De Smet, A., & McGinty, D. (2015). *Getting organizational redesign right*. London: McKinsey Quarterly.

Business dictionary. (n.d.). http://www.businessdictionary.com/definition/line-and-staff-management.html. Accessed 2019.

Business dictionary. (n.d.). http://www.businessdictionary.com/definition/organizational-structure.html. Accessed 2019.

Coenenberg, A. D. (1997). *Kostenrechnung und Kostenanalyse* (3rd ed.). Landsberg, Germany: Verl. Moderne Industrie.

Davenport, T. H. (1993). *Process innovation – Reengineering work through information technology*. Boston: Harvard Business Press.

EN 15221-1. (2006). Facility management. Terms and definition, Austrian Standards.

EN 15221-5. (2011). *Guidance on Facility Management processes,* Austrian Standards.

EN 15221-5. (2018). *Guidance on Facility Management processes,* Austiran Standards.

EN ISSO 9000. (2015). Quality management systems – Fundamentals and vocabulary, Austrian Standards.

Frei, F., Hugentobler, M., Alioth, A., Duell, W., & Ruch, L. (1993). *Die kompetente Organisation – Qualifizierende Arbeitsgestaltung: Die europäische Alternative*. Zü-rich/Stuttgart, Germany: Verlag der Fachvereine Zürich, Schäffer/Poeschel Verlag Stuttgart.

Gareth, M. (1986). *Images of organization*. Beverly Hills, USA: SAGE Publications.

Hammer, M., & Champy, J. (1993). *Reengineering the corporation- A manifesto for business revolution*. New York: HarperBusiness.

Imai, M. (1986). *Kaizen – The key to Japan's competitive success*. New York: Random House Business Division.

Johansson, H. J., McHug, P., Pendlebury, A. J., & Wheeler, W. A. (1993). *Business process reengineering – Breakpoint strategies for market dominance*. New York: Wiley.

2

Kiechel, W. (1993). How we will work in the year 2000. *Fortune, May 17,* 38–52.

Kröger, F. (1994). *Duale Restrukturierung – Wettbewerbsfähigkeit durch west-östliche Arbeitsteilung.* Stuttgart, Germany: Schäffer-Poeschel.

Lechner, K., Egger, A., & Schauer, R. (2001). *Einführung in die Allgemeine Betriebswirtschaftslehre.* Vienna, Austria: Linde.

Morris, D., & Brandon, J. (1994). *Revolution im Unternehmen – Reengineering für die Zukunft.* Landsberg, Germany: Verlag Moderne Industrie.

Peters, T. (1993). *Jenseits der Hierarchien – Liberation Management.* Düsseldorf, Deutschland: Econ-Verlag.

Porter, M. E. (1985). *Competitive advantage: Creating and sustaining superior performance.* London: Free Press.

Prahalad, C. K., & Hamel, G. (1991). *Nur Kernkompetenzen sichern das Überleben, in Harvard Manager,* Nr.2, USA, p. 66–78.

Scheer, A.-W. (1994). *Wirtschaftsinformatik Referenzmodelle für industrielle Geschäftsprozesse.* Berlin/Heidelberg/New York, Germany: Springer.

Schumann, M. (1992). *Betriebliche Nutzeffekte und Strategiebeiträge der grossintegrierten Informationsverarbeitung.* Berlin/Heidelberg: Springer.

Senge, P. M. (1990). *The fifth discipline – The art and practice of the learning organisation.* New York: Doubleday/Currency.

Servatius, H.-G. (1985). *Methodik des strategischen Technologie – Managements – Grundlage für erfolgreiche Innovationen.* Berlin, Germany: Schmidt.

Servatius, H.-G. (1988). *New Venture Management – Erfolgreiche Lösung von Innovationsproblemen für Technologie-Unternehmen.* Wiesbaden, Germany: Gabler.

Servatius, H.-G. (1994). *Reengineering-Programme umsetzen.* Stuttgart, Germany: Schäffer-Poeschel.

Watermann, R. H. (1987). *The renewal factor – How the best get and keep the competitive edge.* New York: Bantam.

Watzlawick, P., Beavin, J. H., & Jackson, D. D. (1967/1974). *Menschliche Kommunikation – Formen, Störungen, Paradoxien* (4th ed.). Bern, Switzerland: Verlag Hans Huber.

Watzlawick, P., Weakland, J. H., & Fisch, R. (1974/1988). *Lösungen – Zur Theorie und Praxis des menschlichen Wandels* (4th ed.). Bern, Switzerland: Verlag Hans Huber.

Wouter, A., Ahlback, K., De Smet, A., Lackey, G., Lurie, M., Murarka, M., & Handscomb, C. (2018). *The five trademarks of agile organizations* – January report. https://www.mckinsey.com/business-functions/organization/our-insights/the-five-trademarks-of-agile-organizations

IT Support

Alexander Redlein and Eva Stopajnik

A. Redlein (ed.), *Modern Facility and Workplace Management*,
Classroom Companion: Business, https://doi.org/10.1007/978-3-030-35314-8_3

Learning Objectives

The students:

- Know how to define ER diagrams to structure RE/FM-related data according to their needs
- Know how to set up an identification coding system for their buildings and equipment
- Know which criteria can be used to select proper IT tools for RE/FM/FS
- Know the key elements of data security and GDPR
- Know the main IT tools to support operative processes within FM and their pros and cons
- Know tools acting mainly as data sources to RE/FM/FS
- Know how to define required integration of IT tools and the main integration technologies
- Understand the concept of data warehouse tools and can apply them to set up IT support for their benchmarking processes

3.1 Introduction

The results of the change management project based on the methodology business process reengineering are the optimised processes and the modified organisational structure but also the necessary IT support. Nowadays, Facility and Real Estate Managers use several tools. Especially when they need graphical information for their daily work, one tool alone is normally not capable of supporting all functionality required. The IT landscape consists of the following subsystems:

1. Computer-aided Facility Management (CAFM) systems support mainly processes in and around buildings.
2. Geographical information systems (GIS) are mainly used for the processes dealing with several properties (e.g. running portfolios of buildings, selection and optimisation of subsidy locations like DM).
3. Enterprise resource planning (ERP) systems are the corporate software solutions covering financial and cost accounting, procurement and warehouse management, sales and distribution.
4. Building automation systems and fieldbus systems manage and control the equipment within the buildings and properties.
5. Tools with specific functionality like Property and Real Estate Management and call centre solutions.
6. Tools that deliver “basic” data, like computer-aided design (CAD) programs
7. Business data warehouse systems deliver management information like benchmarks, but also support the planning processes. Therefore, they use data from different sources and combine them in one data warehouse.

These tools can be clustered in:

- Operational tools covering day-to-day operation
- Management information systems supporting management decisions and the planning processes like budgeting

In the list above, business data warehouse systems represent a management information system, whereas all the others cover daily processes. Some of them also offer report functionality, but are limited to specific areas like technical maintenance or operation. As the tasks are different for an owner, developer, property manager, tenant, etc., the tools applied are selected according to the tasks to be carried out by the company. To guarantee the optimal IT support, the soft and hardware landscape has to support the following requirements (EIB 2002):

- **Process orientation**. The trend from function or department orientation towards process orientation must be considered.
- **Software supporting the whole process**. There is the need of support for the whole process. As we have already mentioned above, RE/FM covers technical but also economic areas. Both parts must be continuously supported to provide optimal operations and a profound view for the management on all results of an action.
- **Optimal support by integration of all necessary tools**. The integration is based on existing tools like CAFM, ERP and building automation. The customer selects the needed functions and decides which software can provide the special functions best. Then these tools are integrated.
- **Open system**. It is important that the resulting integrated IT landscape is open to new integration. It must be capable of adding new functions, either from already integrated tools or new software products. Especially with the upcoming emerging technologies, this point gains even more importance. The landscape has to enable the usage of IoT, ML, etc. to support disruptive change and innovative processes easily.
- **No data redundancy**. In addition to process integration, it is desirable to generate a common database on which these processes are based. It can be necessary to have some identification information redundant in the "distributed" databases, but the attributes should be unique. It is also necessary to define which tool is the data owner. With software as a service (SaaS) and cloud computing using preconfigured solutions out of the cloud, this goal is getting more complicated to be achieved.
- **Base data accessible in all systems, data maintenance in only one system**. The goal is to be able to use base data in all integrated systems, but to maintain the data only in one system. The other systems should automatically be able to use the current data for their tasks.
- **Reduction of maintenance effort**. The fulfilment of the above goal enables the reduction of data maintenance efforts. Information is maintained in one location and automatically updated or directly available for the other parts of the IT

landscape. Selecting cloud and SaaS solution, this fact has to be taken into consideration, as the data exchange may be limited or not available.

- **Data aggregation**. Management is not interested in each transaction. They require aggregated data of a specific structure. CAFM tools are not capable of doing this. ERP systems provide this function, especially the new version based on InMemory technology. Business data warehouse systems offer an even better solution for this problem. They are being integrated into the ERP systems to reduce the effort of data exchange and provide up-to-date information.

3.2 IT Concept

At this stage, based on the required/desirable IT support, the requirements for the existing company including IT like ERP systems for accounting, cost accounting and controlling as well as additional tools like space management have to be deduced. The process flows described in the chapter before give a good basis for the definition of the required functionality. In this phase, the tool to support this activity plus the data processed for each of the process steps has to be defined. Based on this, the IT concept or IT landscape can be defined. It defines which steps have to be supported by which tool and includes the required tools, the interaction of the systems and the required integration of the IT systems.

Additionally, it has to be analysed to which extent standard software products in the field of FM support the required processes and data, or can be adapted to the requirements. In this context, it has been observed that many of the systems available support the proper tasks of FM only to a certain extent and that a general support of all processes can only be achieved by the integration of more than one tool. Therefore, the required integration of tools must also be established at this step. The result is an IT concept to support the FM processes as a whole.

The experience of various practical projects has shown that a more detailed analysis and conception of the processes, the accompanying IT support and the required integration of the tools have tremendously reduced time and money needed during implementation and daily work. This saves costs.

The mere costs of the hardware and software should not be the only basis for the decision of the IT landscape as they are only a small part of the whole implementation costs:

1. Hardware 2–5%
2. Software 10–20%
3. Customizing and training (20–30%)
4. Data collection, validation, maintenance (50–70%)

Using cloud computing and SaaS reduce the initial costs in hardware and software. This increases the importance of proper data, which is the basis for the proper execution of the processes.

3.3 Data Structure

3 Based on the process analysis and the IT concept, the next step is to define the required data and its structure in the form of an entity relationship (ER) diagram. An ER diagram consist of entities representing data objects like a property, a building and relations between them. The next figure gives the possible relations between entities (◘ Fig. 3.1).

There can be one to one, a one to many and a many to many relationship. A specific door key, for example, can only be used by a specific user at a moment. This represents a 1:1 relationship. In contrast, a property can hold many buildings (_:n), but according to the law a building can only be placed on one property (1:_). This represents a 1:n relationship. A floor can have many rooms (_:m), but a room (like an elevator room) can be located at several floors (n:_). This represents an n:m relationship.

Example

An example for an ER diagram in the area of RE/FM is the following: On the right-hand side is the data structure starting from the property down to the room. In this example, we left out the possibility that a room is located in several floors; therefore, there is a simple 1:n relation. This data is normally kept in a CAFM system. The left-hand side represents the data structure of the users of the room. The organisational units using the room are represented by their cost centres. These are grouped together in cost centre groups.

Organisational units equal a cost centre:
- CEO (chief executive officer)
- Financial accounting
- Sales department
- Production (◘ Fig. 3.2)

Also included in the graphic are the different sources or IT systems (ERP and CAFM) where the data should be stored in and maintained. The integration of the tools should make an automatic update possible. In our case, the cost centres representing the user departments are maintained in the ERP system but automatically updated in the CAFM tool where they can be used to label the usage of rooms (◘ Fig. 3.3).

The figure above shows how in the next step the ER diagram can be used to derive a coding system for the different entities like buildings, floors and the equipment located in the building. The graphic shows how an identification code system for RE/FM is set

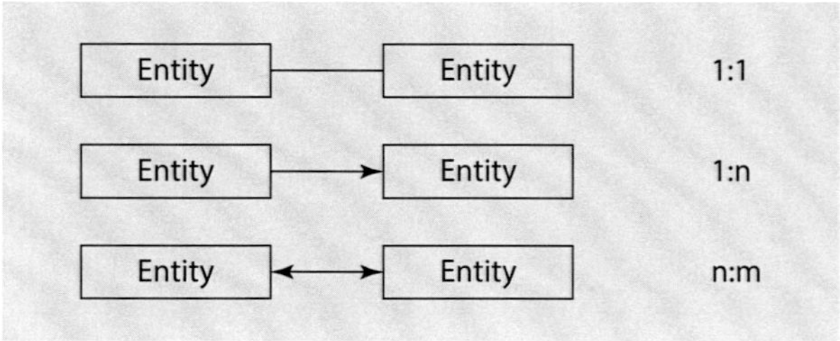

◘ **Fig. 3.1** Types of entity relationships. (Author's own figure)

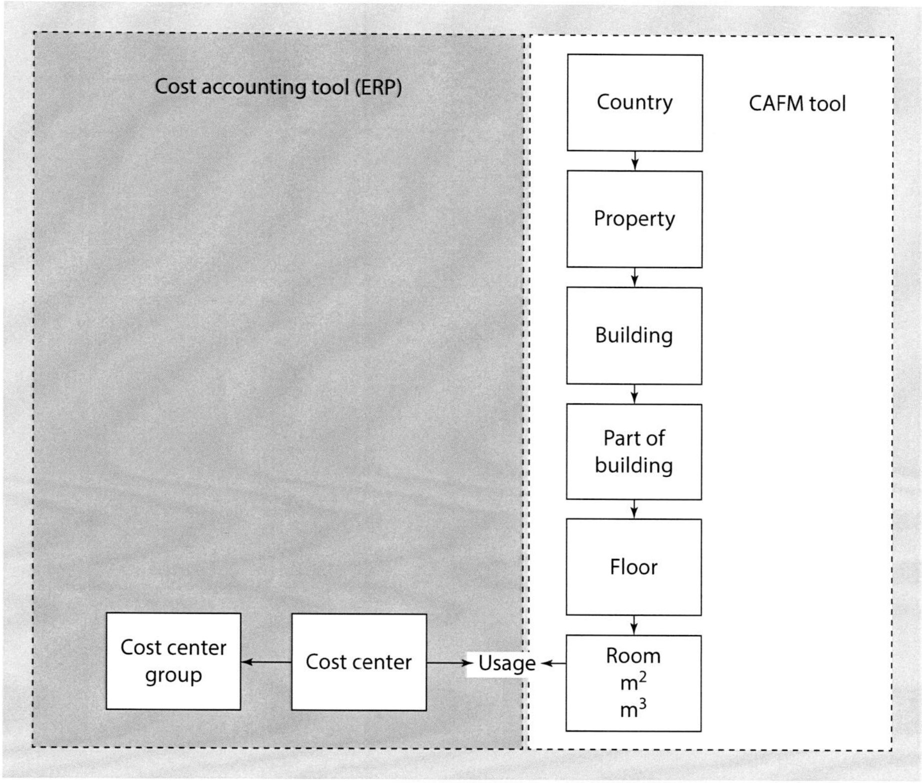

Fig. 3.2 Example of an ER diagram. (Author's own figure)

up. In this example, one level is added to the ER diagram from above: the country. The green area (functional location) equals to our right-hand side of the ER diagram. The first two digits represent the country the property is located in. The hyphen is included to make the code more readable. The next letter represents the property in San Diego. The next digit is the building followed by the floor. The room is represented by another three digits. The new element we see in the graphic is the blue one (installation). On the relation line there is a description of the relation. In this case, it is "installation". That means this equipment is installed or located in this room. The code of the equipment is independent from the code system of the locations (covering the country to the room level). In this case, the equipment is coded according to the Verein Deutscher Maschinen und Anlagenbau (VDMA) which classifies different types of equipment and provides a coding at different levels. This coding is used extensively in German-speaking countries. The next step is to define the required attributes for each of the entities. In the case of a room, the attributes might be:

- Size (in m^2 or sqf)
- Floor type (wood, ceramic tile, etc.)
- User (cost centre of the user to have the relationship implemented)
- Utilisation (office, archive, etc.)

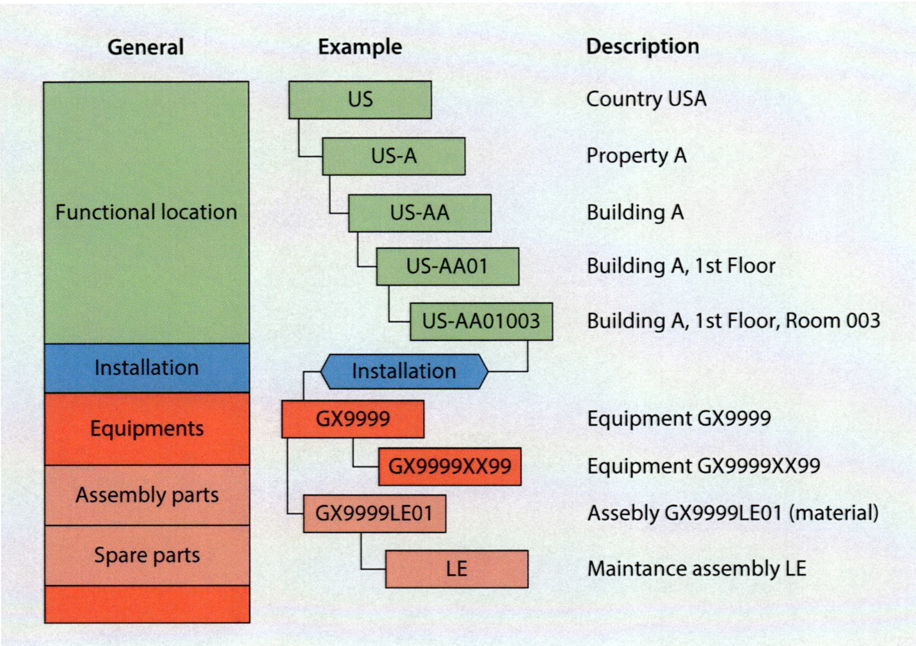

Fig. 3.3 Example of an identification code for buildings and equipment. (Based on graphic by SAP)

If the process and data model, as well as the IT concept, are now completely defined and presented in the necessary structure, then the most challenging and financially complex part takes place: data acquisition and validation. The analysis of the currently available data sources like Excel charts and databases with FM-relevant data is necessary in order to have an overview of the available data, its quality, the data validation and update requirements and the required data imports.

The degree of information detail should not be disregarded. Whether 10 attributes for a room or an equipment are necessary and reasonable depends on the processes, the benefits and the requirements. Graphical data like AutoCAD DXF drawing are still very expensive although new technology like automatic scanning of buildings is coming up soon and decreases the prices. If the relationship between equipment, like the chiller and its power and water supply, or between equipment and rooms, like which room is conditioned by which heating, ventilation and air-conditioning (HVA) unit, is necessary to run the building in an optimised way, the cost increases even more. Data cemeteries are created quickly and are, if at all, cleaned up again only with great effort. According to the information provided by various case studies, the effort of data acquisition, validation and quality assurance accounts for around 50–70% of the total costs of IT projects in the area of RE/FM. However, the percentage varies greatly depending on the type of property (residential property, industrial building) and the type of data collection.

The different possibilities of data acquisition, updating and validation, from manual input to fully automated updates in the FM system, are essential for the up-to-datedness and the effort. Here, the imagination of the user and the technology with all its possibilities has no limits. The procedure should therefore be chosen very precisely. Some fully automatic and therefore expensive techniques have a relatively short return of investment due to high personnel costs.

Due to the direct integration into the system, the available information also has to be completely correct, as an optimisation after it is loaded into the operational systems is more complicated than an optimisation beforehand, for example, due to a consolidation database where database statements can help to check the validity of the data.

3.4 Selection Criteria for IT Tools

In the following, we adhere to the regulations of the European and international building regulations, which define several types of selection criteria:

1. Criteria concerning the company offering the tool, consulting, implementation and training services
2. Technical requirements and selection criteria
3. Process-orientated criteria
4. Cost (investment and operational costs)

In the first step, the potential suppliers have to be selected. Therefore, the following parameters are useful:

- Number of employees
- References
- Experience
- Solution/concept

Example

An example shall show you the importance of the criteria. Two companies joined each other and could not decide on their future FM IT tools. So they asked a consultant to optimise their processes and help them select a proper IT landscape. The consultant was asked in parallel by a CAFM supplier to also represent his software. Since the company that did the merger beforehand was satisfied with the support at the process optimisation, it also handed over the contract for the IT implementation, although the IT provider had never done a project in this region and was not familiar with the industry requirements. As the IT tools had to be enlarged for the specifics and localised, the project not only took much longer but also went over the budget enormously. An additional problem is that many suppliers, especially for FM-specific solutions, are quite small. The start-ups using the newest technologies and providing sometimes disruptive new process models do not have the number of references and the experience in the industry. Another important factor is if the IT provider and the implementation company are the same or if the implementation is done on basis of a "general" tool that several implementation partners can use. In the second case, if the implementation partner does not deliver well or has other problems, the partner can be changed easily. On the other hand, one partner makes the interfaces and communication easier. As you can see, it is not possible to make general suggestions. Only large companies should be engaged or only those having numerous references, because they sometimes may not use the latest technologies or support disruptive change.

After the first step is done and the potential partners are identified, the following criteria are to be evaluated:

- **Software and customising technology**: The software technology and customising possibilities define the usage possibilities, the maintenance effort and general possibilities to a large degree. It also determines the potential for future development. Most programmers today are familiar with JAVA or JavaScript. Therefore, it is easy to hire people and their cost is affordable. ABAP 4 is still the main programming language of SAP. The number of experienced people is rather limited; therefore, the costs are much higher to engage these specialists.
- **Database and database technology**: A database is an electronic system for storing, managing and reading data. It is very common to differentiate databases according to their technological orientation or the type of data structuring into relational database, SQL database, XML (Extensible Markup Language) database or object database. Databases are the most important component of CAFM, GIS and ERP systems. Thus, the technology is of great importance. Today, only systems should be deployed that have a relational database or an object-orientated approach. Standard vendors such as Oracle or Microsoft, or large open software solutions like MySQL, are preferable. But the selection of the database also makes a big difference on costs and maintainability. An access database by Microsoft costs almost nothing but is not really capable of concurrent multiuser use. A Microsoft SQL or Oracle database is much more powerful, but the license costs are also higher. The decision has to be made very carefully considering the future development of the company. So the scalability is very important.
- **Data model**: The data model provided has to support the requirements defined in the previous step. Several tools limit the number of entities and their relations. Some enable the user to define additional attributes or even objects by themselves. Other suppliers only allow changes to be made by themselves. This has an influence on the performance, the validity of the database and the costs.
- **Client server versus stand-alone usage**: An important criterion is whether the program is a single-user system or the software has a client/server architecture. A product that was developed for use as a single-user system usually has short response times and can be individually configured and maintained by the user. There is also a wide range of such tools. However, these products are designed for use on one computer only. Although they can be made available on other computers by technical means, they have the following disadvantages when used by multiple people on different computers, in particular:
  - No central data storage
  - Problems with data security and security
  - No sharing of peripherals
  - No possibility to communicate with other computers

The main problem is data consistency. Since several persons perform changes to the data records in parallel and the software is not designed for such use, data inconsistency and faulty system states can occur. Therefore, client/server systems are more often used. Software has a true client/server architecture when storing and managing the factual data on a centralised database server and allowing users to access it from their workstations (clients) via an appropriate user interface. This concept is designed to allow multiple users to access the software simultaneously (in parallel) and has its own mechanisms to ensure data consistency. When such a system is introduced, both the servers and the client components are installed. The maintenance of such systems is easier, as the updates of the software must usually only be performed at the central server. The client applications remain the same. In some cases, such as a "release" change, however, the clients on the individual user PCs must also be updated. To avoid this, an attempt is being made to use more Internet technology. The clients are no longer their own software tools or the software provider, but instead of a client program, a standard Internet browser is used. When using a web browser, program updates no longer have to be carried out on the user PCs, which considerably reduces maintenance effort. On the other hand, the software providers have to support the used web browser and keep current with the versions of the different browser. The usage of apps on mobile devices also goes into this direction (◘ Fig. 3.4).

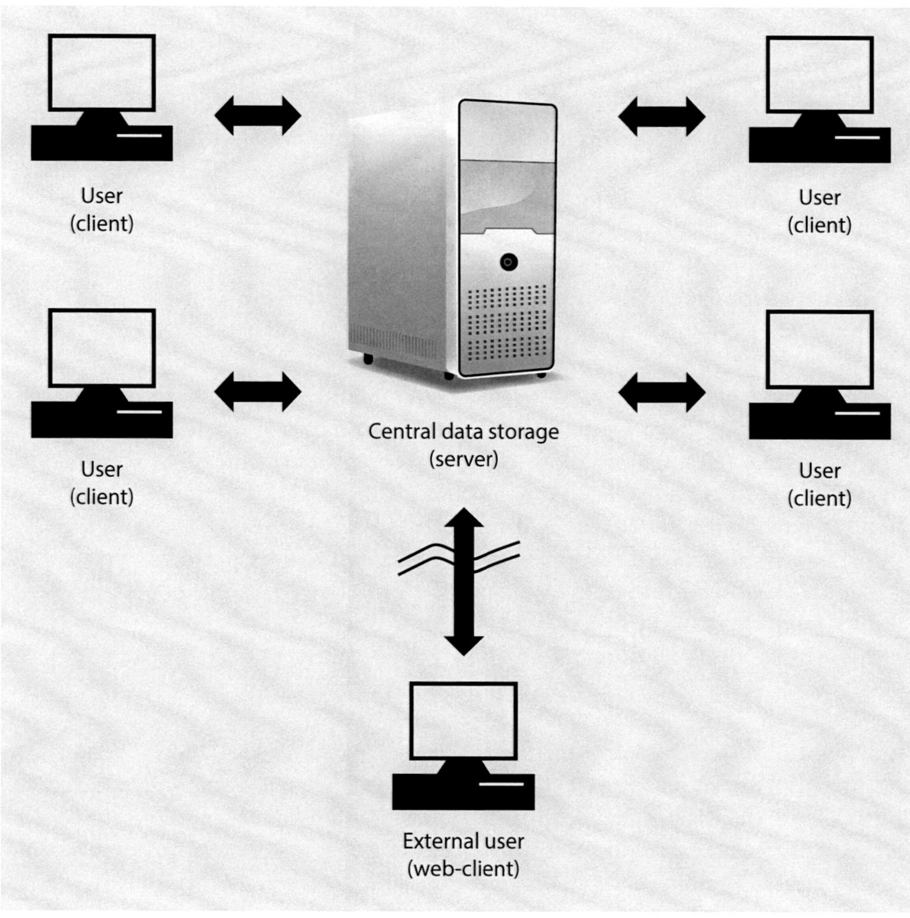

◘ **Fig. 3.4** Client server architecture. (Author's own figure)

- **CAD technology**: As some tools allow to make CAD drawing or at least to change them, the decision has to be made, if it is necessary to make drawing by the user themselves or only to import graphical data to the system. Regarding that fact, the selection can be made as some tools have the full drawing possibilities imbedded, having their origin in CAD, while others only show different views of the buildings' graphic and the link to the database. Their functionality is limited with respect to changes of drawing. In the worst case, this could mean that in case of, e.g. moving a wall, the drawing of the whole floor has to be exported, changed accordingly in an external tool and imported again. Therefore, the exact definition of the required functionality in the area of changes of drawings is very important.
- **Interface technology**: Due to digitalisation and emerging technologies, the interfaces and their possibilities are becoming more and more important. To link systems easily to IoT to gain information about the current status of equipment, to deliver data to ML tools or to "include" them directly cause strenuous effort and therefore costs. One of the keywords in this context is application programming interfaces (API) that allow the direct "control" of functionality of a program by other programs. An API would allow an ERP system to generate a new organisational unit using space (cost centre) in the CAFM tool which can then be used to do space allocation.
- **Internet technology**: This criterion goes hand in hand with the above-mentioned interface technology. It is important to specify the browsers used, as offerings have grown rapidly and different platforms normally prefer specific offerings. Therefore, in most companies several tools are quite heavily spread and need to be supported by the FM IT solution. In addition, the use of apps available on any mobile device is also becoming more and more convenient.
- **Workflow support**: Some of the tools offer workflow systems, which allow to define and configure own workflows. An example is the process to release a purchase order. In most companies, the compliance rule is that when a purchasing employee puts an order above a specific amount in the system, it has to be released by the head of the department. Instead of the person having repetitively to log in the system for release, a workflow can be implemented to send him or her a mail with the information of what has to be released and the direct link to the release. This makes the work of that person easier and speeds up the process. With a workflow engine, these new processes can be defined and supported easily.
- **User access and authorisation concept**: With regard to the security of IT applications, there are basically two areas to be distinguished:
  - The program/application internally
  - The application, the databases and the network externally

The applications usually control the internal access via an authorisation concept. This concept defines the following: who can do what (create, change, read) with which data. Almost all current systems make it possible to assign different user authorisations. The individual user's authorisation determines whether a user has full access or a read-only access to certain types of data that is to certain tables, forms and fields, as well as to specific data records. In practise, this means that an employee who is responsible for a specific building may only change or delete but not create data of his building. The person may have a read-only access to the financial and cost accounting data of all buildings to evaluate the performance of his management tasks. Besides the data access, the functionality to be carried out also may be limited. That means that a person can only execute specific functions in the area of maintenance but not functions in the area of cost accounting. The identification of the users takes place via user name and password. In older programs, the rights described above had to be assigned to each user individually. Newer programs are based on a role concept. The users can be grouped here into groups/roles. Authorisations are then defined per role (role-based authorisation concept). In the second step, users are assigned to this role or to several roles and automatically receive the authorisations of the role or roles (user administration via role-based user groups). Examples of roles are:

- System support
- Master data maintenance
- Maintenance technicians
- Financial accountant
- Controller

- **Data import and export**: Especially in the field of RE and FM, data exchange is an important area. After every completion of a building, the data has to be imported to the systems. In addition, in the case of a refurbishment, the data is then exported, handed over to the planners and construction companies modified by them and imported again after the completion of the project. In the case of small changes like tearing away a wall, the drawings also have to be adapted. This can either be done by the functionality of the tool or the data has to be exported, changed in a CAD tool and imported again. The better the functionality is, the easier the imports and exports are and the less effort has to be made.
- **Reporting functionality and technology**: Since RE and FM is a management task, reporting and support of the planning process are needed intensively. Some of the tools provide big data functionality such as dicing and slicing data. In data analysis, the term generally implies a systematic reduction of a body of data into smaller parts or views that will yield more information. The term is also used to mean the presentation of information in a variety of different and useful ways (Rouse 2018). If this functionality is not given, it is necessary that the data can easily be transferred to real big data systems which support analytics properly.

Along with this more technology-oriented criteria, it has to be ensured that the process flows defined in the optimisation phase are supported properly or can be supported by the use of the workflow possibilities of the IT tools.

The costs (initial investments and operational costs) also have to be taken into consideration. However, the cheapest offer not covering the criteria above is not worth the money. Sometimes the software costs for an optimal solution are high, but the flexibility and possibilities to scale and cover additional functionality in a further step as well as the possibility of innovative service offers for the own employees or the clients can have a higher impact than lower license cost in the beginning. Furthermore, the maintenance costs can change the picture dramatically. This can be the case especially in the area of cloud computing and SaaS. In these cases, it also has to be determined how the data can be exported out of the cloud in case of dissolution of a partnership. Sometimes this "hidden" costs are enormous. Not to be forgotten is the training of the staff that has to carry out the new processes with the new tools. Good training pays off as the churn rate is reduced, and the satisfaction of the staff and the clients is increased. A last criterion is the internal IT requirements of the company. One important issue is the security and safety of data.

3.5 IT and Data Security

3.5.1 General Data Protection Regulation (GDPR)

Several FM processes like space and utilisation planning use data of natural people and process this data in order to, for example, locate the people and to schedule their work. The requirements for data and IT security in these cases are even higher than normal. The General Data Protection Regulation (GDPR) asks for specific measurements to protect the personal data of people. "This regulation lays down rules relating to the protection of natural persons with regard to the processing of personal data and rules relating to the free movement of personal data" (Art. 1 GDPR).

Definition

"'Personal data' according to the law means any information relating to an identified or identifiable natural person ('data subject'); an identifiable natural person is one who can be identified, directly or indirectly, in particular by reference to an identifier such as a name, an identification number, location data, an online identifier or to one or more factors specific to the physical, physiological, genetic, mental, economic, cultural or social identity of that natural person". (Art. 4 Ziff. 1 GDPR)

Definition

"'Processing' means any operation or set of operations which is performed on personal data or on sets of personal data, whether or not by automated means, such as collection, recording, organisation, structuring, storage, adaptation or alteration, retrieval, consultation, use, disclosure by transmission, dissemination or otherwise making available, alignment or combination, restriction, erasure or destruction". (Art. 4 Ziff. 2 GDPR)

To safeguard this data, GDPR asks for restrictions of the data processing.

Definition

"'Restriction of processing' means the marking of stored personal data with the aim of limiting their processing in the future". (Art. 4 Ziff. 3 GDPR)

The goal is also to regulate profiling.

Definition

"'Profiling' means any form of automated processing of personal data consisting of the use of personal data to evaluate certain personal aspects relating to a natural person, in particular to analyse or predict aspects concerning that natural person's performance at work, economic situation, health, personal preferences, interests, reliability, behaviour, location or movements". (Art. 4 Ziff. 4 GDPR)

In the focus are all of the filing systems.

Definition

"'Filing system' means any structured set of personal data which are accessible according to specific criteria, whether centralised, decentralised or dispersed on a functional or geographical basis". (Art. 4 Ziff. 6 GDPR)

Most of the IT tools used in RE/FM include this type of personal data and are therefore to be considered as filing systems in the sense of law.

Consequently, the company processing this type of data has to establish a controller.

Definition

"'controller' means the natural or legal person, public authority, agency or other body which, alone or jointly with others, determines the purposes and means of the processing of personal data; where the purposes and means of such processing are determined by Union or Member State law, the controller or the specific criteria for its nomination may be provided for by Union or Member State law". (Art. 4 Ziff. 7 GDPR)

The controller has to set up a list of processors and recipients of personal data.

Definition

"'Processor' means a natural or legal person, public authority, agency or other body which processes personal data on behalf of the controller". (Art. 4 Ziff. 8 GDPR)

Definition

"'Recipient' means a natural or legal person, public authority, agency or another body, to which the personal data are disclosed, whether a third party or not. However, public authorities which may receive personal data in the framework of a particular inquiry in accordance with Union or Member State law shall not be regarded as recipients; the processing of those data by those public authorities shall be in compliance with the applicable data protection rules according to the purposes of the processing". (Art. 4 Ziff. 9 GDPR)

Apart from the internal FM department, most of the Facility Service companies, and also Property Managers, Asset Managers and so on, are either processors or recipients of personal data, as they need the personal data to carry out their services. A company also has to announce when it is delivering data to third parties.

3

Definition

"'Third party' means a natural or legal person, public authority, agency or body other than the data subject, controller, processor and persons who, under the direct authority of the controller or processor, are authorised to process personal data". (Art. 4 Ziff. 10 GDPR)

All the data can only be processed with the consent of the people of whom data is processed.

Definition

"'Consent' of the data subject means any freely given, specific, informed and unambiguous indication of the data subject's wishes by which he or she, by a statement or by a clear affirmative action, signifies agreement to the processing of personal data relating to him or her". (Art. 4 Ziff. 11 GDPR)

The data of employees can be, e.g. used internally by the FM department for space management, due to the employment contract. If the data needs to be handed over to external service providers, it may be reasonable to include this fact in the employment contract, so that the consent is given. In case of the tenants' personal data, most consent is given due to the Facility Service contracts. However, it would be reasonable to include the consent according to the GDPR in these contracts. In cases of personal data breach, immediate action shall be taken and the relevant people and institutions have to be informed.

Definition

"'Personal data breach' means a breach of security leading to the accidental or unlawful destruction, loss, alteration, unauthorised disclosure of, or access to, personal data transmitted, stored or otherwise processed". (Art. 4 Ziff. 12 GDPR)

These actions have to be included in the RE/FM/FS process flows to ensure that all measurements are set according to the GDPR requirements.

GDPR defines personal data that has to be protected even better:

Definition

"'Genetic data' means personal data relating to the inherited or acquired genetic characteristics of a natural person which give unique information about the physiology or the health of that natural person and which result, in particular, from an analysis of a biological sample from the natural person in question". (Art. 4 Ziff. 13 GDPR)

Definition

"'Biometric data' means personal data resulting from specific technical processing relating to the physical, physiological or behavioural characteristics of a natural person, which allow or confirm the unique identification of that natural person, such as facial images or dactyloscopic data". (Art. 4 Ziff. 14 GDPR)

Definition

"'Data concerning health' means personal data related to the physical or mental health of a natural person, including the provision of health care services, which reveal information about his or her health status". (Art. 4 Ziff. 15 GDPR)

Therefore, the company has to set up binding corporate rules to regulate the processing of the above said type of data.

Definition

"'Binding corporate rules' means personal data protection policies which are adhered to by a controller or processor established on the territory of a Member State for transfers or a set of transfers of personal data to a controller or processor in one or more third countries within a group of undertakings, or group of enterprises engaged in a joint economic activity". (Art. 4 Ziff. 20 GDPR)

Following that, the FM department and the service providers have to set up rules that regulate the processing of personal data. These regulations have their impact on the RE/FM/FS processes and also on the authorisation concepts. In addition, the software tools themselves and the associated databases must be protected against unauthorised use or destruction. The following methods are to be applied for the general protection of data:

- Firewall concepts for the protection of the application and the database
- Encryption within the corporate network
- Virtual private networks for outside access

3.5.2 Firewall

A firewall protects software systems like CAFM tools and their database against unauthorised attempts to directly read or manipulate the data and the application against manipulation or destruction. The programs or databases are located behind the firewall, a kind of "wall" that grants access only to authorised users. This authorisation is controlled in different ways:

- (Encrypted) transfer of a user and password
- Known IP address of the computer
- Announcement of a key (for example, private public key method)

Anyone who cannot authorise will be rejected by the firewall. It makes sense to use the firewall computer only for this service. The computers could otherwise be so busy by the (possibly unauthorised) request and execution of other services, they can no longer provide computer resources for controlling access and forwarding data packets. It can happen that the system is then no longer functional.

3.5.3 Network Protection

Moreover, precautions should be taken in the network itself. "Listening programs" could otherwise "listen in" to usernames and passwords or even to data. With the eavesdropped passwords, an unauthorized system access could then be gained. The easiest way to prevent this is to use encryption programs that make the data transmitted incomprehensible to the listener. For this purpose, small programs are installed on the server as well as on the individual clients to perform this encryption. With the current Windows operating systems or even Linux, such tools are installed by default and only need to be parameterised.

The corporate network is usually also surrounded by a firewall to shield it from unauthorised intruders. While uncritical data can be transmitted unencrypted under certain circumstances in the closed-end/secured corporate network, this should never happen outside this secure network. Pure encryption is not enough to regulate access to the intranet. It must also be ensured that the user/computer is authorised to access the company's intranet. There are two main ways of doing this:

- Tunnelling
- Virtual private networks

Definition

During tunnelling, a secure connection is virtually established between the external client and the tunnel server. The external computer must authenticate itself to the tunnel server, and then the tunnel is set up and the data is transmitted encrypted.

Definition

Another method is the virtual private network (VPN). With the help of this method, the employee works over the Internet (i.e. he uses any Internet access), but then logs in with the help of software installed on his computer. Afterwards, the computer is virtually in the intranet of his company and can use all resources as if he were directly in the company network. Normally, web applications like banking services using an "https" connection and apps on mobile devices support automatically these techniques.

3.6 Implementation

In the next step, the IT concept must be implemented. Tools for project management can support this step. The focus should not only be on the IT systems, but also on the training of the staff that uses the tools afterwards. They should not only be qualified for their tasks in the software but also know the general flow of processes.

Example

An example was a project I did with a large service provider. The call centre agents, and afterwards the maintenance workers, were asked not only to put the failure messages into the system but also to add information of the building, the equipment and the failure reason. As the list of buildings and equipment was very long, the staff started to (permanently) select the first one, as the staff entering the data had no information why this specific data was so necessary. They fulfilled the work properly so the client was happy and had no complaints. Therefore, the management did not realise this was being done. After the first months, the management wanted to use the data to split up the invoices for the client into lump sum and "project-related" sums. The latter was every work done on equipment not under the lump sum contract or work done because of specific failure reasons. But they did not have the data, so the data had to be updated manually.

This shows the importance of training of the functionalities used plus of the process flows in general.

3.7 Operative Software Tools

3.7.1 Computer-Aided Facility Management (CAFM) Systems

The term CAFM is used for software that supports typical FM or FS processes in an integrated way. Especially in German-speaking countries, the software is reduced to tools specifically designed for the use in this area, whereas general IT applications like ERP systems that also support FM and FS processes are not considered as CAFM tools. This use of the technical term CAFM is wrong, since ERP tools and data warehouse systems are CAFM tools that support processes within FM in an integrated way. Sometimes they are even more integrated as pure graphical-orientated tools as they link logistic processes with each other and with financial and cost accounting. However, since the use of the term is quite common, we will also use it in that way.

In general, classical CAFM systems support the following areas:

- Visualisation of areas, their use, occupancy and inventory
- Space management
- Conference room management
- Inventory management
- Move management
- Cleaning management
- Maintenance

3

According to a study of the 500 biggest companies in Austria, Germany and Spain, the most frequently covered areas by CAFM are maintenance and space management, technical documentation, cleaning management, layout allocation plans and cost accounting. The results for Austria and Germany are quite similar. In Spain, CAFM systems cover more areas; most CAFM systems there include inventory, capacity planning, energy management, legal compliance and call centres (◘ Fig. 3.5).

The basis for process support is the usage of alphanumeric and graphical data, i.e. of factual data and maps. Modern systems provide a fixed link between graphical objects in maps and alphanumeric database contents (factual data). In this way, room plans are managed, whereby the individual objects of these plans can also have database information in addition to their graphic representation. The user can either search in the database and get the rooms highlighted in the graphic or "double-click" on a graphical item and get additional information out of the database. As an example, the user could "ask" the system to highlight all rooms with more than 30m² or those having a workplace available. Also the highlighting of the graphics according to usage or floor types is possible. An example for database data is the "double-click" on a piece of furniture and getting the information of the supplier, the data of purchase, etc. out of the database.

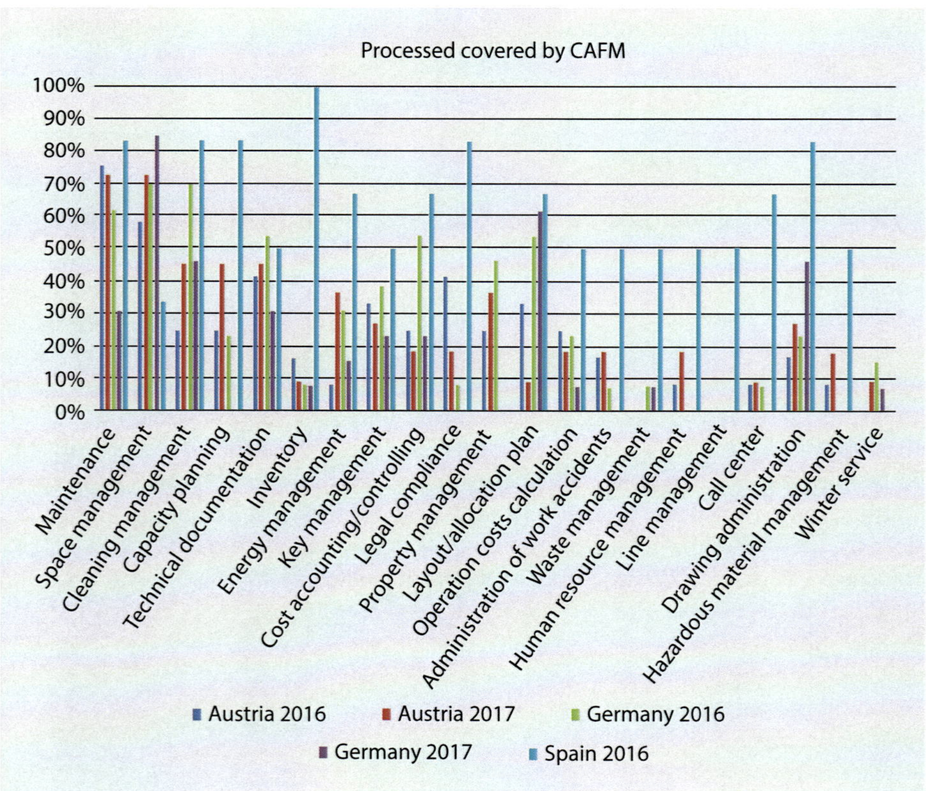

◘ **Fig. 3.5** Processes covered by CAFM. (Author's own figure)

Another important structural element provided by CAFM tools are polylines. These lines consist of several corners and are always closed to identify areas or better spaces. Examples of these spaces can be rooms or floors. When polylines are used in drawings, CAFM tools can provide very easily reports of elements located within these polylines. So a list of furniture within a room can be listed. Or when the room stamp is located in the room (space), the data is automatically linked with the room. There is an additional functionality connected with the polylines. When an element is taken to another "space", then a report can be generated to list all elements that were moved.

To use this functionality in the first step, the digital drawings of the buildings must be read into the CAFM systems. The CAFM tools have import routines for this purpose, which make it possible to import structured drawing exchange format (DXF) or AutoCAD® proprietary drawings (DWG). The structure can differentiate between:

- Carrying walls
- Easy to remove walls
- Windows
- Doors
- Furniture

The elements are structured by the use of DXF layers. Especially in the last three groups, the elements consist of several parts (lines, curves, etc.) and attributes like fire protection, data and suppliers. To structure these the block structure of DXF can be used. It groups different drawing elements together. These blocks can also have attributes. They can be used to specify fire protection values, suppliers, etc.

During the import routine, the data of the graphic is imported directly to the CAFM drawing and linked automatically with a database table that takes up the corresponding attribute information.

The following figure describes this in detail (◘ Fig. 3.6).

All the room attributes are automatically delivered to the table room and all furniture attributes are delivered to the furniture table. This is the basic data set for a move list. The data can then be used for the different modules of the CAFM software to provide process support for the areas mentioned above. In many cases, the modules can be customised, i.e. adjusted to the customer's requirements through parameter settings. By suitable selection of the modules and subsequent customising, the CAFM tools can cover the specific needs of the different companies. The functionality covered by each program is different.

For example, some of the tools have a full CAD editor included, such as Allfa. Some have only basic drawing functionality, like Planon. The assignment of the individual functions to the basic and additional modules is also very different. The functionality in the area of interfaces, like interfaces with fieldbuses and IoT devices, is very diverse too. The products vary tremendously in support functionality.

In general, CAFM products have different "product philosophies": The software products can be classified primarily with respect to their flexibility. The bandwidth ranges from "A" to "Z".

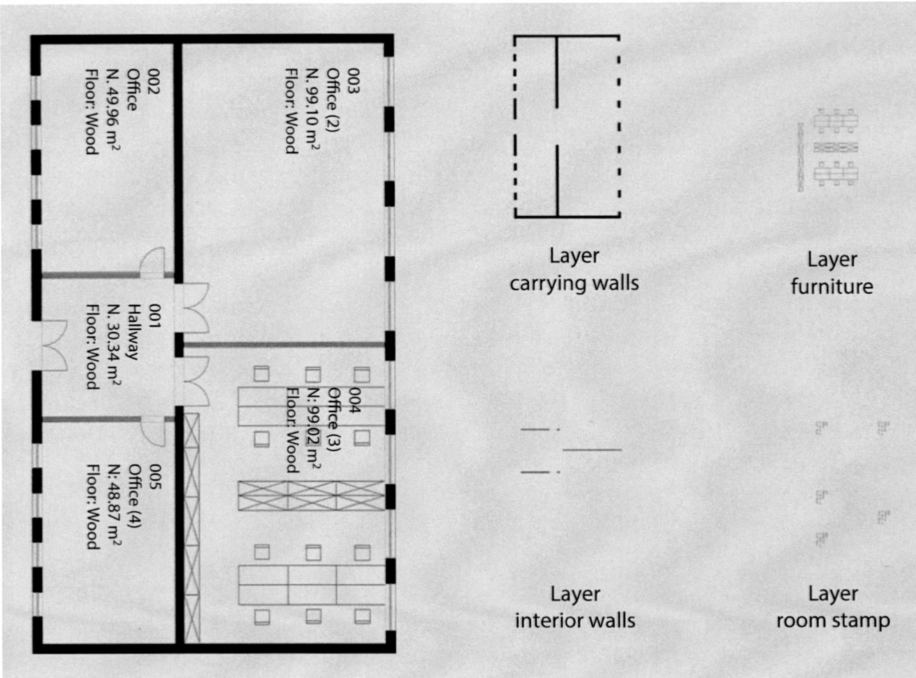

Fig. 3.6 Floor plan, consisting of several layers like carrying, wall, furniture, room stamps, etc. (Author's own figure)

"A" are the flexible tools:

Comparable to an AutoCAD® in the CAD world, these software products provide basic functions. Examples are reports about the objects that are inside a polyline or the automatic link between elements of the graph and database entries. The remaining functionality is implemented either by the customer or by the implementation partner. The functionality can therefore be optimally adapted to customer needs. However, the implementation partners usually also provide "standard functions", which are then adapted to the customer requirements in a second step. This procedure corresponds to the programming of add-ons in the area of AutoCAD®. These systems are very flexible and can easily be adapted to changing needs in the course of the project. Such software systems are also well suited for a gradual introduction.

An example of such tools is Archibus, an AutoCAD® attachment, also from the United States. In Europe, this product has a fairly wide distribution with several local implementation centres.

"Z" are the CAFM standard software products:

These tools are comparable to an ArchiCAD® or Allplan/Allplot® in the field of architectural CAD (CAAD) applications. They offer standard processes that can be customised to a certain extent to the needs of the customer. They support to some extent the change of the process flow and allow the adding of new database fields to the given master data hierarchies and display these fields in the corresponding masks.

For some very rigid products, even these adaptions can only be done by the software manufacturer.

Examples of such CAFM standard software tools are:

- Allfa by Nemetschek: This tool is based on the Allplan/Allplot® CAD tool and largely supports all standard FM functions.
- Fame is a well-known and widespread CAFM tool in Germany.
- Peregrine Facility Centre is a former IT help desk solution that has been expanded to cover most FM functions.
- Planon originates from the Netherlands and is also more likely to come from maintenance and troubleshooting, but has been expanded to provide a holistic coverage of FM functionality.

"M" are software products that have both "A" and "Z" characteristics:

These tools support standard processes, but can be adapted to a large extent to the needs of the customer. They are not as flexible as "A" tools and not as rigid as the "Z" products. The supported process portfolio is usually lower than for products in category "Z". But without additional programming, they offer more process support than the tools in category "A".

Examples are:

- BuiSy is manufactured by a German software company, which is also strongly represented in FM consulting.
- Speedikon FM is a product based on CAD software. This software largely supports all the standard FM processes required.

In general, one cannot say whether a product of category "A" or one of category "Z" is the better solution. It depends very much on the requirements of the company.

The following graphic shows the most frequently used CAFM systems. The people interviewed for the survey were chosen from the 500 biggest companies of each country. A survey with smaller companies might show different results. According to the surveys, about 50% of companies currently use a CAFM system. The most common systems are Pit FM/Grüner and Aperture. In Germany, BuiSy by Conject and Speedikon are also often used. The other categories mainly include Loy&Hutz vFM and waveware, IMS, S-Motive, FAMOS, VisionR, ISPRO, MicroStation, Hollaus and others. The average satisfaction with the CAFM system ranges between 1,7 in Austria in 2013 and 2,6 in Germany in 2017. It is quite amazing that Aperture still has such a large usage, as the core FM functionality has not really been updated for several years (▣ Fig. 3.7 and 3.8).

3.7.2 Enterprise Resource Planning (ERP) Systems

These tools support the management of all resources within a company. Therefore, they support both the administrative and core business processes. They are often referred to as enterprise standard software. They offer support in the following areas:

- Financial accounting including financial reporting
- Asset accounting and management
- Cost accounting (including cost centres, cost elements, internal orders, etc.)

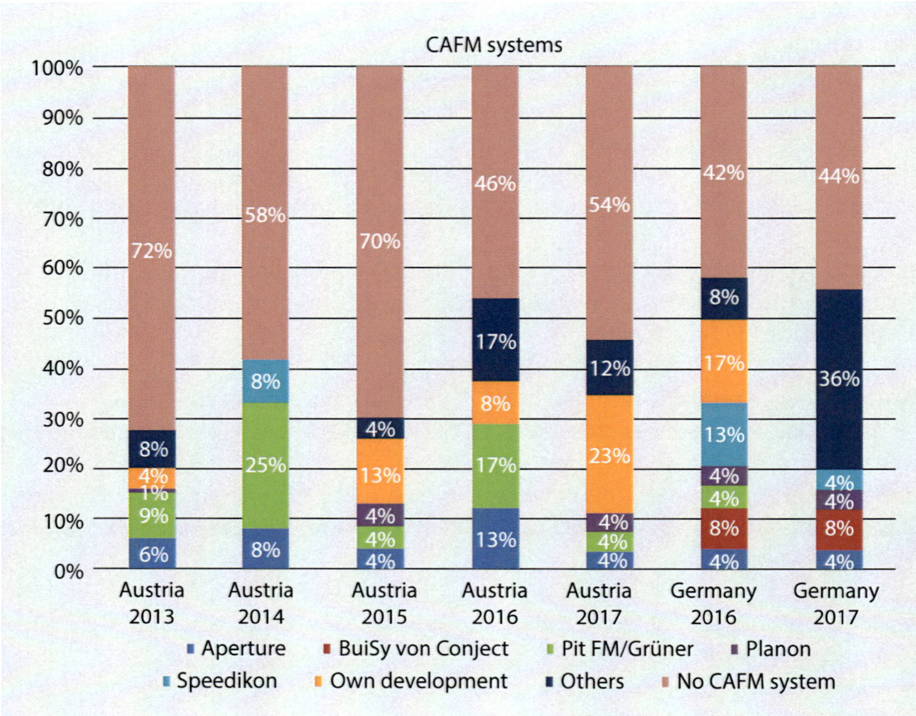

Fig. 3.7 CAFM systems. (Author's own figure)

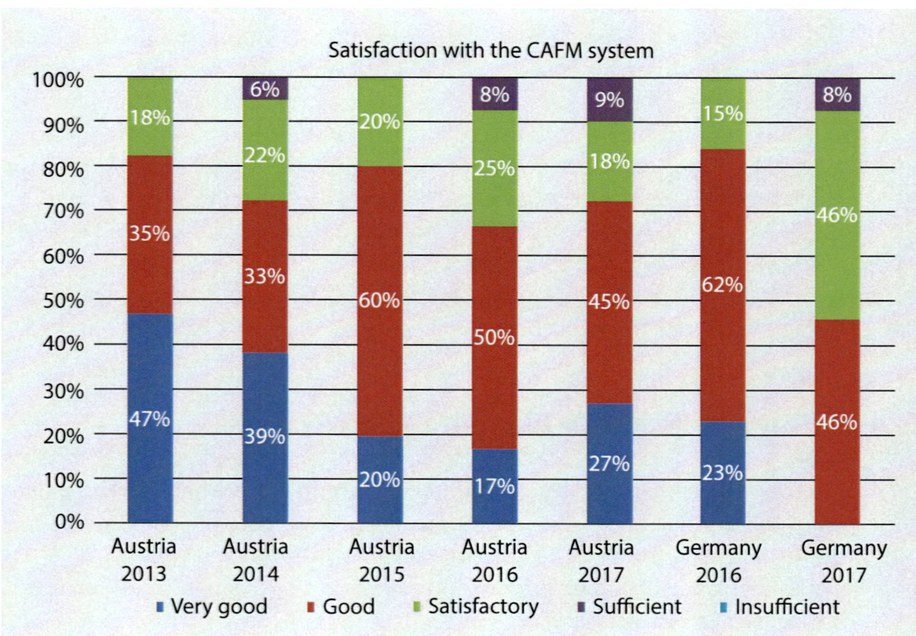

Fig. 3.8 Satisfaction with the CAFM system. (Author's own figure)

- Production planning including maintenance
- Material management including procurement and warehouse management
- Distribution
- Marketing
- Human resources
- Quality management

Most of these systems are real-time systems, linking logistic processes like material management, production and sales directly with the value flow to financial and cost accounting. A simple example is stock management. If a person carries out a goods issue, at least three process steps take place in parallel in such an integrated system:

- The storage quantity is reduced. In addition, a procurement order may be triggered if the stock falls below a certain value.
- In financial accounting, a posting is triggered in which the warehouse account is reduced and the consumption account "consumption of stock material" is increased.
- In cost accounting, a cost collector, for example, a cost centre or an order, is debited with the costs.

Examples of functionality in ERP systems that support Facility Managers in their daily work are:

- Material management including procurement and warehouse management
- Maintenance (preventive maintenance and/or troubleshooting and help desk)
- Project management (the systems at least provide cost collectors; some even support the creation of network diagrams that are integrated into material management and human resources)
- Workflow (static and ad hoc workflow support)
- Quality control
- Asset Management

In addition to supporting day-to-day operations, ERP systems provide management information. Examples of day-to-day processes as well as management support can be found in the following areas:

- **Maintenance/repair**: The basic data for preventive maintenance, such as maintenance intervals, activities to be performed or material required, can be mapped in ERP systems. However, the graphical representation of the buildings and the installation sites of the plants is not available in ERP systems. This functionality may cover complementary software products, such as CAFM systems.
- **Asset management**: The tasks to manage assets like the creation of assets, assets under construction, and the deprivation of assets are covered by the ERP systems. The localisation of assets and asset components are supported by CAFM systems. The ERP systems thus provide the basis for the analysis of the assets and the inventory.
- **Human resources**: After the decision is made that a new person should be hired, the personal data is entered into the ERP system. The person also needs a workplace environment. However, the functionality of ERP systems is not sufficient to

ensure the procurement of a workplace and the other resources required. To support these process steps, therefore, other tools are used, such as CAFM systems, which are based on the information provided by the ERP systems.

- **Tenant management**: Also, the sales processes are supported by ERP systems. Sometimes additional functionality and data are required to start the sales and especially the invoicing process. Examples of required functions or data are plans of rental units and basic information (m^2 per use) for the leases. The generation of invoices, the dunning process, etc. are covered by the ERP systems directly.
- **Financial accounting and accounting**: From the operative work, the figures for the financial accounting and the information in the balance sheet and the profit and loss account are generated. This data supports basic decision-making in the area of RE/FM.
- **Cost accounting**: The financial accounting entries also affect the cost accounting. The cost accounting should have a greater importance in RE/FM, as it allows cost transparency. With their help, the "total" costs of operating a property can be shown. The respective share per square meter or even a better use can also be determined. These values represent the basis for decisions on further action.
- **Controlling**: Basic data for cost allocations, cost drivers, non-monetary basic data for key figures, etc. must be transferred to the ERP system by complementary software products. Complementary products, such as CAFM tools, have better functionality for delivering data about the space and asset usage of tenants, organisational units, etc. The cost accounting provides some of the information needed for a management information system. In addition to the cost information, data on usage, quality standards and customer satisfaction must be available to make management decisions. Most of this data is also available in the complementary tools. Therefore, an integration of these tools is very important and provides a "common ground" for benchmarking.

According to surveys, about 70–80% of companies use ERP systems to support processes within RE/FM. In Germany, the percentage is a little lower but still around two-thirds of all companies use ERP systems. It is readily apparent from the above that integration between at least the CAFM and the ERP systems is required. The ERP systems can optimally cover the monetary and cost accounting functions and manage the cost data. The CAFM systems support the FM-specific activities and manage the object-related data. To support the entire operational process – both technical and economic – process integration is required to ensure a continuous workflow and ensure data consistency (◘ Fig. 3.9).

Examples of ERP tools used are SAP ECC (ERP central component), BAAN, Oracle Applications and Microsoft Dynamics. In addition to these international providers, there are still products that are more local and only represented in a few countries. The results of the figure below are based on the 500 biggest companies of each country. A survey with smaller companies might show different results (◘ Fig. 3.10).

The average satisfaction with the ERP system lies between 1,9 in Austria in 2014 and 2,7 in Romania in 2013. The graphic below shows that more than 50% of ERP users rate their system with very good or good. Only in Romania in 2013 the users are less

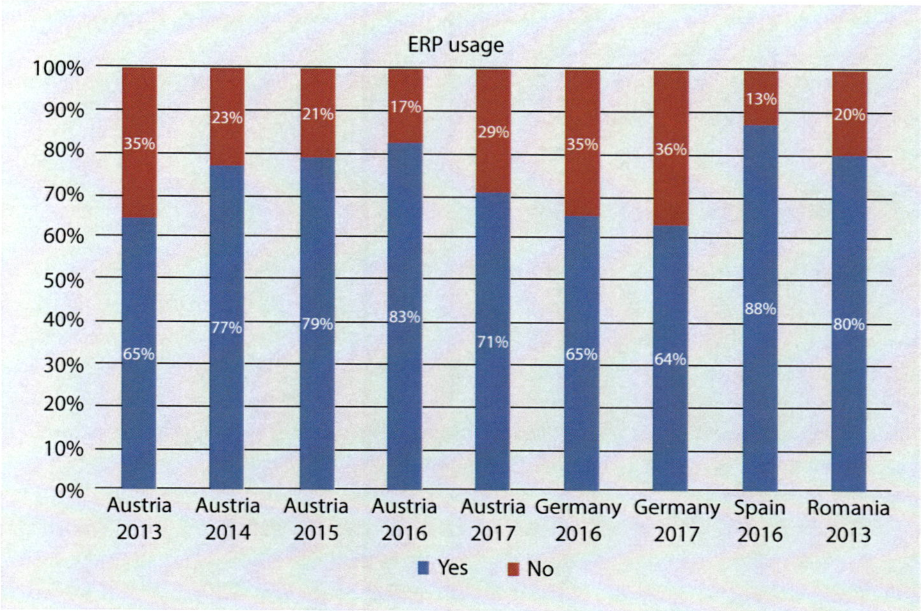

Fig. 3.9 ERP usage. (Author's own figure)

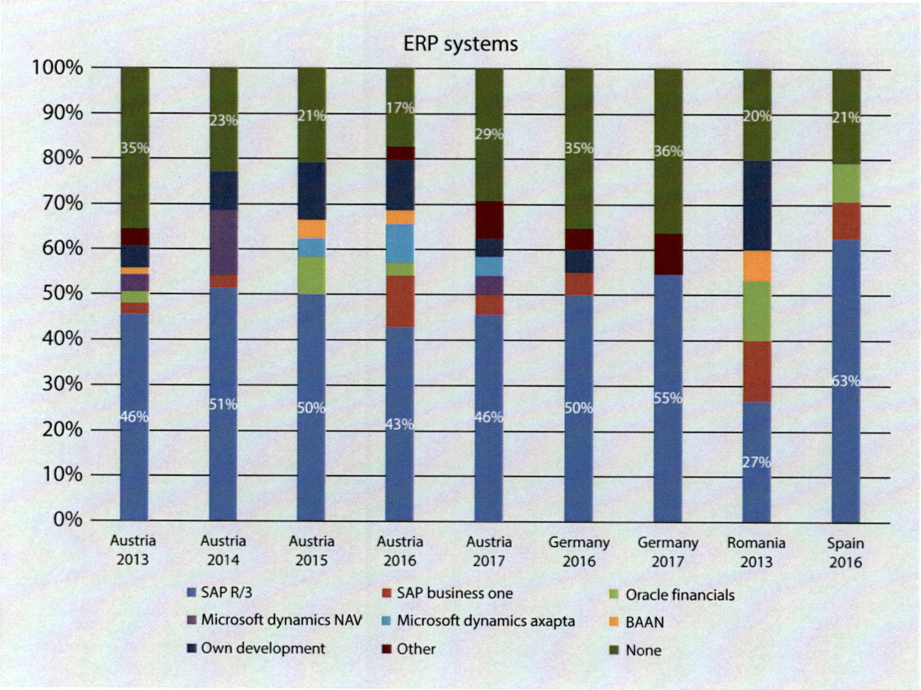

Fig. 3.10 ERP systems. (Author's own figure)

satisfied. This could be connected to the usage of other systems, such as in-house developed systems (■ Figs. 3.11 and 3.12).

The companies analysed use their ERP systems mainly for financial activities, accounting, costing and controlling, procurement, maintenance, HR and distribution.

3

3.7.3 Building Automation

The building automation or control system is used to control the technical facilities of a building, such as heating, air-conditioning and ventilation. Some of these systems also support troubleshooting and even include help desk functionality. In case of failures, these systems can, for example, send messages via email or short message service (SMS). Some building management systems also support preventive maintenance. Since many of these systems today use fieldbuses or even IoT to facilitate communication between the individual devices, they can also be referred to as a "building network" (Kranz 1997).

Building control systems visualize also the facilities and their operational status. For this purpose, often own drawings of the building and the plants are created or programmed. The use of drawings in the drawing exchange format (DXF), which are based on the digital building plans of the architect and also contain all the necessary elements, is not yet widely used in building control systems. However, this approach to visualisation would bring significant cost savings. Another approach would be the integration of building management systems and CAFM systems. CAFM systems provide the

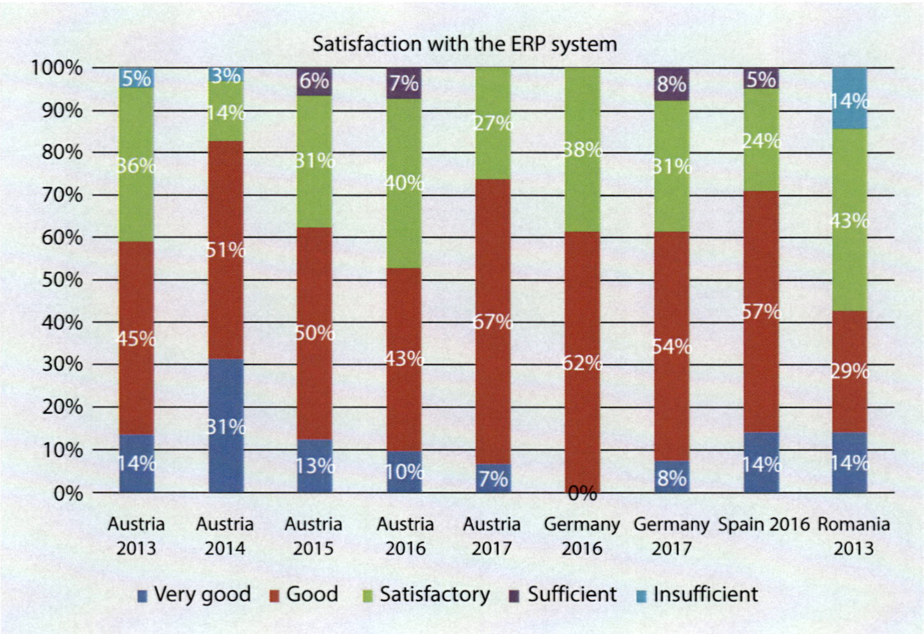

■ Fig. 3.11 Satisfaction with the ERP system. (Author's own figure)

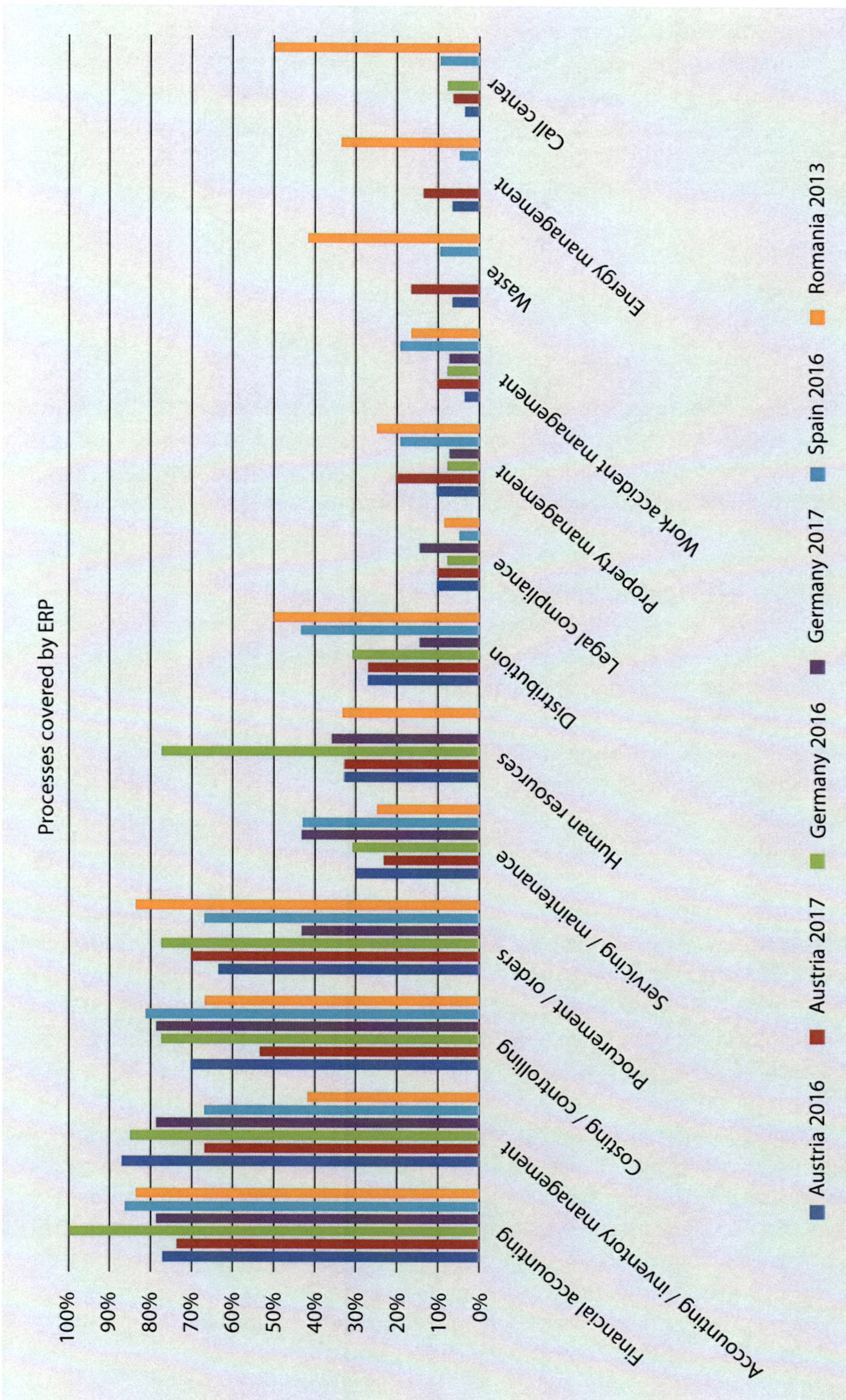

Fig. 3.12 Processes covered by ERP. (Author's own figure)

functionality required for visualisation. The building management system supplies the current data of the building, which are then displayed by CAFM tools.

The building management system mainly contains building data in the area of technical equipment. Most of the information is technical or quantity-oriented. Examples are operating hours, downtime, meantime to repair or meantime between failures, maintenance activities, etc. The systems manage only a small amount of cost data, but also include data for the maintenance process, such as:

- Supplier
- Manufacturer
- Operating status
- Counter readings, operating hours
- Fault messages

The integration of building control systems with ERP or CAFM systems would improve the IT support of operational processes, especially in the area of troubleshooting and visualisation. New building automation solutions support a direct data flow from the devices to a big data system where analytic tasks can be carried out.

3.7.4 Geographical Information Systems (GIS)

Unlike CAFM systems that manage building-related data, GIS manage data about the properties and land. For example, they deal with the following information:
- Plans of properties and the buildings, infrastructure on it
- Information of the land register about area, owner, charges, etc.
- Information about the surrounding land
- Zoning
- Demographic data

With the help of GIS, property data can be managed and made available for processes. GIS are used when a company owns a large number of properties and needs to manage them efficiently; otherwise this property information can also be managed in a CAFM system.

Similar to the CAFM systems, data structures and data sources also play a major role in the GIS. Property data can be obtained from companies, for example, geometers. Public agencies such as surveying offices also offer data in the form of digital land registers (DLR). These include the information about the plots, the borders and the altitude. The availability of DLR varies from country to country. While in Germany some countries still cannot provide vector graphics digitally for large areas, in Austria coverage is around 95%. In addition to the DLR, there is still the digital land register. Both data sources have data structures that should be used in GIS tools to facilitate data reconciliation (Longley 2001). New European legislation asks the public authorities to provide all data already paid from tax income free of charge. This makes the access to data easier and in a lot of cases free of charge. A lot of use cases are now possible with almost no investment:
- Precious and in-depth data for the evaluation of property
- Search for location according to income, unemployment rate, etc.
- Zenith angle and course of the sun for a specific plot

3.7.5 Special IT Tools

Because CAFM, building control, GIS, and ERP systems cannot support all the functionality needed, additional products are available to support specialised areas. Such special functionalities are, for example, property management, maintenance/servicing or help desk solutions. However, it must be analysed whether the desired process support cannot be found in the ERP or CAFM systems and is sufficiently covered there, since the use of external tools can quickly lead to high costs due to the integration requirements and the associated costs.

3.7.6 Tools as Sources for RE/FM Relevant Data

Most of the software tools described so far require a large range of basic data for process support, such as digital building plans, organisational data and asset information. In order to obtain this information, one usually has to gather the resulting data of the planning phase from the planning tools or other data sources validate them and bring them in a structured form. Examples of tools that deliver data for the utilisation phase are:

- **Computer-Aided Architectural Design (CAAD) and Computer-Aided Design (CAD)**

Computer-aided (architectural) design software products are used by architects and civil engineers. At the end of the planning activity and construction phase (after the inventory plans have been created), all the data for the building operation is available from the point of view of the buildings and the equipment. This information is not needed entirely for the management. Therefore, in the first step the maps of the buildings are imported to these tools. Most of them have the functionality to import DXF or building information model (BIM) drawings. For further process the DXF drawings must be structured in a proper way. On the graphic side there are mainly three elements provided for this:

- Layers: for a main structure into walls, windows.
- Blocks: for detailed structure of single elements.
- Polylines: identify areas like rooms floors. CAFM tools can provide very easily reports of elements located within these polylines.

To these blocks additional information like room number, square meters, manufacturer, maintenance contracts and cleaning effort can be added. This information can either be imported to the system or generate of data included in the drawing like square meters.

BIM already know building objects like a floor, a room and openings (e.g. doors, windows). If the CAFM or ERP system can import BIM models, all the objects used in the design and construction phase are also available in the CAFM or ERP system. The data is then used for the processes to be carried out with the IT tools used during utilisation. The additional management information such as maintenance contracts, maintenance plans and usage period is sometimes missing in the planning data, but can be easily supplemented. All this information and the updates done in the IT tool used during the utilisation phase are the basis for refurbishment.

- **Digital product catalogues**: These databases can provide additional information such as lifetime, maintenance and cost over building components.
- **Digital land register**: The digital land registry contains information about the owners of a property, uses, charges, etc.
- **Digital cadastre**: The digital cadastre includes property plans, building outlines and data such as lot number, area, etc.

When these sources are used, the implementation effort can be greatly reduced as the cost of data collection drops sharply.

3.8 IT Landscape and Interfaces

Some areas of FM processes are well covered by the IT tools described above. However, many processes can only be partially covered by one tool alone. Between the individual process steps, the user must change the system. Often this also means that she or he must enter information repeatedly. This circumstance leads to increased efforts and costs and also a high probability of error. Another problem is the fact that the information about the same object is distributed over several systems and therefore the data is often inconsistent and not up-to-date. Now, if decisions are made based on the data that is in a system, it can lead to errors.

To solve these problems, it would be necessary to integrate the individual tools. Various analyses have shown that a continuous workflow is possible and that about 80% of the standard processes could be continuously supported if the existing software tools were integrated with each other. Some examples of such process support by several tools together are shown in the following diagram (◘ Table 3.1):

To cover the space management, maintenance and property management processes properly, more than one tool is necessary. In the case of maintenance, the CAFM tools

◘ **Table 3.1** FM processes and activities covered by different tools (table compiled by authors)

IT tools	CAFM	ERP	Building automation
Maintenance	Location available in drawings, schemata	Contractual information, tasks, cost	Status of equipment and building
Space management	Space information in drawings, usage	Cost information, cost allocation	Usage data (number of users, linkage to HVA)
Property management	Rental unit drawings, usage	Rental agreement, invoicing, dunning	Usage data

provide the location of equipment, which is used to find the equipment in the property in the case of failure handling and inspection or maintenance tasks. The CAFM tools also deliver the m2 to charge the costs properly to the users or to set up and update the tenant agreement in case of property management. The ERP system is rather used to store contractual information, as the procurement of services is supported by these types of tools. As ERP systems also carry out the cost allocation to the final users, this part of the cost accounting process is covered by these types of tools. Building automation tools provide mainly the current status of equipment, which can be used for monitoring but also as a trigger for failure handling or preventive maintenance. As can be seen from these examples, the interaction or even better integration of different tools providing different information but also supporting different parts of the process is vivid and makes the execution of the processes more smoothly.

3.8.1 Manual Replication or Traditional Batch Methodology

A pure data exchange, for example, through a database link, is the simplest and most cost-effective method of integration. Therefore, this method is used very frequently. But very often data is still taken manually from one system (sometimes even in paper form) and then manually or automatically read into the other systems where the data is needed. This process is usually time consuming and costly. Only in a few cases – rather stable data – this procedure is sufficient.

Integrations based on the technology described above present some problems:

- **Pure data exchange**: This integration only supports the pure data exchange. No additional logic can be implemented. Also, the timeliness of the data is not guaranteed, because this method usually exchanges the data only at certain times (in batch). In between, the data is inconsistent. This method also causes problems for complex systems such as ERP systems. These systems have a complex database structure, so it can easily lead to errors in data exchange, which in extreme cases can lead to the destruction of the system. In the case of updates of the ERP system quite often, also the data structure changes which demands for an update of the data exchange procedure.
- **No process support – pure data interface**: With this method, there is no process support and no guarantee of the workflow beyond the limits of the individual tools.
- **Data redundancy**
- **Data exchange between more than two systems**: The classic method can only integrate systems in which the required functionality for the integration already exists; otherwise the functionality has to be implemented in every system. If more than two systems are to be integrated with each other, interfaces must be implemented on a one to one basis. This means that additional programs must be created for each link of one program to another. Thus, in the case of three systems, six interfaces must be implemented; in the case of 5 systems, 22 interfaces have to be implemented. Another type of integration, for example, via a "message handling agent", would drastically reduce the effort since in this case only one interface would have to be maintained for each system.

3

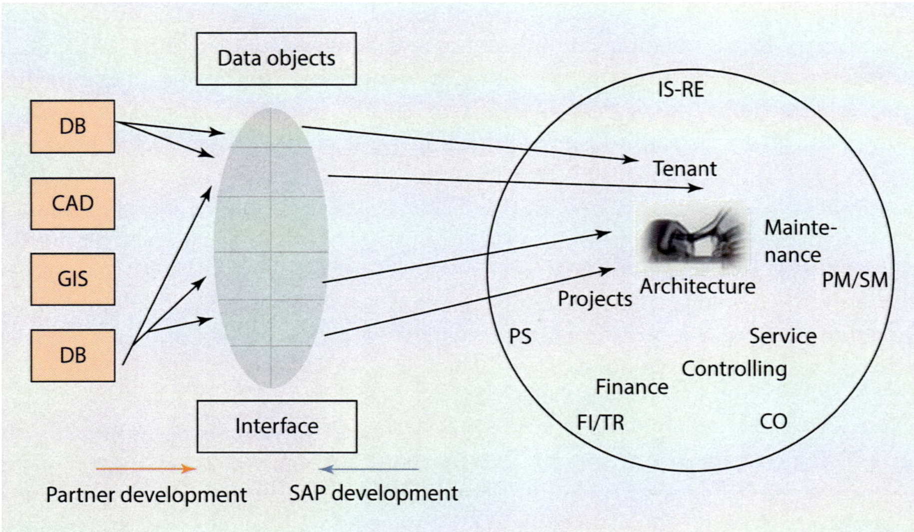

Fig. 3.13 Cost allocation process supported by ERP and CAFM system. (Based on SAP Online Help for release 4.6 C)

- **Software updates**: For every software update, the interfaces to all other programs would have to be updated. For four integrated systems, this means 12 interfaces have to be adapted. The same applies if a new system has to be integrated.
- **Basis for a management information system** is not available, as the different data is stored separately and no data consistency is guaranteed

The concept of a "middleware" solves these problems and inadequacies. This type of integration is usually not associated with much extra effort these days, since there are middleware solutions already available either for general purposes or even for use in the field of FM, which allow a cost-effective implementation. Nevertheless, it should always be checked whether the effort is worthwhile, or if the functionality can be covered by fewer systems or an organisational solution can be found (Fig. 3.13).

3.8.2 Middleware

The core element of the integration concept is a middleware, an online process interface implemented as proprietary software. It has the following tasks:

3.8.2.1 The Middleware Connects the Databases

This tool automatically updates the relevant data in the various databases, ensuring data consistency in all systems at all times. This mechanism is the prerequisite for consistent data in the various "sub-" systems.

3.8.2.2 The Middleware Has Its Own Functionality

If a relevant process step is executed in one of the programs, the program sends a "message" or "triggers" the middleware. The middleware "interprets" the message or trigger and automatically performs the necessary steps. These steps can be:

- Get data.
- Process and manipulate data.
- Update data in all tools affected by the changes.
- Start processes in the other tools.

The middleware itself has the information about which tools are affected, where to retrieve the relevant data and which steps – from a simple data transfer to a complex data processing – are to be executed. The middleware can also trigger processes in the other tools (workflow support). Using this method, bidirectional standard interfaces can be implemented, for example, between different ERP modules and CAFM as well as BA (building automation) systems. In the case of ERP, in addition to the own middleware provided by most of these tools solutions from various third-party providers can be used. In the case of SAP this would be either the exchange infrastructure SAP XI or the Leonard environment.

3.8.2.3 Customising

The middleware can usually also be parameterised so that it can be adapted to the different needs of the company without any programming effort.

The use of middleware also simplifies release changes, since only the interface to a tool needs to be changed, the remaining interfaces remain the same. Even extensions can be implemented more easily, since only the logic and the data exchange are extended, but existing interfaces do not have to be adapted.

From the user's perspective, the middleware behaves like a component of the operating system. Only in the case of failure will the scope of the functionality become recognisable to the user (◘ Fig. 3.14).

When integrated with ERP systems, such process interfaces are used primarily in the following areas:

- Cost accounting
- Human resources
- Asset accounting
- Corporate Real Estate Management
- Maintenance/repair

With the application of the middleware concept, the process shown in the next figure using the functionality of different IT tools can be realised. The ERP system is used to maintain the cost centres of the departments using the space. The middleware makes sure that all changes to these cost centres are automatically updated in the CAFM system. In the case a new department is founded, a new cost centre is generated in the ERP system and automatically generated by the middleware also in the CAFM system. If an existing cost centre is renamed, this change is automatically updated in the CAFM

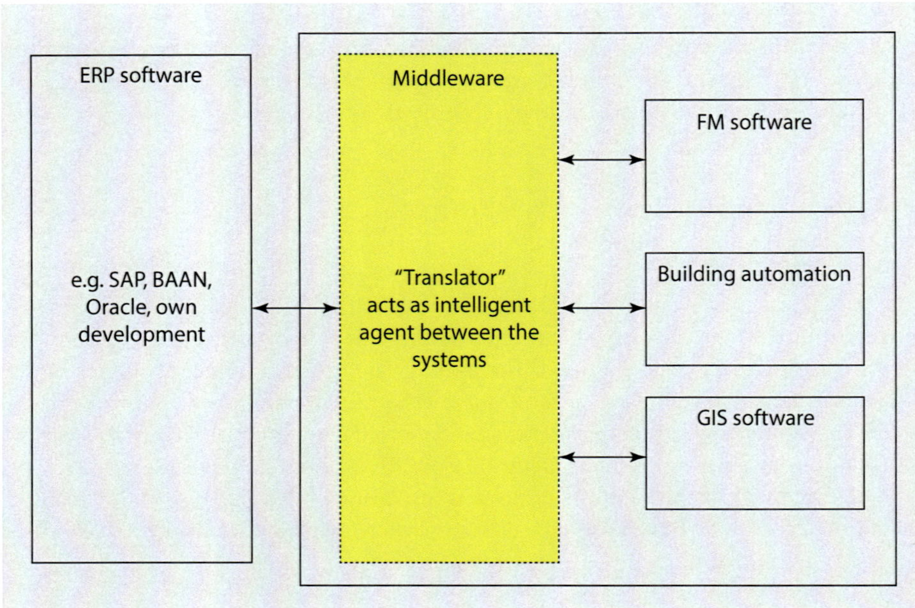

Fig. 3.14 Middleware concept. (Author's own figure)

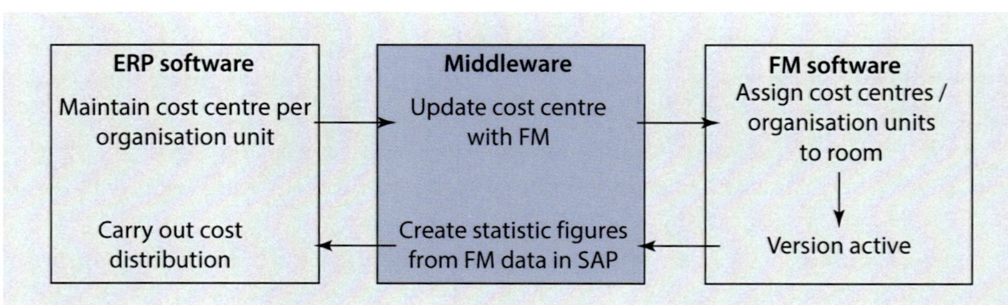

Fig. 3.15 Example of database link between ERP system (SAP) and CAFM tool. (Based on SAP Online Help for release 4.6C)

system too. This secures that all department information are up to date in both IT tools. When a move is carried out in the CAFM tool, the current square meters used by the departments are delivered automatically (after the move is done) to the ERP system and used there for cost distribution according to the used space. Due to the middleware, only existing departments equal to ERP cost centres are in the CAFM tool and the cost distribution is always accurate (Fig. 3.15).

A detailed analysis of the process steps, the localisation of the steps in the individual tools and the definition of the data to be updated is a prerequisite for the design of the process integration. There are companies available to carry out this work. But you should make sure that the consultants know all the relevant products and their functionality. Specialists who only know one product will always try to implement all functionality there.

3.9 Strategic IT Tools: Benchmarking

The previous subchapter explained the integration of IT systems to support operational processes. The main focus of these tools is on the optimum support of the operative processes. What is lacking is the full support, especially of Facility Management. In this context it is necessary that the required management information as well as tactical and strategic process support is available and given. The operational IT systems with their different reporting possibilities can help and provide exact analyses, e.g. about especially sensitive fields. Also, the exact analyses of repairs of certain sensitive parts can be presented and facilitate further decisions. However, special tools are required to, for example, put costs in relation to space, to slice and dice data, etc. Tools offering this functionality are, for instance, pivot tables.

The above-described concept enables a consistent data structure above the limits of the different operational tools and enables subsequently the generation of benchmarks, which form the basis of the benchmark process. The goal of the benchmarking process is to identify "best practice" and to learn from those who perform the best (Kaplan and Norton 1997; Binder 1989; Schulte and Pierschke 2000 S. 242 ff.).

The benchmark process consists of three stages:

1. The standardised calculation of structured key figures of operational data
2. The internal comparison of this key figure and the external identification of best practice examples
3. Drawing conclusions and implementing organisational learning and knowledge enhancements

The standardised and automatic calculation of benchmarks is only possible if a consistent data model exists. However, a necessary prerequisite for using a consistent data model is an exchange mechanism between the application and the database, which can only be achieved by an enterprise application integration (EAI) system, described above. But the data is still stored in the different tools.

The data warehouse concept is best suited for combining different sources into a single object model, processing all necessary data and aggregating the information for strategic analysis. The data warehouse concept as the basis for a management information system (MIS) brings together the information sources of all IT systems involved (◘ Fig. 3.16).

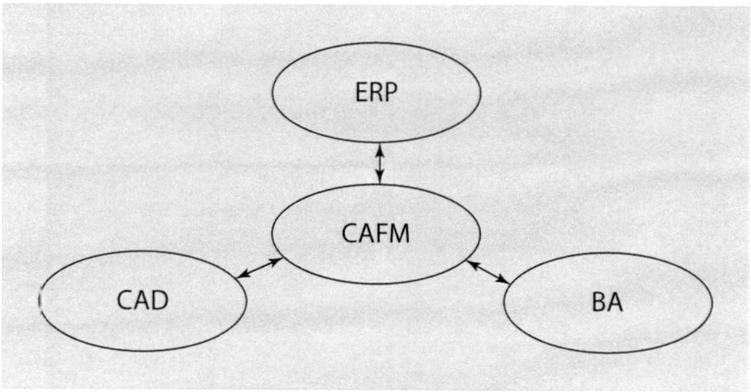

◘ **Fig. 3.16** Integrated operative IT landscape. (Author's own figure)

Despite the discussion on European standardisation of FM benchmarks (EN15221-7 2012), a major problem has not yet been adequately addressed: the complexity of the data needed to identify the metrics and the delivery of this basic data. When determining key figures, it should be noted in particular that the calculation of these figures must not be too complicated to be carried out. If too many detailed data are needed, the execution is almost impossible. The underlying problem shows the following aspects:

- The data must be structured and standardised.
- Only if, e.g. the cost types which are charged to the properties and buildings are structured in the same way for all the participants of the benchmark process, then and only then a comparison in the sense of apple to apple is possible.
- A data structure that can provide the necessary information must be implemented in the overall IT system. Most of the required data and functions already exist, but are distributed in different systems.
- All information must be merged into one system.

The data warehouse concept is ideal for this purpose. The following subchapters present the concepts, which enable a solution for an automatic calculation of the necessary figures.

3.9.1 Data Structure and Standardisation

Data structures and standardisation are important in every area of IT support. However, these are not available in the FM because different business areas are involved in this area. In some countries, some parts of the data structures are governed by standards or by law, such as a building code and the EN15221–7. For some areas or countries no structure exists at all.

Therefore, the biggest problem is that no common structure has yet been established. The EN15221–7 is the best guideline that exists at the moment and can be used as a starting point. Based on the exact definition of key figures of the EN (for example, cleaning costs per m^2), a useful structure must be set up in the organisation and later implemented in the different IT tools. For this purpose, it is necessary to identify the different sources in a first step.

According to several case studies carried out by the authors, the data sources are structured as follows:

- Property and building related
- Cost-relevant
- Quality relevant
- Other (e.g., organisation type)

Some of the data sources were mentioned already in the ► Sect. 3.7 and will be discussed in more detail below.

3.9.2 Property and Building-Related Data

- Net/gross floor area, main usable area, rentable area, etc. in m^2 (sum per building or per user)
- m^2 cleaning area (sum per building or per user)
- m^3 interior (cubature), ventilated room, etc. (sum per building or per user)
- Type of area (office, apartment, etc.)
- Building equipment in general (for example, heating, ventilation, cooling, wiring)
- Number of jobs
- m^2 per workstation
- Technical equipment of workplaces

In Germany and Austria, there are national standards such as EN15221–7, DIN 277 or ÖNORM B 1800, which specify these terms and the calculation of the associated key figures.

3.9.3 Cost-Relevant Data

Most metrics are based on cost information. These data, such as energy costs (e.g. oil or gas), cleaning costs, etc., should be available to the organisation in detail. Posting all invoices in one account and then posting them to one cost centre is insufficient for Facility Management. Minimum requirement is a detailed cost element and cost centre structure (Kemmetmüller 1986).

Based on the definition of the benchmarking system, a costing model needs to be defined. It must be based on the definitions of the relevant standards, for example, DIN 276, ÖNORM B 1801 T1, ÖNORM B 1801 T2 or ÖNORM A 4000, EN15221–7. In addition, the company's controlling needs must be taken into account

The main task is to introduce a simple process of posting incoming invoices in financial accounting and cost accounting. The data from this process can then be aggregated and used directly for the calculation of key figures. A detailed structure allows better insights, but makes bookkeeping and cost accounting more labour-intensive and error-prone. However, a structure with insufficient detail makes it impossible to fulfil the controlling task. The happy medium must be found:

- The structure must be detailed enough to provide a good basis for the calculations of the key figures and thus to enable controlling.
- It has to be lean enough to keep efforts and error rates low.

Also, a cost awareness in the business organisation at the level of the departments should be created. This can be achieved by offsetting the consumed Facility Services either directly through consumption (for example, via direct activity allocation or activity-based costing) or indirectly via cost distribution based on used m2 or a comparable measure (Seicht 1997, S148 f.).

- **Cost Element Structure**

Cost elements are defined according to the definition of standards (like the EN15221–7) or the industry standards mentioned. The following is a possible but very detailed structure for the cost element "Energy":

Cost Element: "Energy"

1. Subgroup 1. Electricity
    - 1.1.Type of costs 1. Low summer rate
    - 1.1.Type of costs 2. Low winter rate
    - 1.1.Type of costs 3. High summer rate
    - 1.1.Type of costs 4. High winter rate
    - 1.1.Type of costs 5. Top rate
    - 1.1.Type of costs 6. Rental fee for counter
    - 1.1.Type of costs 7. Fees for the use of the electricity network

1. Subgroup 2. Liquid or gaseous fuels
    - 1.2.Type of costs 1. Gas
    - 1.2.Type of costs 2. Oil

1. Subgroup 3. Hardly flammable fuels
    - 1.3.Type of costs 1. Brown coal
    - 1.3.Type of costs 2. Wood

1. Subgroup 4. Alternative energy sources
    - 1.4.Type of costs 1. Solar energy
    - 1.4.Type of costs 2. Geothermal energy

1. Subgroup 5. Water

Many systems support a hierarchical grouping of cost elements. This enables a detailed evaluation in subareas, for example, in controlling the energy sector, the hierarchy also supports aggregated evaluations, that is, the cost element group level. By using these cost elements, an invoice from a vendor can be posted directly to a (cost) account in financial accounting, and in cost accounting, it can be booked to a cost centre with the correct cost element.

- **Cost Centre Structure**

There are two different types of cost centres, which are normally used in RE/FM: on the one hand cost centres that represent the different buildings or building classes and on the other hand the cost centres denoting the different organisational units. Examples are:

Example

Building structures	Cost centre structure
Location A	Cost centre group A
Building 1	Cost centre A-1
Building 2	Cost centre A-2
Location B	Cost centre group B
Building 1	Cost centre B-1
Building 2	Cost centre B-2

Organisational units equal to cost centre
- Board
- Marketing department
- Sales department
- Production

If it is necessary to record the income per object, it is required to use internal orders as cost objects instead of cost centres.

3.9.4 Financial and Cost Accounting Bookings

3.9.4.1 Basis for Benchmarking

Each incoming invoice is posted to the corresponding P + L account from the perspective of general ledger accounting/financial accounting (Frick 1991). From a cost accounting perspective, the expense must be posted either to a cost centre assigned to a building or, if it is a direct expense for an organisational unit, to the cost centre of the organisational unit (Kemmetmüller 1986).

Internal costs spent for a specific organisational unit, for example, the direct cost of the refurbishment work of an employee asked for by a specific department, are also posted to the cost centres of the department (Seicht 1997, S. 148 f.).

With this approach, building-related costs are accumulated to a very detailed degree to individual cost centres (belonging to a building or an organisational unit). In a next step, the costs of projects (auxiliary cost centres) can be charged to the cost centres of the buildings. If they are connected with services delivered to the departments directly, they are charged directly to the organisational unit. The costs now incurred by the individual cost centres form the basis for the calculation of the key figures (benchmarks).

3.9.4.2 Cost Transparency

Activity that is executed directly for a specific organisational unit results in a direct settlement. The remaining costs, which are charged to the building cost centres, are distributed on the basis of the square meters used to the cost centres of the departments.

3

Another step would be the use of process cost accounting. In this case, a work centre would be burdened with a fixed, building-related amount (resulting from the activity-based costing). All additional services would then be charged per "call of the service" (Wöhe and Doring 2000, S1187 f.).

Another approach is profit centre accounting, which is a widely used concept for Facility Management, as it takes both cost and revenue sides into consideration (Seicht 1997, S. 378 f.).

3.9.4.3 Quality-Relevant Data

The building and cost data are highly dependent on the features, the standard and the quality levels provided. To allow a comparison, values for the features of the building, e.g. the service levels have to be included in the analysis. This information can be obtained from service-level agreements (SLA).

3.9.4.4 Other Data

Other data also affect the values of benchmarks and must be considered in the system to ensure correct analysis of the data. Examples can be found in the EN15221–7 or in the CREIS model. The data can either be obtained by aggregation of building-related data or determined by additional analysis and imported into an information system.

Examples of such data are:

- Organisation type (hierarchy levels, etc.)
- Central purchasing/decentralized purchasing
- Central copy service/decentralized copy service

3.9.5 Management Information System

3.9.5.1 Data Warehouse Concept

Facility Managers analyse data based on a specific problem. For example, a Facility Manager examines the cleaning costs of different buildings in relation to the region/location, building structure, cleaning company and the time spent. Parts of the information are available in the ERP system like the costs and the different contract types. Other data may be stored in the CAFM system such as the location and region. To enable this analysis, the data has to be combined from the different sources and stored in a structured database in one system. The goal of the data warehouse concept (see ◘ Fig. 3.17) is to bring coherent information from different sources into one system and to generate a "unified" object (see also ◘ Fig. 3.18). This object can contain either some specific information or all data from all relevant systems (Grabatin 2001, S. 107 f.).

In our example the sources would be:

1. ERP
2. CAFM
3. Maintenance tool

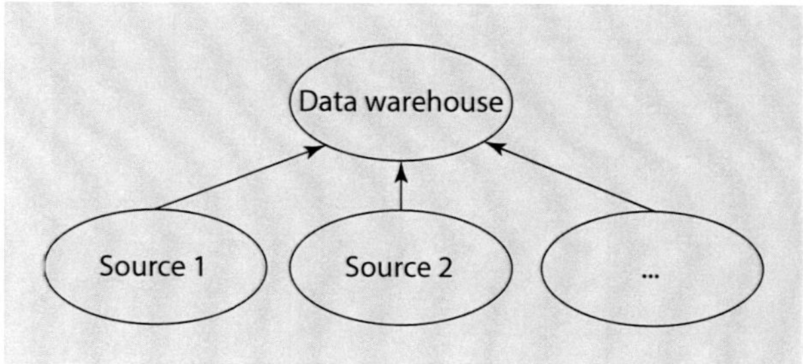

Fig. 3.17 Data warehouse concept. (Author's own figure)

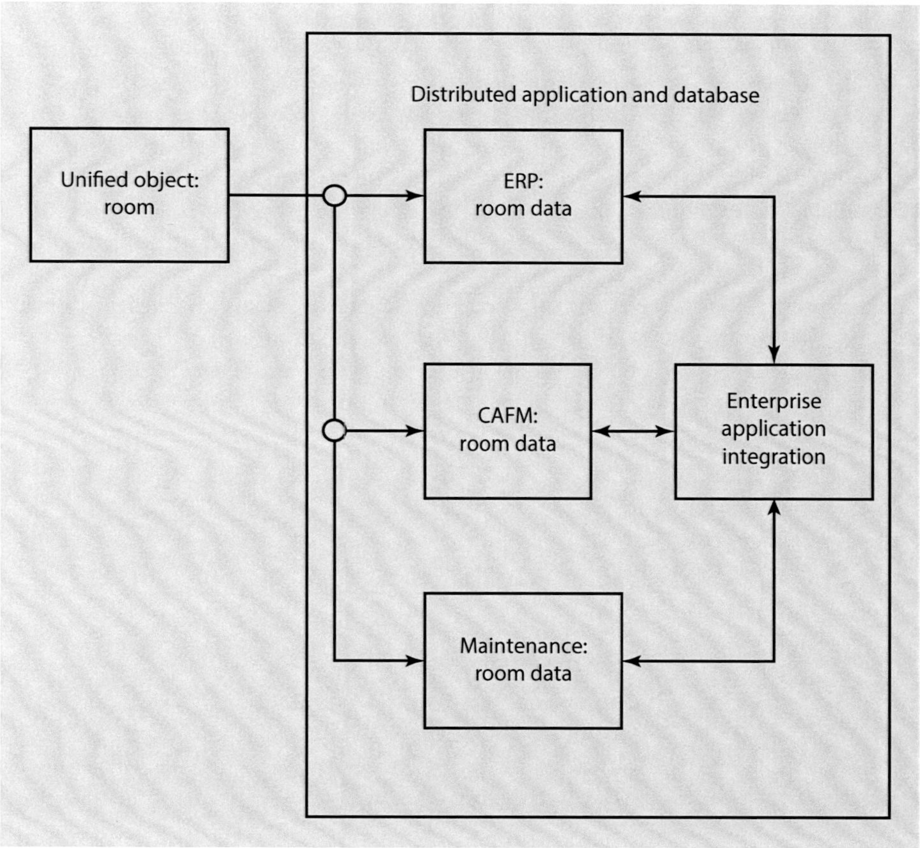

Fig. 3.18 "Unified" object. (Author's own figure)

The data warehouse brings together the information of the different tools and "unifies" them in one system, so that the management can use all different aspects in one system.

The multidimensional structures of the database usually follow the STAR scheme, which is optimised for evaluations and analyses. The STAR scheme consists of the fact table, which is in the centre of the scheme and holds the main information to be analysed as well as the foreign keys of the dimensions. The dimensions are the points of the star and represent different "views" on the fact table. An example can be that the tenant's payments are stored in the fact table. One view can be the time, as costs normally vary over the time. Another view can be the tenants', type of contract, etc., as these dimensions influence the earnings of the tenants. The next figure gives an example of a simple STAR scheme (■ Fig. 3.19).

3

This multidimensional data structure enables flexible ad hoc questions and answers with a broader scope than in traditional information systems. These instruments are very powerful, thanks to an intuitive data analysis that does not follow a predetermined structure. New ideas and hypotheses can be quickly verified. If necessary, detailed data is accessible.

Analysing a complex question with a traditional online transaction processing (OLTP) system can take a few days, even if the base data already exists. Although a SQL database is standardised and allows for various queries and analyses, its table structure, views and joins make this type of data processing very time consuming. Online analytic processing systems (OLAP) such as data warehouse instruments have the so-called Info Cube – the data cube – and an easy-to-use query language. They facilitate navigation in the multidimensional database and support functions for presenting the results. The Info Cube is the centrepiece. The data structure of the "Info Cube" is structured so that the data can be structured and processed according to the required criteria, and different types of analysis can be carried out.

The manipulation of the data structure during operation mainly changes the dimension and aggregation of the basic data. The most used functions are:

- **Drill down**: For management tasks, it is often necessary to accumulate data. Sometimes it is necessary to get more detailed information. "Drill down" means changing to a less abstract level.

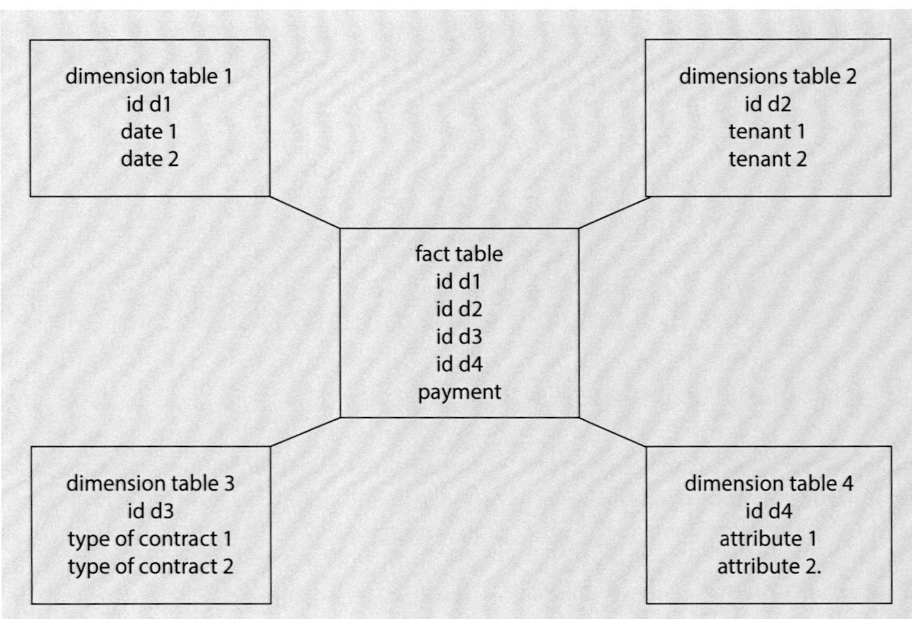

■ **Fig. 3.19** STAR scheme to analyse tenant's earnings. (Author's own figure)

- **Roll up**: This means being able to arrive at a more abstract view in the opposite direction.
- **Slicing**: "Slicing "is to select a piece of the data cube. It is also referred to as rotation, because a series of different pieces viewed from different angles correspond to a rotation of 90 °, but without re-sorting the data.
- **Data dicing**: "Dicing" means that after selecting a position on the "Info Cube" in one of the dimensions, the required data of the matrix is reduced to the relevant information.

3.9.5.2 Data Warehouse System for FM

We can now apply the tools and their functionality described above to generate an FM management information system. To make this possible, it is necessary to carry out the following steps:

The definition of the sources and the data has to be included, such as:

- **Source 1** is an ERP system used for financial and cost accounting. Necessary data are costs as well as revenues associated with the buildings/facilities.
- **Source 2** is a CAFM system that is used for space planning. Necessary data are building-related data such as floor space per building (group).
- **Source 3** is a BA system that provides up-to-date data from equipment (◘ Figs. 3.20 and 3.21).

The context and interdependence of the different data of the individual sources must be specified. The Info Cube contains all the data and displays it according to the requirements either as they were uploaded or as a result of a formula.

Example

In this example, the STAR scheme consists of the fact table with the cost information. The STAR scheme has four dimensions:

- Building (type, volume, m2/floor, etc.)
- Interior design parameters (floor and wall type, HVA, etc.)
- Location of the facilities (climate zone, urbanity, etc.)
- Time

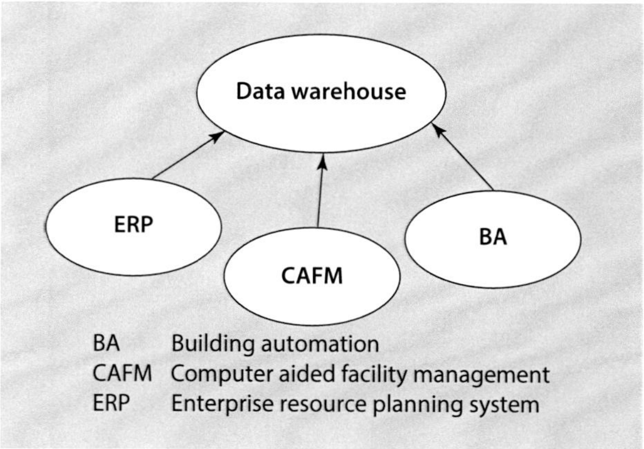

◘ **Fig. 3.20** Example of a management information system in the area of RE/FM using the data warehouse concept. (Author's own figure)

3

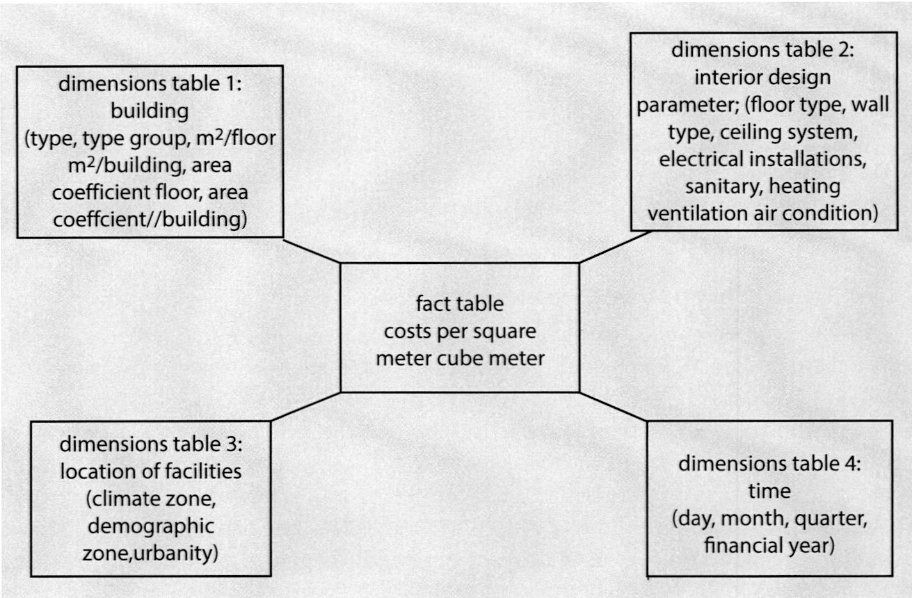

Fig. 3.21 STAR scheme for benchmarking. (Author's own figure)

Fig. 3.22 Structure of the MIS. (Author's own figure)

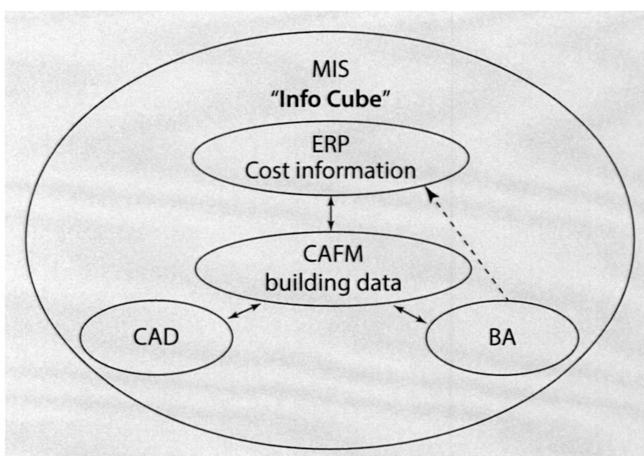

As a precondition, the building objects of the different IT systems providing the data must be linked, which means that there must be a 1 to 1 connection of the building IDs in the different systems (applications).

When the datasets are uploaded to the data warehouse, the necessary data is then available in one system with the necessary accuracy and details from all the different subsystems.

When using the data warehouse concept and after having carried out the preparatory steps, a Facility Manager receives all desired benchmarks without any additional effort. An example is an Info Cube, which shows the cleaning costs per square meter as shown in the Fig. 3.22 below:

- The cleaning costs are queried by the ERP system.
- The area information is available in the CAFM instrument.
- The value "cost per square meter" is calculated and displayed per building in the Info Cube.

3.10 Conclusion

As stated above, the calculation of benchmarks can be performed in an efficient manner if the following three conditions are met:

- Efficient IT support of the operational FM business processes that provide the baseline data for benchmark calculation. As shown, this requirement can only be met if standard software instruments are integrated with an enterprise application integration (EAI) instrument, such as middleware.
- The comparison is only possible if the basic data is available in a suitable, standardised manner for all organisational units participating in the benchmarking process. Therefore, a standardisation of cost accounting and the building-related data must be done. The building-related data can be structured according to national standards. Due to deviations of the national standards, correction coefficients have to be developed in order to use benchmarks at an international level.
- The calculation of benchmarks can only be performed by an instrument that is suitable for handling, aggregating and processing all data. The data warehouse concept fulfils these desired features and can easily retrieve and process the structured data generated by operational FM processes.

The concept supports the search for best practice examples. Analysing the data, best practice examples can be identified. By analysing the data of the operational processes on a detailed level, concepts can be identified which enable the best practice (▶ Chap. 4). These results can be used to learn from the best.

Review Questions

1. Name the elements of an ER diagram and give a practical example of an ER diagram in the area of RE/FM?
2. Give an example of an identification code for FM.
3. Name the main selection criteria for IT tools and group them.
4. What are the main elements of data security?
5. What is the GDPR and what relevance has it to RE/FM/FS?
6. What are the IT tools that support operational RE/FM/FS processes? Which functionality do they cover?
7. What technology is normally used to integrate IT tools? What are the necessary information needed to set up an optimal process support over the limit of the different IT tools?
8. What is a data warehouse tool? How can it be used in the area of RE/FM/FS?

3

References

Binder, S. (1989). *Strategic corporate facility management*. New York: McGraw-Hill.
EIB. (2002). Finanzbericht: Finanzausweise der EIB-Gruppe, Luxenbourg.
EN 15221-7. (2012). *Guidelines for performance benchmarking,* Austrian Standards.
Frick, W. (1991). *Bilanzierung,* Wien.
Grabatin, G. (2001). *Betriebswirtschaft für Facility Management: betriebswirtschaftliche Grundlagen, Einführung in kaufmännische Prozesse, wie Rechnungswesen und Controlling, für die Dienstleistung Facility Management*. Wuppertal: TAW-Verlag.
Kaplan, R., & Norton, D. (1997). *Balanced Scorecard. Grundlagen, Computerunterstützung, Einführungsstrategie*. Stuttgart, Schäffer-Pöschl Verlag.
Kemmetmüller, W. (1986). *Einführung in die Kostenrechnung*. Wien: Service Fachverl.
Kranz, H.-R. (1997). *Building control. Technische Gebäudesysteme: Automation und Bewirtschaftung* (2nd ed.). Renningen-Malmsheim: Expert-Verlag.
Longley, P. A. (2001). *Geographic information systems and science*. Chichester: Wiley.
Rouse M. (2018). *Slice and dice*. https://whatis.techtarget.com/definition/slice-and-dice
SAP Online Help for release 4.6 C.
Schulte, K.-W., & Pierschke, B. (Eds.). (2000). *Facilities management*. Köln: R. Müller.
Seicht, G. (1997). *Moderne Kosten- und Leistungsrechnung. Grundlagen und praktische Gestaltung*. Wien: Linde.
Wöhe, G., & Doring, U. (2000). *Einführung in die allgemeine Betriebswirtschaftslehre* (20th ed.). Vahlen-Verlag, Munich.

Benchmarking

Karin Schaad and Susanne Hofer

A. Redlein (ed.), *Modern Facility and Workplace Management*,
Classroom Companion: Business, https://doi.org/10.1007/978-3-030-35314-8_4

Learning Objectives

Students should know the following:

- The phases and different types of benchmarking and how to select the proper ones for their use case.
- The difference between process-step- and cost-based benchmarking.
- The advantages and disadvantages of this management tool.
- The value of benchmarking for companies.
- Gain an insight via practical knowledge of cleaning and catering key figures.

4.1 Introduction

Benchmarking is an often-used term in the business context of the last decades. There are different definitions of the term in the contemporary literature. According to the Business Dictionary (2019), benchmarking is defined as follows:

Definition

A measurement of the quality of an organization's policies, products, programs, strategies etc., and their comparison with standard measurements, or similar measurements of its peers. The objectives of benchmarking are to determine what and where improvements are called for, to analyse how other organizations achieve their high performance levels, and to use this information to improve performance (Business Dictionary 2019).

A similar definition comes from the European Standard of Facility Management for Performance Benchmarking EN 15221-7 (2011, p. 6).

Definition

"Benchmarking is the process of comparing strategies, processes, performances and/or other entities against practices of the same nature, under the same circumstances and with similar measures".

The term benchmarking comes from the Anglo-American language area and is derived from the noun benchmark, which can be translated as "with reference point or fixed point" (Brasat 2012; EN 15221-7, 2011). The term consists of the word components bench, which means seat or workbench, and mark, which means to mark. Metaphorically speaking, it is a marking on a workbench that serves, for example, to cut tubes to the same length (Fromm 1994 cited in Tucher von Simmelsdorf 2000). In the figurative sense, benchmarking refers to a reference point that is to be striven for. Benchmarking thus represents the endeavour to achieve a certain position or performance (Siebert, Kempf & Massalski, 2008). The relatively new term has its origin in land surveying for height and direction comparisons, but it also appeared in other areas such as the performance measurement of IT components (Brasat, 2012). In the 1980s, the concept of benchmarking became established for the first time in economics. When Robert C. Camp reported about the benchmarking activities of Xerox, the Xerox case was considered to be a prime example of benchmarking. However, the methods used in benchmarking originated much earlier. The first targeted application took place in 1916, when Henry Ford successfully transferred the assembly line principle from a large slaughterhouse to the automotive industry (Brasat, 2012). The description of the benchmarking concept by Xerox-Manager Camp (1989, p. 10), as "continuous process of measuring products, services and practices against the toughest competitors or those companies recognized as industry leaders", is until today one of the best known. And yet, a generally accepted definition of benchmarking, especially of its scope, still does not exist today (Brasat, 2012).

About the objective of benchmarking, the EN 15221-7 (2011, p. 4) stated that:

Definition

Benchmarking is part of a process which aims to establish the scope for, and benefits of, potential improvements in an organisation through systematic comparison of its performance with that of one or more other organisations. It is a tool in common use across industries worldwide, but has often been misused and misunderstood within Facility Management.

After clarification of the definition, scope and target of benchmarking, the following chapter describes the typical characteristics.

4.2 Benchmarking: Modules and Range

Against the background that benchmarking is characterised by a variety of characteristics and that there is no universally valid definition, Spendolini has developed a grid system based on a company survey for the definition of benchmarking, which allows different definitions. ◘ Fig. 4.1 shows Spendolini's benchmarking menu with its specific building blocks, which can be combined to create different definitions. The content and the focused area (blocks 5 and 6) can be quite different (depending on the objective), whereby the procedure is always systematic and process-oriented (blocks 2 and 3) (Brasat 2012). With regard to the objectives (blocks 4 and 9), a distinction can be made between the measurement and learning perspectives. The former refers to the relativisation and positioning of one's own performance in comparison to others; here we also speak of the quantitative level, whereas the latter places the learning from others in the foreground, the so-called qualitative level. According to Brasat (2012, p. 46), benchmarking can generally be summed up as "a systematic process that is characterized by its proactive character with a continuous focus on best values for objectification and performance improvement".

The comparison of one's own strategies, products, methods and processes can take place both within the company between different subdivision, as a so-called internal benchmarking, and also outside the company with direct competitors or even companies outside the industry as a so-called external benchmarking (Spengler, 2009). ◘ Fig. 4.2 shows the range of the benchmarking horizon. External benchmarking distinguishes between horizontal benchmarking, comparison with an organisation at the same industry,

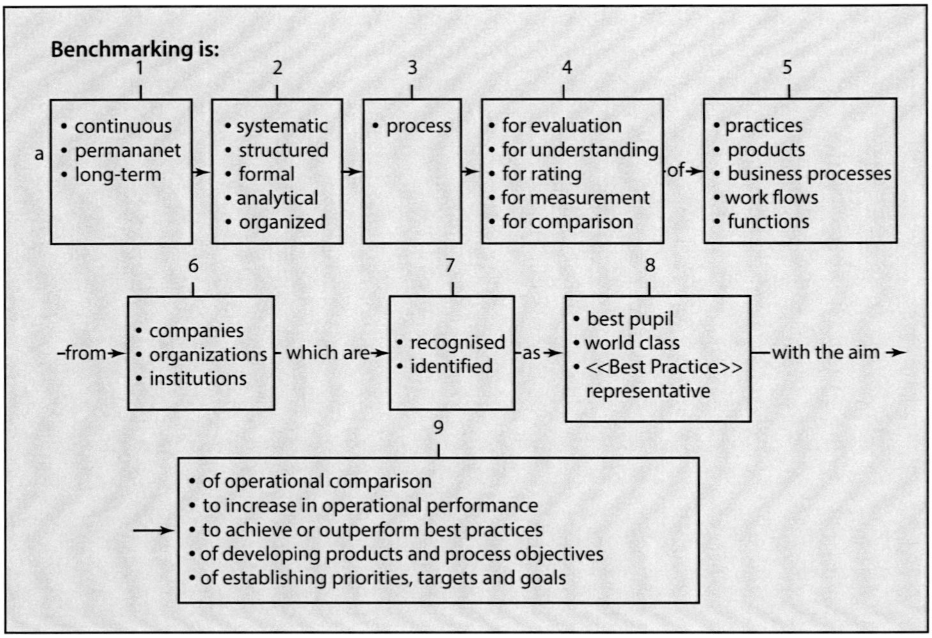

Fig. 4.1 The benchmarking menu according to Spendolini (1992, p. 10)

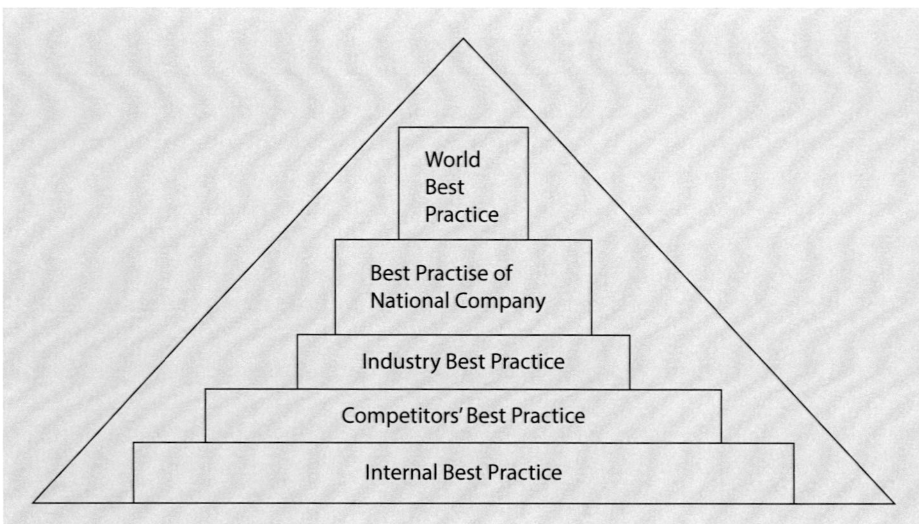

Fig. 4.2 Comparative horizons of benchmarking (Kasilingam, 1999 cited in Barber, 2004, p. 303)

■ **Table 4.1** Morphological box (Horvath and Herter, 1992)

Parameter	Specification of the parameter			
Object	Products	Methods	Processes	
Target size	Expenses	Quality	Customer satisfaction	Time
Comparison partner	Other business areas	Rivals	Same industry	Other industry

governmental or political level; vertical benchmarking, comparison with an organisation at a higher or lower industry, governmental level; and intersectoral benchmarking, comparison with organisations in other sectors (Grieble and Scheer, 2000).

4.3 Benchmarking: Types and Phases

There is no clear definition of benchmarking types in the literature. However, according to Horvàth and Herter (1992), the core elements, object, partner and target size, can be used as a basis for systematisation (see ■ Table 4.1). The benchmarking object describes the area to be analysed. Comparisons are possible for entire companies, company sub-areas, strategies and products up to individual processes and activities that are carried out in the company. The criterion comparison partner describes the search field in which – from the perspective of learning – a successful practice is to be identified. The criterion target size describes the measured quantity such as costs, revenues, consumption quantity or time to be measured (Brasat, 2012).

From this systematisation two types of benchmarking are widely used in the area of FS (Abel et al. (2004): process-step-based benchmarking and cost benchmarking.

4.3.1 Process-Step-Based Benchmarking

Based on Abel et al., (2004), Hofer (2013, p. 259) defined:

» The process-step method leads to a high level of detailed knowledge in terms of processes and key performance indicators. The use of this method requires a big effort by the participating partners, as the collection of data corresponding to individual processes is labour-intensive, time-consuming and quite often interdisciplinary. On the other hand, gathering detailed information about a process flow is the only way to identify best practice as it guarantees the comparability of the information. A positive side-effect is that the information generated about FS processes is suitable for quality management and its functions as well.

4.3.2 Cost Benchmarking

According to Abel et al., (2004) and based on Hofer (2013, p, 259):

> Compared with the process-step-based method, this type of benchmarking comes up with less meaningful results, as it provides a comprehensive overview of the general situation with respect to FS. The information gained through cost benchmarking can also be used to decide which processes are worth investigating further. The side-effect here is that this method can be used as a basis for a cost allocation system. (Abel et al. 2004).

In the light of their different – yet complementary – advantages, a combination of those two benchmarking methods should be used for sustainable improvement of Facility Management organisation.

4.4 Benchmarking: Phases

In the literature, there are a variety of models about the benchmarking process with regard to its phases, which should serve as structural frameworks. Some well-known models are the Camp (Camp, 1992) 10-phase scheme, the Karlöf/Oetsblom (Karlöf, Daschmann & Oetsblom, 1994) 5-phase scheme, the Pieske (Pieske, 1997) 8-phase scheme and the Böhnert assignment of the 17 core activities. The heterogeneity of the models in terms of the number of phases is mainly due to the different prioritisation and subdivision of activities, although in terms of content the models are very similar. It should be noted that it is advisable to consider the phases and their depths individually, depending on the circumstances of the business (Brasat, 2012).

In the following, the benchmarking phases are explained using Camp's 10-phase scheme as an example (see ◘ Fig. 4.3).

Example

During the planning phase (1) the benchmark is determined, (2) comparable enterprises are identified and (3) the data and data collection methods are defined. This is followed by the analysis phase, where (4) the current performance gap and (5) the future performance level are determined. This is followed during the integration phase by (6) communication of the results and (7) definition of the functional objectives. During the action phase, (8) the action plans are then developed, (9) the results are monitored and (10) the benchmark is adjusted, until the leadership position is reached in the maturity phase and the process can be integrated into the actions (Camp, 1989, p. 19).

These schemes show that benchmarking is a plannable process with different phases, which should be adapted to the individual circumstances of the business. Camp's theory from the late 1980s seems to be the basis for the EN 15221-7 and its phases.

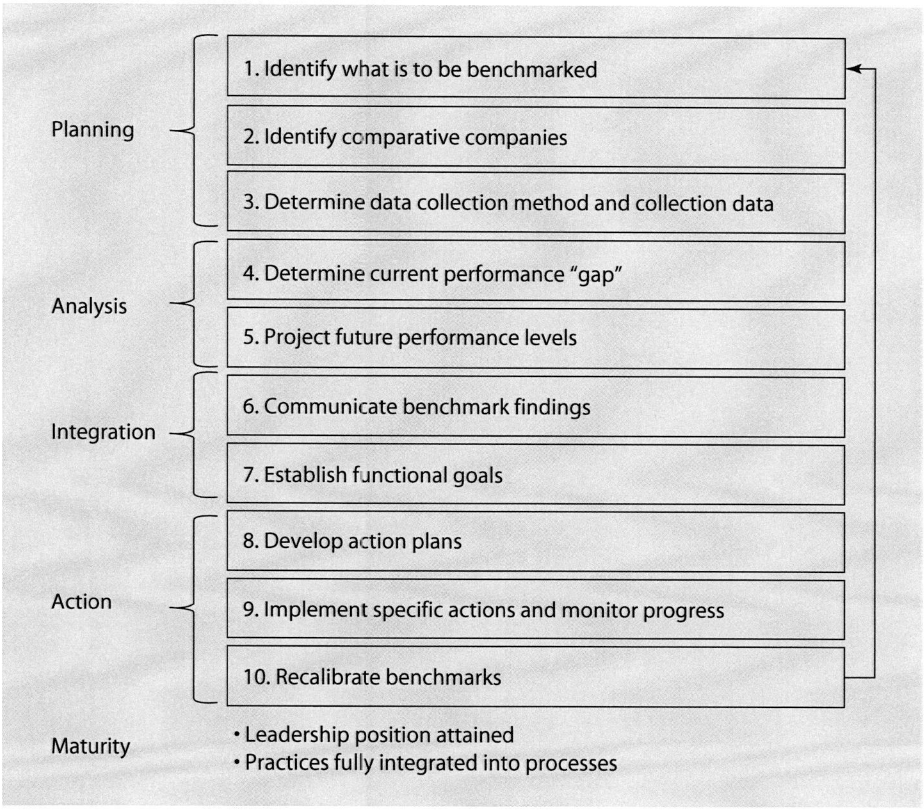

Fig. 4.3 The 10-phase scheme according to Camp (1992)

4.5 Benchmark Process According to EN 15221-7

According to EN 15221-7 (2011, p. 16), a benchmarking project can be divided into three phases: preparing, comparing and improving.

Example

During the preparing phase (1) the objectives are set by defining the purpose and scope of the benchmarking exercise. Further, (2) the methodology is determined by describing the indicators and benchmarks. And (3) partners are selected, which agreed on a code of conduct. During the comparison phase (4) data is collected and validated and then (5) analysed whereupon (6) gaps become apparent by comparing and explaining the data. Subsequently, (7) the report findings are communicated and discussed. During the improving phase (8) an action plan is developed by defining tasks and milestones, and (9) the plan is implemented – adjusted if necessary – and monitored. At the end, (10) the process is reviewed and recalibrated and the successive process steps are run through again (see below figure).

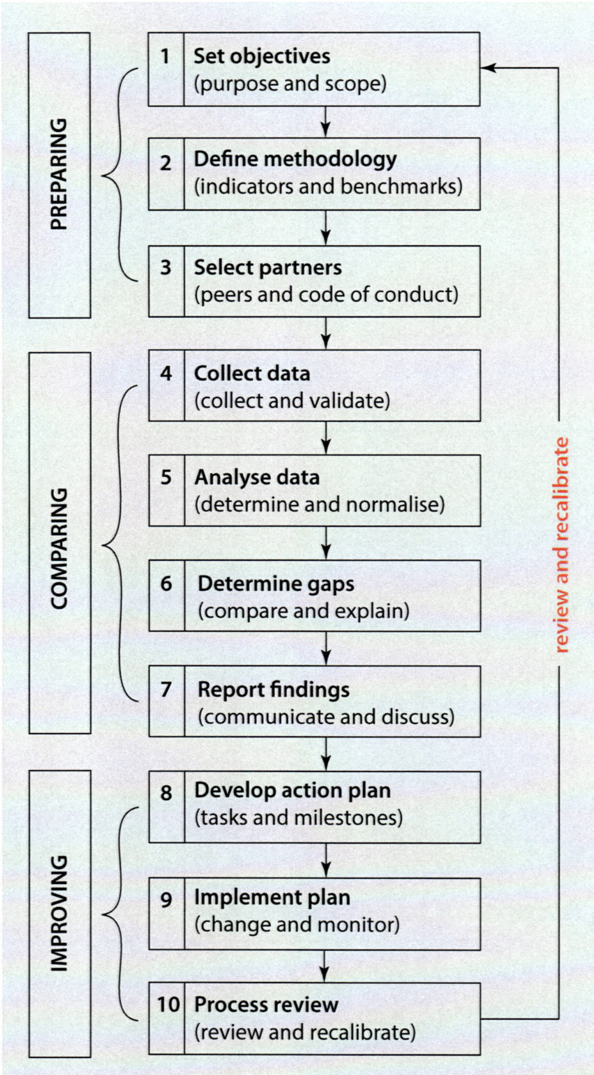

Benchmark process (EN 15221-7, 2011, p. 16)

FM as a management discipline should be linked to economic issues. Benchmarking with the steps described above provides the management with a tool and information on how to improve the overall FM services and performances in terms of costs, space and processes in order to deliver best value for money (Wauters, 2005, p. 151). According to Madritsch (2009, p. 63), benchmarking is used very little as a tool, despite it showing great potential for cost savings and optimising operating costs without compromising – rather the opposite – on quality of services (Hofer, 2013).

With increasing competition, benchmarking as management tool for evaluating processes in relation to best practice or best prices is gaining importance. The benchmarking process evaluates "who achieves best value-for-money and how they are doing it" (Wauters 2005, p. 143).

4.6 Benchmarking Methods: Advantages and Disadvantages

According to Hofer (2013, p. 258) and Dieckmann (2003, p. 6), the advantages of FM are as follows:

- In-depth analysis of key figures and their derivation.
- Intra-organisational, interdisciplinary discussion to generate the requested data.
- Better understanding of one's own processes.
- Experience of IT-supported calculation tools.
- Getting to know other organisations.
- Anonymous comparison with other benchmark participants.
- Exchange with benchmark participants in general.
- Identification of improvement potential.
- Delivery of basics for the implementation and optimisation of standard processes.
- Delivery of basics for the definition of internal objectives.
- Providing indications for reasonable use of resources, such as personnel.
- Reference values for budget processes
- Factual-based argumentation for or against a change.

According to Hofer (2013, p. 259) and Dieckmann (2003, p. 6), the disadvantages or challenges of reasonable benchmarking include the following:

- Use of methodology in a similar manner by partners is unknown.
- Data validity (wide scope of interpretation and wide scope of accounting entry).
- Comparability of the comparison group.
- Consequent evaluation of the underlying processes:
  - Adequate size of comparison group to evaluate the best in class benchmark.

Besides the challenge of getting comparable data, the confidentiality of data needed to get usable results often makes meaningful benchmarking almost impossible. In addition, collaborating organisations can generate a competitive edge because they are likely to have internal access to confidential data suitable for benchmarking. Another way of gaining comparable data for organisations willing to collaborate is through loose interest groups (e.g. Hotellerie-Benchmark, see ▶ Sect. 4.7.1), initiated through associations, or research projects. Another group of institutions with an interest in the benchmarking of organisations are financers and insurers or controlling authorities (Dieckmann, 2003).The lacking data and missing research activities are accompanied by an increased demand for transparency and clarification, by the Facility Managers themselves. These were the reasons for the benchmarking project Hotellerie-Benchmark being established (Baacke, 2019) in 2010, which continues still today.

4.7 Example FM/FS Benchmarking in Swiss Hospitals

The examples described below are based on the papers "Catering Benchmark of Swiss Hospitals" by Züger and Hofer (2015) and "Method to Benchmark Cleaning Services in Swiss Hospitals" by Honegger, Betschart, Züger & Hofer (2015).

Example

4

According to the Organisation for Economic Co-operation and Development (OECD) ranking, the Swiss healthcare system is one of the world's most expensive systems. Its comparatively high costs can be tied to its striving for excellence as well as to the perceived easy accessibility and patient friendliness. In 2012, in order to promote efficiency and effectiveness and achieve more transparency, Switzerland introduced the DRG (diagnosis-related group)-based remuneration system, factoring in country-specific factors. According to Lennerts and Janish (2012) and Zehnder (2012), FM is responsible for about 30% of the total costs of a hospital. Thus, the soft and hard services as described in the EN15221-4 account for roughly one-third of the total hospital costs.

According to the research done by Züger and Hofer (2015) and Hofer, Honegger & Züger (2013), benchmarking activities in general are still very rare, especially for food services as well as within the healthcare FM sector. Furthermore, one of the most important facts within benchmarking is the continuum; hence, data should be comparable over the years. This means benchmarking has to be done continuously.

4.7.1 Catering Benchmark

The phases are according to EN 15221-7 (see benchmarking process).

4.7.1.1 Preparing Phase

According to the FM costs described above, catering costs rank second. Catering is known to be an important image factor for hospitals. To raise the efficiency and effectiveness of catering services, a benchmarking platform for Swiss hospitals was developed. The results provide a comprehensive overview of the current situation of Swiss hospital catering and trends which are applicable to multiple hospitals have been identified.

Example

In the early years of the Hotellerie-Benchmark, catering provided findings for 23 key benchmarking figures based on 39 hospitals. Twenty-two of the base numbers, including floor space measurements and data about staff and turnover, could be extracted from already existing annual reports, cash systems, menu ordering systems and other accounting reports. The last key figure, "cost of meals per patient per day", could then be calculated using a specific method, which is described in detail in Hofer et al. (2013).

In order to set up their catering benchmark in hospitals, the researchers applied a descriptive survey research design. A vast amount of data was collected using the previously

◘ **Table 4.2** Benchmark participants 2014 (Züger and Hofer, 2015)

	Acute hospitals	**Psychiatric hospitals**	**Rehabilitation clinics**	**Home for elderly**
Number of participants	33	1	4	1

designed online benchmark platform. Since the benchmark tool was to be used by the FM practitioners at the participating hospitals, the researchers chose a pragmatic approach.

In order to allow the participation in the benchmark of healthcare institutions from different healthcare segments, a convenience sampling strategy was applied. In 2014, 39 participants benchmarked their figures of the previous year. The participants were clustered according to their segment as shown in ◘ Table 4.2:

4.7.1.2 Comparing Phase

After data collection, the data provided by the participants was put through a validation process and then analysed in a descriptive way. The key figures were defined "to form a reflection of each other to ensure the quality of the basic numbers" (Züger and Hofer, 2015).

Clustered results of the following years for over 50 participants (acute hospitals, psychiatric and rehabilitation clinics as well as home for elderly) can be found at ► www.hotellerie-benchmark.ch.

- **Key Figure 1: Cost per Meal**

According to the researchers, it was interesting to see that 39 healthcare institutions, accounting for almost 30% of all acute hospitals in Switzerland, participated in the catering benchmark in 2014. The key figures shown below are a selection out of the most useful benchmarks. Values shown as 0.00 are missing values, meaning that the participating institution was not able to provide the basic number needed to calculate this key figure. The blue line shows the basic population; the other coloured lines show the differentiation into reference groups.

The following graph shows the on-going process very well (◘ Fig. 4.4).

- **Key Figure 2: Cost per Patient**

As shown in ◘ Fig. 4.5, the average costs of meals per patient per day is CHF 37.12, the minimum is CHF 23.72 and the maximum is CHF 51.24. These figures show that the cost range is quite wide. ◘ Fig. 4.6 shows the change over the years and the clusters (small/green, medium/yellow and university hospitals/orange). This key figure can be an indication of what catering options healthcare institutions provide to their patients. It is calculated with a specific data collection, as mentioned above, as no calculation or not a standardised one of these costs is currently in place in Swiss healthcare institutions. Patient catering is a top priority customer segment in healthcare institutions.

Comparing these two figures, costs have been reduced and stabilised over the years. The institutions optimised the process on different levels but kept the food quality or enhanced the quality due to a strong quality management.

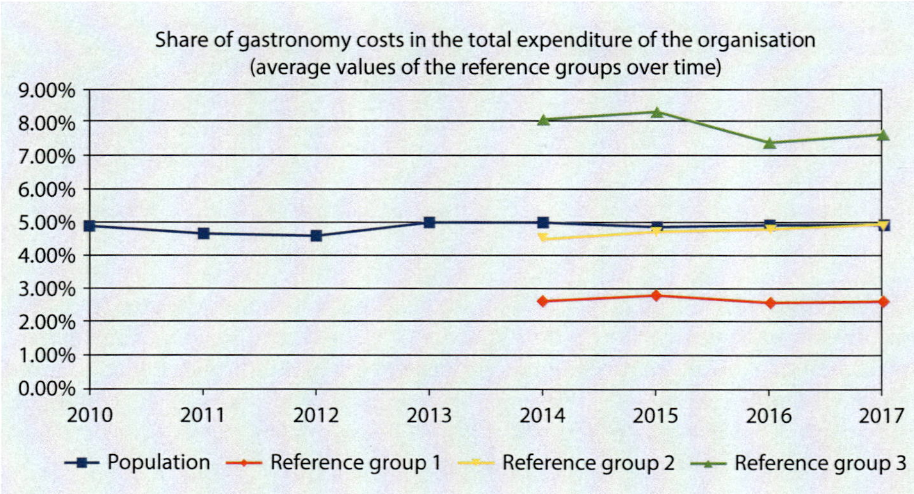

Fig. 4.4 Overall food cost compared with the total expenditure of the institution over the years (authors own figure)

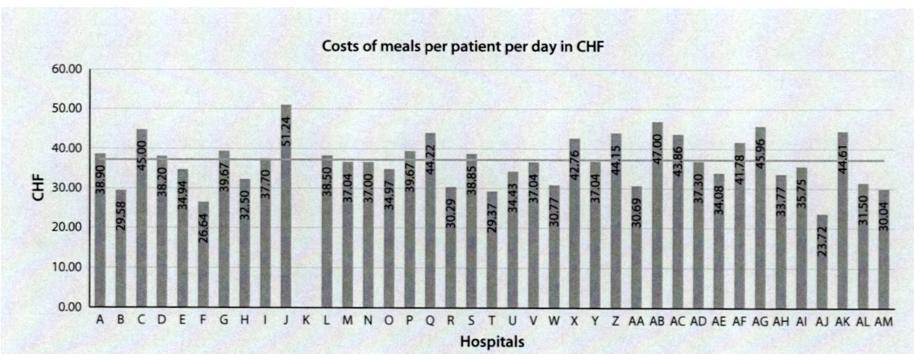

Fig. 4.5 Costs of meals per patient per day in CHF (authors own figure)

■ Key Figure 3: Food Costs

Figure 4.7 displays the food costs (unprocessed food) as a percentage of the total catering turnover in CHF. The formula behind it is [total food costs of catering] / [total catering turnover (patients, external catering, restaurant)]. The average food costs are 35.79% of the total catering turnover. The minimum is 12.32% and the maximum of a healthcare institution in this benchmark is 93.20%, which is of course an outlier and has to be eliminated.

As the reference groups (small, medium or university hospitals) and the qualitative requirements specified by the management are missing, the figure of institution A or B, etc., can be seen as an in-house performance figure rather than a comparison to the best.

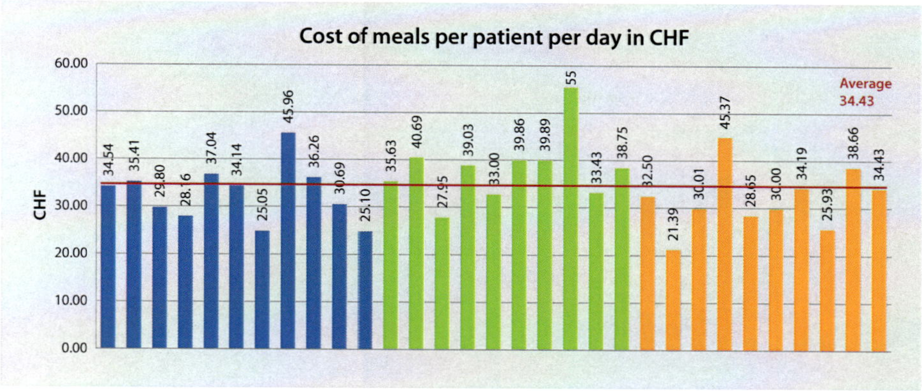

Fig. 4.6 Costs of meals per patient per day in CHF some years later and divided into groups (authors own figure)

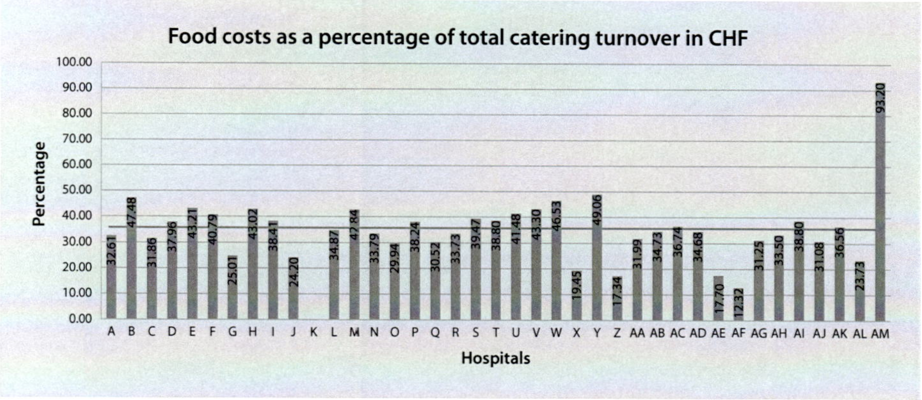

Fig. 4.7 Food costs as a percentage of total catering turnover in CHF (authors own figure)

Key Figure 4: Turnover

The personnel and food costs as a percentage of the total catering turnover in CHF are shown in Fig. 4.8. The formula of this key figure is: [total personnel and food costs of catering] / [total catering turnover (patients, external catering, restaurants)]. Included in this graph are the results of Fig. 4.7 plus personnel costs. To produce meals, the overall cost factor contains the cost of goods and personnel expenses. Both highly depend on purchasing behaviour (raw material/food or convenience products), which affect the cooking processes and thereby the cost for cooking staff.

In general, figures above 100% mean that expenses cannot be covered by the revenues. The average personnel and food costs make up 96.94% of the total catering turnover. The minimum is 44.62% and the maximum is 164.64%. It must be kept in mind that personnel and food costs are the two major cost blocks, but not the only ones which need to be covered by the total catering turnover.

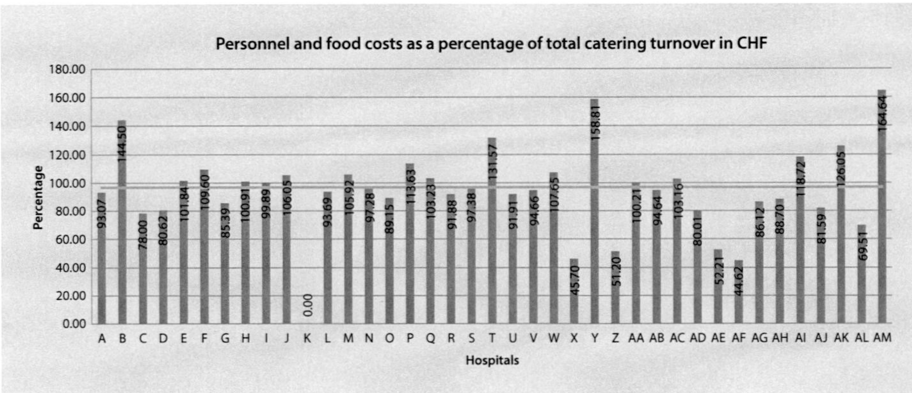

Fig. 4.8 Personnel and food costs as a percentage of total catering turnover in CHF (authors own figure)

To have a closer look at the personnel costs, different graphs can be drawn. The most important one is Fig. 4.9, reasons for absenteeism. Such information gives an assessment about the work moral and the kind of leadership; hence an action plan can be taken into consideration.

- **Key Figure 5: Profitability**

Institutions with figures over 100% are making a loss, which means personnel and cost of goods are higher than their revenues.

So far, there are no indications about the processes, the salary differences, the kitchen equipment and the amount of food waste. Food waste is defined as produced menus which are not consumed due to overproductions, mis-orders, incorrect production volume, etc. (Fig. 4.10).

As example, each hospital knows its amount of food waste produced by patients due to mis-orders (Fig. 4.11). With such kind of information, the institution can take an action plan into consideration to avoid or reduce food waste, hence enhance profitability.

4.7.1.3 Improving Phase

So, with different key figures drawn from the evaluation, the processes can be optimised to become profitable. Each institution has to analyse/interpret its results and compare different variables to make the weaknesses visible.

These insights can be very helpful for FM practitioners as a basis for decision-making. The numbers come in handy when calculating the cost of external services, when optimising services, when planning the refurbishment of existing facilities or developing new catering facilities. The various key figures can also be used by Facility Managers as an argumentation aid when discussing matters on a strategic level.

The numbers of healthcare institutions participating in this benchmark are evidence that the method developed for benchmark catering in Swiss hospitals works in practice.

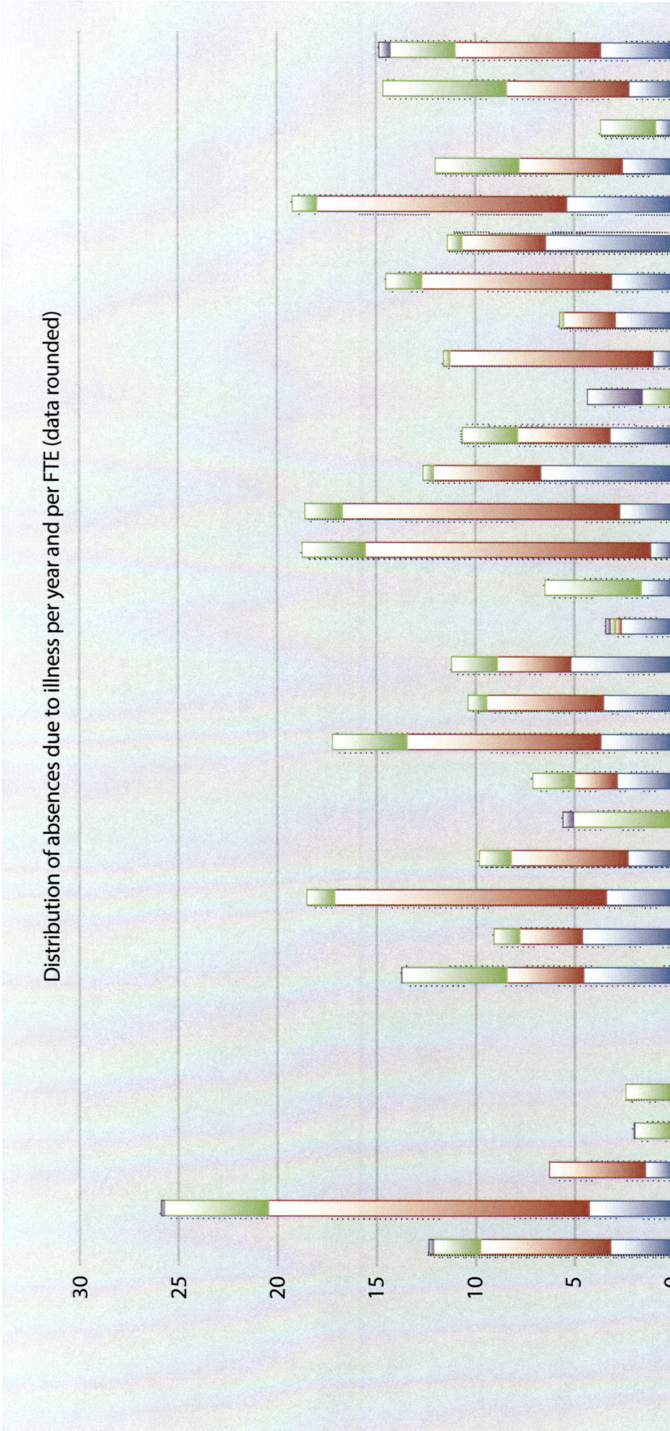

	Average	A (ZV, kR)	B (ZV)	C (ZV,rU,kR)	D (ZV, rU)	E (ZV, rU)	F (ZV, rU)	G (ZV)	H (ZV, rU)	I (ZV)	J (ZV, rU)	K (ZV, kR)	L (GV, rU)	M (GV)	N AG (GV)	O (GV)	P (GV, kR)	Q (GV, kR)	R (GV, kR)	S (GV)	T (GV)	U (GV, rU)	V (SK, rU)	W (SK)	X (SK, rU)	Y (SK, rU)	Z (SK, kR)	AA (SK, kR)	AB (SK)	AC (SK, kR)	AD (SK, kR)	AE (SK)
Sick due to pregnancy	0	0	0	0				0	0	0		1	0	0	0	0	0	0	0	0	0	0	3	0	0	0	0	0	0	0	0	1
Accident	2	5	0	2	2			5	1	1	2	5	2	4	1	2	0	5	3	2	1	3	2	0	0	2	1	1	4	3	3	3
Long-term illness	7	16	5					4	3	14	6		2	10	6	4	0	0	14	14	5	5		10	3	10	4	13	5	0	6	7
Short-term illness	3	4	1	0				5	5	3	2		3	4	4	5	3	2	1	3	7	3		1	3	3	6	5	3	1	2	4

Fig. 4.9 Factors to increase the personnel costs (sick leaves) (authors own figure)

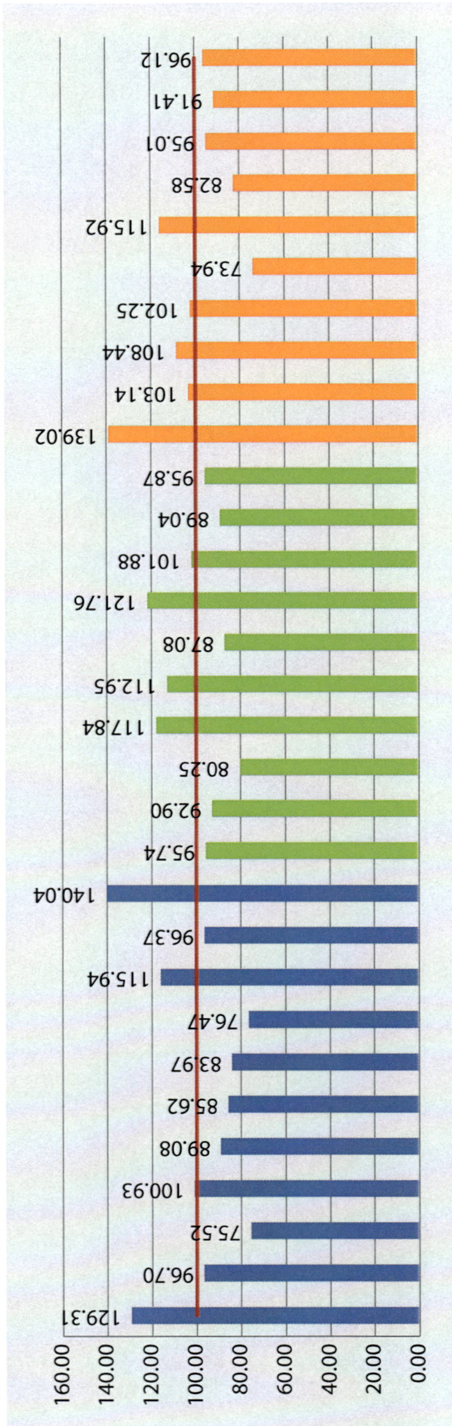

Fig. 4.10 Profitability (authors own figure)

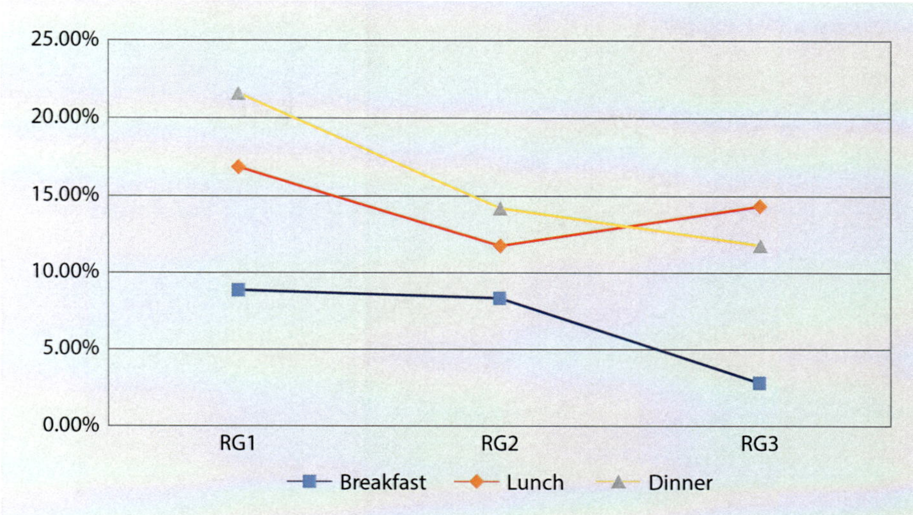

Fig. 4.11 Unprofitability, food waste according to the reference groups and the three main meals (authors own figure)

The benchmark platform is therefore going to be used on a yearly basis with an increasing number of participants. In addition, various insights can be drawn from specific key figures as well as by combining sets of key figures as shown in the graphs above.

The findings provide essential key figures for the soft service part of FM and as such contribute to the FM knowledge base (van der Zwang, 2007).

In the next step, the number of key figures will be extended to additional interesting areas of a catering department in healthcare institutions such as food waste. In addition, other benchmarks for FM topics in healthcare institutions will be developed, such as cleaning, and will be based on the methodology of this catering benchmark.

4.7.2 Cleaning Benchmark

4.7.2.1 Preparing Phase

Example

The second example about the benchmarking of cleaning services was a follow-up of the first example, the successfully implemented catering benchmark in Swiss hospitals. The seven hospitals which agreed to participate in the cleaning benchmark were accessed through existing connections. A purposive, non-probability sampling technique was applied. According to Honegger, Betschart, Züger and Hofer (2015) cleaning activities which are typical in Swiss hospitals were represented, including both hospitals with in-house and outsourced cleaning services. The following table provides an overview of the key parameters of the seven participants:

Table 4.3 Key parameters of sample hospitals (all acute care) (table compiled by authors)

	Hospital 1	Hospital 2	Hospital 3	Hospital 4	Hospital 5	Hospital 6	Hospital 7
Number of Beds	377	264	607	479	156	210	8'29
Inpatients	18'406	66'799	36'406	20'005	47'347	14'676	34'441
Inpatient days	106'744	72'586	25'1653	126'405	53'151	65'503	265'818
Number of staff (FIE)	1'325.40	927.00	3'418.70	1'886.00	680.00	1'293.70	ns
Number of staff (head-count)	1'940.00	1'268.00	4'361.00	753.00	1'005.00	1'958.00	3'429100

4

The aim of this study was to develop a method to facilitate the benchmarking of cleaning activities in Swiss hospitals. Not only will the benchmarking results provide Swiss hospitals with valuable data but they will also add to the understanding of the particularities of Swiss hospitals. The following paragraphs display some benchmarking data of the seven hospitals initially involved. The results are based on the hospitals' 2012 figures.

The key figure (Fig. 4.12) as shown below illustrates that, with an average of only 1.54%, cleaning costs do not account for a major part of the total hospital costs. However, in spite of their comparatively low impact on hospitals' total costs, cleaning services are often encouraged to reduce costs when it comes to cost-cutting demands.

As specified already in the first example above, to avoid inaccurate comparisons, clearly defined key figures, calculated using clearly defined base numbers, are essential for benchmarking activities. According to Honegger et al., (2015), "usable base figures were obtained from the data on existing sources of process and cost information, such as inventory control systems, payroll accounting and human resource statistics". According to them, key figures were selected and developed, taking into account the requirements of the cleaning managers at the participating hospitals and are based on the conducted semi-structured expert discussions. These resulting key figures provide decision-makers with argumentation aids based on improved process and cost transparency.

An example of how these figures were defined is given by the relatively simple key figure "total cleaning cost", as shown in Table 4.3.

As data had to be comparable, the question of work performances was essential and gives reasons why a hospital with mediocre accounting figures could become best in class when the work performances were much higher than elsewhere.

According to the researchers, one of the challenges in defining the key figures was the different systems used in the hospitals. Every definition needed several versions,

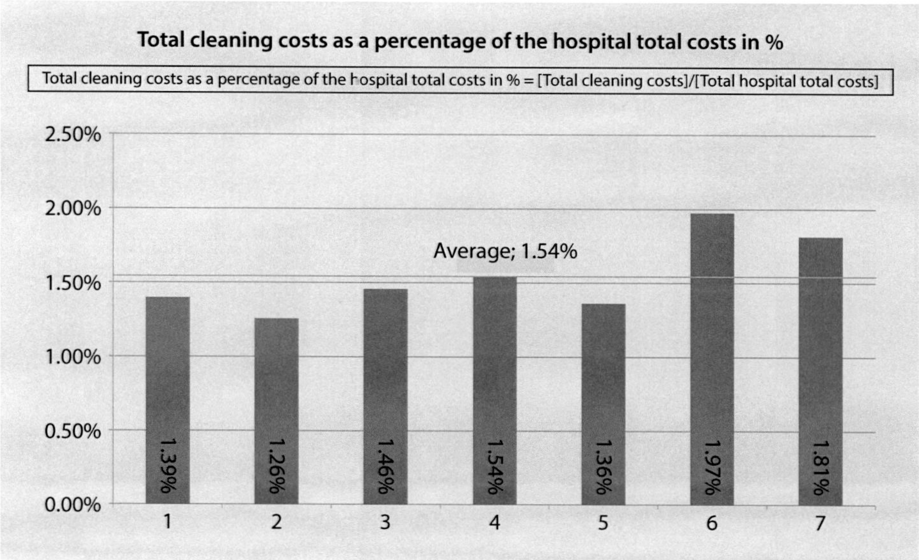

Fig. 4.12 Benchmark results: total cleaning costs as a percentage of the hospital total costs (authors own figure)

Table 4.4 Example key figure definition (Honegger et al., 2015)

Name of key figure	Total cleaning cost
Formula (use of base numbers)	Personnel cost + material cost + cost purchased cleaning – Cleaning revenue
Definitions	Personnel cost = cost of staff working exclusively for the cleaning department (includes social benefits) Material cost = cost of materials used for the cleaning itself (not including cleaning material used by other hospital staff; a list showing examples of materials which costs are integrated and delimited is provided) Cost purchased cleaning = cost for cleaning services provided by external providers Cleaning revenue = revenue obtained for cleaning services provided to external clients

until it was understood in the same way by all the participating hospitals. Often, there was no applicable common ground and a feasible definition for the base number in question had to be developed, leaving "the least possible room for misinterpretation" (Fig. 4.13).

The methodology adopted facilitated the development of 21 clearly defined base numbers leading to 12 informative key figures. The focus was on topics that included cost data, such as cost of staff or ratio of skilled to unskilled employees as well as floor

4

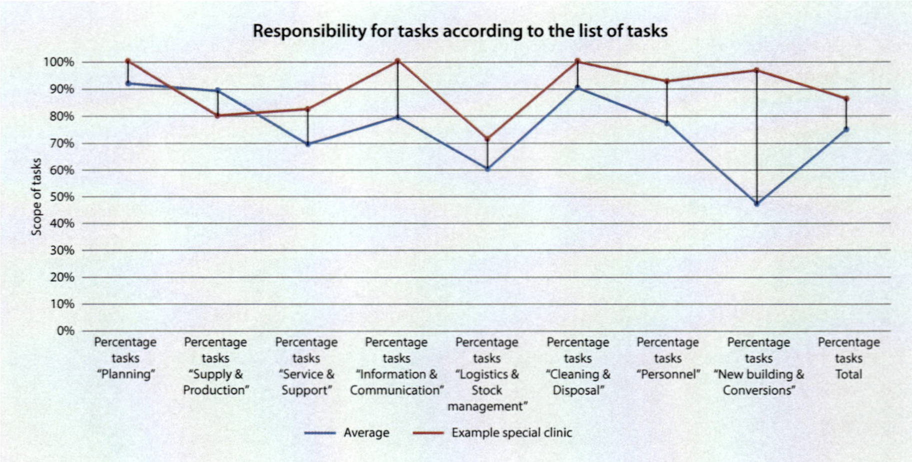

Fig. 4.13 Qualitative performance catalogue (authors own figure)

space to be cleaned. To allow the comparison of cleaning data across hospitals of different sizes, most of the key figures represent relative data.

Cleaning costs need to be assigned to the cleaning tasks being carried out. To do so, a catalogue of weighted cleaning tasks was developed by Honegger et al., (2015). This tool, defining a total of 234 tasks, gives an overview of the tasks carried out by cleaning services. The tasks differ in terms of resources used to carry them out.

Example

For example, cleaning patient rooms is more relevant than cleaning parking space. To factor this in, following intensive expert discussion, all tasks were assigned to a weighting. The weights of the tasks are determined by the necessary resources in terms of relevance, cost and time/frequency. The catalogue is part of the cleaning benchmark and each participating hospital has to mark the tasks being carried out by their cleaning department. This standardised procedure leads to a hospital-specific number of tasks with a total weight expressed in points, the so-called "task points". This process allows us to examine total cleaning costs in relation to the task points scored across hospitals.

4.7.2.2 Comparing Phase

Figure 4.14 displays the key figure "material costs as a percentage of total cleaning costs". This information shows that material costs only count for a small part, on average 5.21%, of the total cleaning costs, as staff costs are relatively high in Switzerland. Differences between the hospitals are based on the different cleaning techniques used. Hospitals 4 and 5 invested in new cleaning equipment affecting their 2012 numbers, which explains why they are above average.

As mentioned above, staff costs in Switzerland are relatively high. Fig. 4.15 shows average hospital staff costs in Swiss francs per full time equivalent (FTE) working in the cleaning department. The average across participating hospitals is around 73,000 Swiss francs, which is about 77,000 US dollars (based on the exchange rate from 05/26/2015).

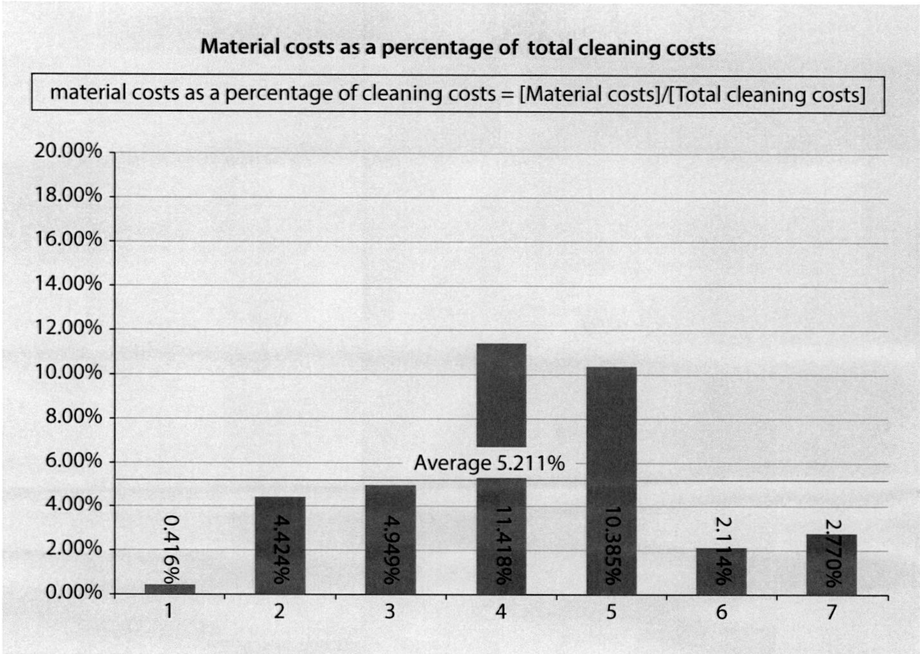

Fig. 4.14 Benchmark results: material costs as a percentage of total cleaning costs (authors own figure)

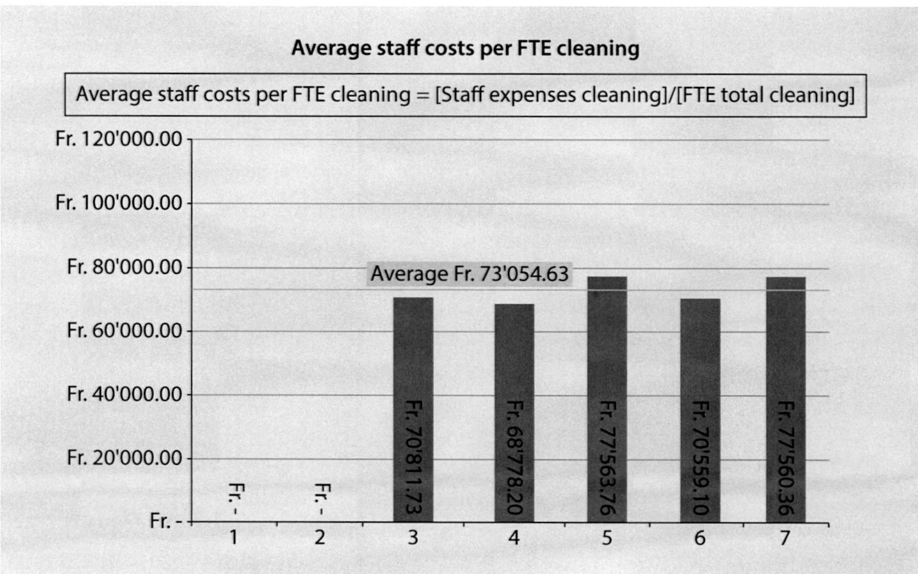

Fig. 4.15 Benchmark results: average staff costs per FTE cleaning (authors own figure)

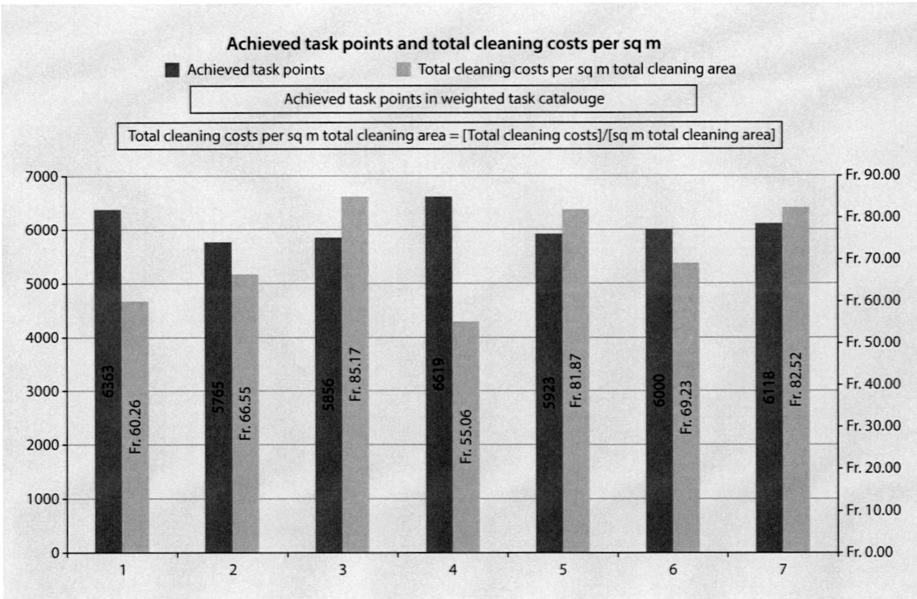

Fig. 4.16 Benchmark results: achieved task points and total cleaning costs per m² (authors own figure)

Hospitals 1 and 2 have outsourced their cleaning services and could not obtain wage data from the external service provider. Differences are presumably due to the staff structure based on the employee's age, skills, gender and number of years of employment.

Figure 4.16 shows the central information, the task points assigned from the weighted task catalogue and hospitals' total cleaning costs per m^2.

The data shows that there is no obvious correlation of high total costs with the task points assigned, as hospitals with relatively high task points can also score relatively low on total cleaning costs, such as hospital 4. The range is relatively broad, ranging between 55.06 and 85.17 Swiss francs. These results are currently being researched, as it is important to understand the reasons behind them. Nevertheless, the existing benchmark results based on the developed method enable for the first time a high level of transparency on which to base an investigation behind the data in further steps.

4.7.2.3 Improving Phase

Honegger et al. (2015) have found the cleaning services in hospitals are a complex matter. Through the benchmarking method, further hospital specifics such as number of buildings, number of hospital beds and number of internal patient transfers which trigger resource-intensive cleaning tasks are obtained. They put the benchmarking results into perspective, as they make it possible to explain differences in the results and to start an optimisation.

4.8 Conclusion

The response to the benchmarking possibilities provided in the examples above has been very positive. Participation provides clear structures to raise the cost transparency in FM in hospitals and to effectively compare cleaning structures and costs across Swiss hospitals. The examples above cover phases 1 to 7 of the EN15221-7. Based on the results, the action plans for each hospital have to be derived to optimise their internal operation in their field.

The findings of this reporting platform provide FM managers with argumentation aids when discussing effectiveness and efficiency issues on a strategic level and add to the knowledge of how FM costs emerge and are justified.

In order to raise efficiency and effectiveness as well as provide excellent service, Facility Managers need tools such as the benchmark platform described above. The developed benchmarking method can be used in every industry to ensure efficient and effective support services. But it must be stated very clearly that to compare key figures is not benchmarking. First of all, in the "preparing" phase the objectives must be set, the methodology like the type of benchmarking is applied, the key indicators to be compared need to be defined, and proper partners are to be selected either within the own industry or even from other industry sectors. In the next step, the "comparing phase" based on a detailed definition of the data (what are the services, the costs, etc.), the data collection, validation and gap analysis can take place. Based on the data gained, reporting can be done to enable the last phase, the real "improvement".

As described in the chapter, IT support tools can help with the data structuring, collection and validation, but this only supports a part of the whole benchmarking process.

Review Questions

1. Define benchmarking.
2. What do you understand about comparative horizons of benchmarking?
3. Come up with the explanation of parameters' specification.
4. What is the difference between Camp's 10-phase model and the EN 15221-7?
5. What are the pros and cons of benchmarking?
6. What are the five major benefits of being a part of a benchmark community?

References

Abel, J., Pfründer, U., & Lennerts, K. (2004). *Benchmarking in 13 German hospitals, Process-step based benchmarking vs. cost benchmarking – Results of the OPIK Research Project*. Karlsruhe Germany: University of Karlsruhe. Retrieved from http://www.tmb.kit.edu/966_1928.php

Baacke, L. (2019). *Hotellerie-Benchmark*. www.hotellerie-benchmark.ch. Schaffhausen, Switzerland.

Barber, E. (2004, May). Benchmarking the management of projects: A review of current thinking. *International Journal of Project Management*, 22(4):301–307.

Böhnert A. A. (1999). *Charakteristik eines aktuellen Managementinstruments*. Gefälligkeitsübersetzung: Benchmarking: characteristics of a current management tool.

Brasat, N. (2012). *Internes Benchmarking in Handelsunternehmungen als Basis wertorientierter Unternehmungsführung*. Deutschland: München und Mering.

4

Business Dictionary. (2019, July 29). *BusinessDictionary*. Retrieved from http://www.businessdictionary.com/

Camp, R. C. (1989). *Benchmarking: The search for industry best practices that lead to superior performance*. Milwaukee: ASQC/Quality Press.

Camp, R. C. (1992). Learning from the Best Leads to Superior Performance. *Journal of Business Strategy 13*(3), 3–6.

Dieckmann, M. (2003). Benchmarking als Best Practices-Börse für Spitäler. *Competence, 11*, 5–9.

EN 15221-7. (2011). *Facility Management – Teil 7: Leitlinien für das Leistungs-Benchmarking*. Brussels, Belgium: Comité Européen de Normalisation.

Fetter, R. B. (1991). *Diagnosis related groups: Understanding hospital performance*. INTERFACES, 21(1), 6–26.

Fetter, R. B., Thompson, J. D., & Mills, R. E. (1976). A system for cost and re- imbursement control hospitals. *Yale Journal of Biology and Medicine, 7*(3), 97–114.

Grieble, O., & Scheer, A.-W. (2000). *Grundlagen des Benchmarkings öffentlicher Dienstleistungen*. Saarbrücken: Veröffentlichungen des Instituts für Wirtschaftsinformatik.

Hofer, S. (2013). *Facility management in Swiss Hospitals*. (Doctoral dissertation). Charles Sturt University, Badhurst, Australia.

Hofer, S., Honegger, F., & Züger, G. (2013). A method to benchmark Swiss Hospital catering. *International Journal of Facility Management, 4*(3), 3.

Honegger, F., Hofer, S., Züger, G., & Betschart, M., (2015). A method to benchmark cleaning services in Swiss hospitals [Paper]. In *IFMA Academic & Research Track Proceedings World Workplace Conference in Denver. World Workplace Conference*, Denver, 2015. Georgia Institute of Technology.

Karlöf B., Daschmann H.-A., & Östblöm S., (1994). *Das Benchmarking-Konzept*, Verlag: Vahlen, Aufl. 1, München Deutschland.

Kasilingam R. G. (1999). *Logistics and Transportation*: Design and planning, Springer Verlag, Aufl. 1, Berlin, Deutschland.

Lennerts, K., & Janish, K. (2012, November). System zur gerechten Kostenaufteilung. *Kma guide, 17*, 121–123.

Madritsch, T. (2009). Best practice benchmarking in order to analyse operating costs in the healthcare sector. *Journal of Facilities Management, 7*(1), 61–73.

Pieske, R. (1997). *Benchmarking in der Praxis*, Verlag: Mi-Wirtschaftsbuch, München Deutschland.

Siebert, G., Kempf, S., & Massalski, O. (2008). *Benchmarking: Leitfaden für die Praxis*. München: Carl Hanser Verlag.

Spengler, G. (2009). *Strategie- und Organisationsentwicklung: Konzeption und Umsetzung eines integrierten, dynamischen Ansatzes zum strategischen Management*. Berlin: Springer.

Tucher von Simmelsdorf, F. W. (2000). *Benchmarking von Wissensmanagement*. Wiesbaden: Deutscher Universitätsverlag.

van der Zwang, J. (2007). *The challenges, possibilities and limits of existing and future European Standards in the Area of Facility Management*. Milano: CEN European Comittee for Standardization.

Wauters, B. (2005). The added value of facilities management: Benchmarking work processes. *Facilities, 23*(3/4), 142–151.

Zehnder, A. (2012, April). Viele, viele Fragezeichen. *kma, 17*, 66–68.

Züger, G., & Hofer, S. (2015). Catering Benchmark of Swiss Hospitals [Paper]. In *IFMA Academic & Research Track Proceedings World Workplace Conference in Denver. World Workplace Conference*, Denver, 2015. Georgia Institute of Technology.

Digitalisation

Alexander Redlein and Claudia Höhenberger

A. Redlein (ed.), *Modern Facility and Workplace Management*,
Classroom Companion: Business, https://doi.org/10.1007/978-3-030-35314-8_5

Learning Objectives
Students should know the following:
- All four industrial revolutions.
- The goals of digitalisation.
- How digitalisation influences RE/FM/FS.
- The most important emerging technologies in RE/FM/FS.
- The most affected services by digitalisation.
- Based on detailed examples, how to depict the changes in specific FS due to emerging technologies.

5.1 Introduction

A traditional textbook on Real Estate and Facility Management would end here with a conclusion and an outlook into upcoming trends. As this is a textbook on "Modern Facilities and Workplace Management", the new kid on the block has to be included: digitalisation. Yes, several big players consider the trends connected with digitalisation as not relevant for the industry. This is also shown by studies of several international consulting companies like EY (Herrenkohl et al. 2017). All of those stated that the industry does not really care about properly preparing itself for the changes (Nagl et al. 2017). However, digitalisation is not really a new kid on the block. What does digitalisation actually mean? First of all, there are similar words that we should define before we go into more details:

According to **Gartner's IT Glossary**, "digitalisation" is the "process of changing from an analog to a digital format", which means the conversion of analog texts, pictures or sounds into a digital format, that can be processed by a computer (Blieberger et al. 1996, p. 18).

Digitalisation is the use of digital technologies to change a business model and to provide new revenue and value-producing opportunities. It is the process of moving to a digital business (Gartner IT Glossary 2019).

For some executives, it is about technology itself. For others, "digital" means a new way of engaging with customers. And for another group, it represents an entirely new way of doing business. None of these definitions is necessarily incorrect. Nevertheless, such diverse perspectives often trip up leadership teams (Dörner and Edelman 2015).

The term "digitalisation" used nowadays is linked to the term "4th Industrial Revolution". Klaus Schwab was one of the first to use this term in his 2016 publication presented at the World Economic Forum in Switzerland.

In that publication, he defines the following "revolutions":

> "The agrarian revolution combined the efforts of animals with those of humans for the purpose of production, transportation and communication. Little by little, food production improved, spurring population growth and enabling larger human settlements. This eventually led to urbanisation and the rise of cities.
>
> Industrial revolutions began in the second half of the 18th century. These marked the transition from muscle power to mechanical power.

The first industrial revolution spanned from about 1760 to around 1840 and was triggered by the construction of railroads and the invention of the steam engine. It ushered in mechanical production.

The second industrial revolution, which started in the late 19th century and into the early 20th century, made mass production possible, fostered by the advent of electricity and the assembly line.

The third industrial revolution began in the 1960s. It is usually called the 'computer' or 'digital revolution' because it was catalysed by the development of semiconductors, mainframe computing (1960s), personal computing (1970s and 80s) and the internet (1990s). This revolution is linked with the term digitisation, as it is first necessary to convert analog signals into digital ones that then they can be processed by computers.

The fourth industrial revolution began at the turn of this century and builds on the digital revolution. It is characterised by a much more ubiquitous and mobile internet, by smaller and more powerful sensors that have become cheaper, and by Artificial Intelligence and Machine Learning.

Digital technologies that have computer hardware, software and networks at their core are not new, but in a break with the third industrial revolution, they are becoming more sophisticated and integrated and are, as a result, transforming societies and the global economy. This is the reason why Massachusetts Institute of Technology (MIT) Professors Erik Brynjolfsson and Andrew McAfee have famously referred to this period as "the second machine age". They state in their book, that the world is at an inflection point where the effect of these digital technologies will manifest with "full force" through automation and the making of "unprecedented things"." (Schwab 2016, p. 11).

> "In the fourth industrial revolution, digital connectivity enabled by software technologies is fundamentally changing society. The scale of the impact and the speed of the changes taking place have made the transformation that is playing out so different from any other industrial revolution in human history." (Schwab 2016, p. 109).

Klaus Schwab further states that the fourth Industrial Revolution is "marked by the emergence of new business models, the disruption of incumbents and the reshaping of production, consumption, transportation and delivery systems. On the societal front, a paradigm shift is underway in how we work and communicate, as well as how we express, inform and entertain ourselves" (Schwab 2016, p. 7).

This means that the RE/FM industry shall not limit the fourth Industrial revolution to the "usage of new emerging technologies", but consider it as a game changer with respect to:

- **Customer orientation**: Our clients are used to getting services and products customised to their needs and demands. One size fits all is from yesterday.
- **On demand**: We are used to getting feedback immediately, not only during working hours.
- **Human touch**: People, at least not all of them, do not want fancy technology; they want convenience. Especially during my visits in Stanford I learned from always

being asked by the mechanical engineering design thinking team: What does the client really want? Will they be afraid of all this technology?
- ***Wow* effect**: Customers want to be surprised, they already know the common services and products; thus they look for the extra mile, the personalisation, etc.

Technology is an enabler. But what are the emerging technologies? In his book, Klaus Schwab quotes the survey report "*Deep Shift – Technology Tipping Points and Social Impact*" which was published in September 2015. He refers to 22 technologies changing business – as well as the private world dramatically in the next few years:
1. Implantable technologies
2. Our digital presence
3. Vision as the new interface
4. Wearable Internet
5. Ubiquitous computing
6. A supercomputer in your pocket
7. Storage for all
8. The Internet of and for things
9. The connected home
10. Smart cities
11. Big data for decisions
12. Driverless cars
13. Artificial intelligence and decision-making
14. AI and white-collar jobs
15. Robotics and services
16. Bitcoin and the blockchain
17. The sharing economy
18. Governments and the blockchain
19. 3D printing and manufacturing
20. 3D printing and human health
21. 3D printing and consumer products
22. Designer beings
23. Neurotechnologies

The list above and its examples are universally common; consequently, it is hard to apply them directly to our industry. Therefore, several years ago, the TU Wien started a research project to analyse the impact of digitalisation on the Real Estate and Facility Management industry. According to the results, digitalisation has an impact on two main areas:
1. Changes in the core business, like new ways of working, modify the demand for infrastructure and services dramatically.
2. Emerging technologies: For example, Internet of things (IoT), big data and artificial intelligence (AI) allow disruptive and much more efficient ways of service provisioning. Therefore, the service provision itself is changed by digitalisation.

This chapter focuses on the second area: the use of new technologies to optimise FS provision. The next and final chapter will provide an insight into the domain of workplace management as it brings all the chapters of the book together to "one final product", the work environment, to make people but also their employees successful.

Let us now focus on FS operation. Many studies analyse the impact of digitalisation on work processes. These studies assume that digitalisation will have the greatest effect on routine tasks or tasks that can be accurately defined allowing a code to be developed capable of taking over these tasks. Drastic changes are predicted and so shifts in skills will be required (Nagl et al. 2017; Stopajnik and Redlein 2017a; Frey and Osborne 2013). The study of Frey and Osborne (Frey and Osborne 2013) forecasted the probability of computerisation for over 700 occupations in the United States. They estimate that 47% of all jobs will probably be substituted by computers. The background of their study was an analysis of the technological progress in machine learning and mobile robotics. Furthermore, the study of Stopajnik et al. (Stopajnik and Redlein 2017a) pointed out the huge impact of digitalisation on the FS industry. Typical FS activities (EN 15221-4 2018) are more likely to be automated than other activities. To give an example, Frey and Osborne determined a 50% probability of automation for installation, maintenance and repair work, a 66% probability for janitors and cleaners and last but not least a 94% probability of first-line supervisors for housekeeping and janitorial workers being substituted by computers (Stopajnik and Redlein 2017a; Frey and Osborne 2013).

The existing studies show the changes caused by digitalisation in the whole RE/FM/FS industry and the whole economy itself, but not on the level of effected tasks of employees or new technologies that are to be implemented by companies (Stopajnik and Redlein 2017b; Frey and Osborne 2013). So they cannot be used for an estimation of the changes due to digitalisation in RE/FM and FS operations. Most notably, the proof of the feasibility of technologies in the area of FS cannot be done (Herrenkohl et al. 2017). But an estimation of relevant technologies is necessary to determine how these technologies will change the industry. This chapter is based on the results presented in the IEEE and EFMC 2019 publications.

Learning outcomes:

Students shall be capable of answering the following questions:

1. What are the relevant smart building technologies for optimising the Facility Service provision?
2. What are the services mainly affected?
3. Which technologies influence the primarily affected services and how?

5.2 Relevant Emerging Technologies

To answer these questions a quantitative literature review of almost 600 case studies was carried out. The goal was to analyse and evaluate international use cases of smart building technologies already implemented or to be implemented in the near future within different Facility Services. The goal was not only to forecast the impact of digitalisation in the FS sector, but also to provide best practice use cases. The EU standard 15221-4 was used to cluster the effected FS, as it is the only standard accepted by more than one country. The smart building technology categories were coded according to the suggestions of Klaus Schwab.

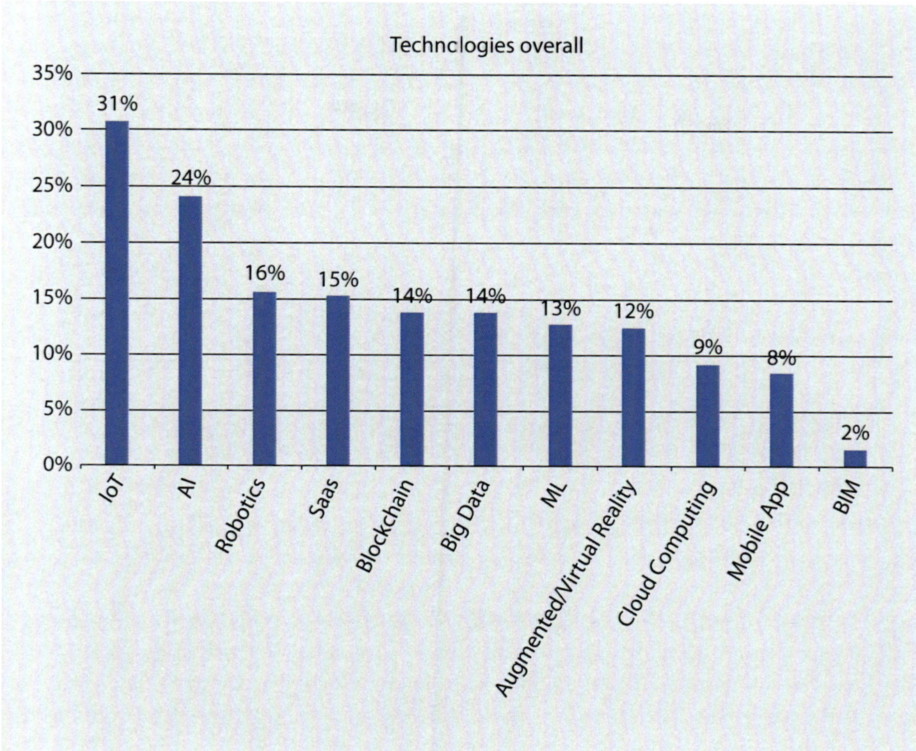

Fig. 5.1 Technologies grouped by category and occurrence within the case studies as a percentage of all cases analysed (595) (authors own figure)

The results of the quantitative literature review regarding the relevant smart building technologies are shown in **Fig. 5.1**. The figure shows the occurrence rate of the smart building technologies within all the reports analysed as a percentage of all analysed use cases.

Software as a service (SaaS) and clcud computing were not within the scope of the pre-study as it is more a way to provide software, rather than a tool in itself.

5.2.1 SaaS

Definition

Software as a Service (SaaS) is a software distribution model in which the respective software is provided, maintained and operated as a service. (Matt 2009).

Software as a service, or SaaS, is a way of providing cloud-hosted application to Internet users. It is a software deployment model, where a standardised software is provisioned over the Internet for the consumers. There is no tailoring of the software to fit the end user, like with the application service provider (APS) model. With SaaS, cloud-based applications run on distant computers and servers that are operated and owned by others (Mäkilä et al. 2010). These are connected to the users' computer via the Internet and are usually accessed via a web browser. SaaS is mainly used as an enabler for other technologies, as a way for end users to, for example, easily access and share data collected by IoT devices. Pooling the data from thousands of users allows the software provider to strengthen their AI and ML algorithms by increasing the sample size for pattern recognition.

5.2.2 Cloud Computing

Definition

Cloud Computing is the delivery of virtualised IT resources over the Internet. It is computing as a service, delivered on an on-demand, pay-per-use basis, through a cloud services platform. (HPE 2019).

Cloud computing, which is often simply referred to as "the cloud", describes the delivery of on-demand computing resources via the Internet on a pay-for-use basis (IBM 2019). This includes everything from data centres to applications. The underlying concept of cloud computing was introduced in the 1960s by John McCarthy (Jadeja and Modi 2012). He described a computer model that would be organised as a public utility. The first widely available cloud computing solution was Amazon EC2 developed in 2006. Cloud computing deals with storage services, data access, software and computation that may or may not require end user knowledge of the physical location and the configuration of the system, which is delivering these services. It refers to the hardware and software required to run the system in the data centres, as well the applications delivered as services over the Internet (Fox et al. 2009). In cloud computing the solutions can be customised more to the needs of the company. Quite often, this methodology is used to outsource the ownership and operation of the company's hardware and software to an external service provider. In this case, the applications can be customised in the same way in the same level of detail as they were hosted on premise, which means in the company's own IT centre. Like SaaS, cloud computing enables other technologies by providing data storage.

In the following analysis, the two software platforms, SaaS and cloud computing, are not included as they support all smart building technologies, while here only the technologies themselves are analysed.

As can be seen in ◘ Fig. 5.1, IoT is mentioned the most, followed by artificial intelligence (AI), robotics, blockchain, big data and machine learning (ML). Augmented and virtual reality and the use of mobile apps follow next. Normally, BIM would not show up as an important emerging technology, as it only occurs in less than 2% of the cases. It is included in the figure only to show the difference in importance to the other "emerging technologies" compared with the technology BIM. The relevant emerging technologies are now presented in detail not according to the occurrence rate of the technologies within all the reports analysed, but along the dataflow. So we will start with IoT as data delivery and go ahead with mobile apps as a first "user" of the IoT data. In the next step, the storage of the IoT data in big data tools and their analysis with the help of ML and AI are done. Then we will go into details with robotics, blockchain, augmented and virtual reality. All of these emerging technologies will be listed with their definitions, the history of their development and some practical examples in how far they can be used in the RE/FM industry.

5.2.3 IoT

Definition

IoT enables physical objects to see, hear, think and perform jobs by having them "talk" together, to share information and to coordinate decisions. (Al-Fuqaha et al. 2015).

This means, IoT devices can communicate and interact with one another and the Internet. They can be remotely monitored and controlled. Each of them has a central processing unit (CPU) which represents a small embedded computer that can carry out programs directly, as well as a worldwide unique ID, so that it can be directly addressed.

The concept of IoT (Internet of things) was first thought of by Mark Weiser in his 1991 seminal paper "The Computer for the 21st Century". He called this construct "ubiquitous computing" and predicted that in the future, computers would be everywhere, without limitations in location, format and size (Weiser 1991). The term IoT was coined by Kevin Ashton in 1999 in a presentation where he came up with the idea of combining RFID technology and the Internet to improve supply chain management (Ashton 2009).

In all the publications, the smart building technology IoT is mentioned the most. The reason for this is the enormous price reduction of sensors and IoT devices within the last years. The availability of self-sufficient devices that produce the energy they need by themselves and can be easily connected to the Wi-Fi of the buildings also enables the use of IoT (Xu et al. 2014). IoT devices are mainly used to get current information about a building or its infrastructure and equipment. This information can be status information like temperature and humidity in a room, or usage data like number of people in a room and operating hours of an equipment. It is important to have this current and operational information, but how can we use it? There are two main ways. First, the CPU on the IoT can directly trigger "actions", for example, it can send an email to a ticket system or directly to the responsible employee in case of a critical value being exceeded. A practical example would be a classroom with an IoT device measuring the temperature and humidity. If the temperature exceeds a specific limit, the IoT device will automatically send an email to the responsible person. The person can now use a mobile app to monitor all emails and start handling the situation, before the teacher or the students are harmed. The other usage is to send the data to a big data system for further analytics.

5.2.4 Mobile App

» App is short for "application," which is the same thing as a software program. While an app may refer to a program for any hardware platform, it is most often used to describe programs for mobile devices, such as smartphones and tablets.

The term "app" was popularised by Apple when the company created the "App Store" in 2008, a year after the first iPhone was released. As the iPhone and App Store grew in popularity, the term "app" became the standard way to refer to mobile applications. Programs for Android and Windows Phone are now called "apps" as well. Mobile apps can only be obtained by downloading them from an online app store. Most devices automatically install apps when downloaded, which creates a seamless installation process for the user. Some apps are free, while others must be purchased. However, mobile apps are typically much cheaper than PC applications. Part of the reason mobile apps are cheaper than desktop applications is because they are often less advanced and take less resources to develop. Apps are limited to the capabilities of the mobile operating system (such as iOS or Android) and therefore may not offer as much functionality as a desktop program. For example, a word processor for Android will most likely have significantly less features than a word processing application for Windows. Most apps are designed to be small, fast, and easy-to-use. Unlike desktop applications, apps are intended to be used on-the-go and are developed to advantage of a small touchscreen interface. (► techterms.com n.d. Christensson 2012)

Now, the IoT device can send an email that can be opened with a mobile app or the data, generated by the IoT devices, can directly be monitored in a specific app. For example, new smart home devices like television sets and washing machines can be directly monitored and controlled by apps. This is also possible with HVA devices or even photovoltaic power plants on the roof of houses. More sophisticated apps also allow routing of service technicians, maintenance order handling, etc. Even some core functionality of ERP and CAFM tools are now accessible via mobile apps to support employees who work mainly out of the office. As the computing power of the mobile devices is steadily increasing, the possibilities of mobile apps is too. But in most cases, there is still a backend application and the mobile app is primarily supporting operational processes. This leads to the second path of data, from IoT devices into big data systems.

5.2.5 Big Data

Definition

Big data is high-volume, high-velocity and/or high-variety information assets that demand cost-effective, innovative forms of information processing that enable enhanced insight, decision making, and process automation. (Laney 2001).

Big data is applied to datasets that grow too large to handle with traditional database management systems. Their size is beyond the ability of commonly used storage systems and software tools to store, capture, manage and process the data within a tolerable time frame (Kubick 2012).

Single datasets can easily reach many petabytes (1 PB = 1000 TB) in size. The main issue arising in big data management comes from the storage and searching capabilities, sharing, analysing and visualising the data. These challenges are summarised by the three V's: volume (the size of the data batch), velocity (how fast data is changed and created) and variety (how many different formats and types of data and users are involved) (Russom 2011).

The origins of big data go back to the 1970s when the first data centres were created and relational databases were first developed. By 2005, it became apparent that humans create vast amounts of data at an unprecedented rate. YouTube and Facebook had commenced operations the year before and other services would soon follow. Hadoop was created as an open-source framework to store and analyse big sets of data (Dontha 2017). The price reduction in storage space also helped to popularise the technology. Applications for big data include all areas where vast amounts of data are generated. In our industry, this is mainly done via IoT sensors delivering current status data of the building and its equipment. As described in the chapter IT, data warehouse systems and big data systems can be used to analyse the data in detail, to calculate automatically benchmarks and to a specific extend to set control actions based on the results of the previous steps. As the data volume is really huge, additional tools are used to analyse the data. Examples are AI and ML.

5.2.6 Artificial Intelligence

Definition

AI is the theory and development of computer systems able to perform tasks normally requiring human intelligence, such as visual perception, speech recognition, decision-making, and translation between languages. (Oxford University Press 2017).

AI has its beginnings in World War II when British and Polish scientists developed a machine that was able to crack the German Enigma code. Their computer, called Bombe, laid the foundation for what is now known as machine learning and artificial intelligence.

By the 1950s British mathematician Alan Turing, who had worked at Bletchley Park during the war and was one of the people heavily involved in the creation of Bombe, started to explore the mathematical possibilities of artificial intelligence. His paper "Computing Machinery and Intelligence" argued that humans use reason and available information to solve problems and those machines could be built to do the same (Ray 2018). In order for Turing's vision to become reality, computers had to become more powerful than they were in 1950. Mainly, they needed the ability to store commands and not just execute them. The proof of concept for AI was initialised by Allen Newell, Cliff Shaw and Herbert Simon, "logic theorist". This program was designed to mimic human problem-solving skills and was presented in 1956 (Anyoha 2017). Artificial intelligence is very common today. Applications include the analysis of data generated by IoT devices, pattern recognition and prediction of upcoming events, like machine part failures. An additional and very promising area are chatbots and speech recognition. These AI tools enable an entirely different level of "control" over the building by using the voice as direct communication method. An example is Alexa® or Google Home®. Both devices are not only loudspeakers but also have a ML application included. This means they screen the conversation in the room the whole time they are active to recognise the command that "activates them". When, for example, someone says "hey google", followed by the command "play abc radio station", Google Home will turn on the radio station. The same happens if the television set is linked to Alexa® or Google Home®. The devices will switch them on or change the station based on oral commands. This increases commodity. People do not have to stand up and look for a remote control or a mobile device to control the different smart home devices. However, the devices screen the conversation the whole time to recognise commands, which stresses again the importance of the GDPR (see ▶ Sect. 3.5.1 GDPR). The same systems are being used more and more in the office environment to control the building or even order drinks.

The next chapter is about chatbots.

5.2.7 Chatbots

Definition

A chatbot is a domain-specific conversational interface that uses an app, messaging platform, social network or chat solution for its conversations. Chatbots vary in sophistication, from simple, decision-tree-based marketing stunts to implementations built on feature-rich platforms. They are always narrow in scope. A chatbot can be text- or voice-based, or a combination of both (Gartner IT Glossary 2019).

Chatbots can be used to answer questions of clients either on the phone or via email. Examples are questions of tenants, for instance, if the cost of waste is included in the operational costs or not. The answers are in the easiest cases given, based on a database with questions and answers. More sophisticated systems can search for answers by themselves in knowledge databases or connect answers in different ways. Simple versions of these chatbots with limited feasibilities are available for around 100 Euro or Dollars.

Another game changer will be the use of AI in self-driving cars going along with the expansion of the shared economy. According to Cambridge Dictionary, a sharing economy is "an economic system that is based on people sharing possessions and services, either for free or for payment, usually using the internet or a platform to organise this" (Cambridge University Press, 2019). This means people will not go for the ownership of goods or services but pay for the use of it.

Example

A practical example is if you do not buy a car but pay for mobility to a platform like Car2Go or DriveNow. If this car now drives autonomously, the requirements for parking lots, charging infrastructure, etc. need to be changed. The cars will move around 80 to 90 percent of the time instead of standing 90 percent of the time, which is on average now. The number of cars and parking lots will reduce dramatically. There will be additional empty space, for example, in the basements, which can then be used for many other different purposes.

However, let us come back to the analysis of the big data systems by AI or the "subtechnology" ML.

5.2.8 Machine Learning

Definition

In machine learning, a computer first learns to perform a task by studying a training set of examples. The computer then performs the same task with data it has not encountered before. (Louridas and Ebert 2016).

Machine learning (ML) has its roots in early computer sciences. Bayes' theorem from 1812 as defined by Pierre-Simon Laplace describes the probability of an event happening based on prior knowledge of conditions that might be related to the event. Mathematicians laid the foundation for modern machine learning, including Adrien-Marie Legendre who developed the least squares method for data fitting in 1805 and Andrey Markov's analysis techniques called Markov's chains. By 1948 computers were developed that stored their programs in the same memory used for data storage. Alan Turing's work, which was pivotal for artificial intelligence, was published. In 1951, the first neural network was built by Dean Edmonds and Marvin Minsky. This was the first computer-based simulation of the way an organic brain works. In 1996, Deep Blue beat Gary Kasparov in chess. By 2006, neural net research is rebranded as "deep learning". Machine learning is widely used. Computers learn from experience, which means they modify their processing based on newly acquired information. Advanced ML algorithms are comprised from many technologies, including neural networks, natural language processing, deep learning, etc. These are used for supervised and unsupervised learning and operate guided by lessons from existing information (BBC 2019).

This means the use of ML changes the behaviour of computers dramatically. When we use a "classical" application like Word or Excel, all functionality is programmed by a human being. So it comprehensively knows how the program will act in specific situations. This is different with ML. ML applications develop their own "code". They learn from data and try to identify clusters that are used to decision-makings in the future. In RE/FM we can therefore use ML to find patterns in the big data "lakes" we generate by using IoT sensors, providing a picture of the current status and the operating data of equipment. In the last year, AI/ML tools made great progress in this area. They are mainly used to analyse the data generated by the IoT devices and identify patterns (Moreno et al. 2014). The capabilities of big data and AI/ML tools in this area have increased. Several device producers like Fujitsu include AI/ML features already in their devices. Examples are surveillance systems that can automatically inform security personnel of dangerous and unusual events, like cameras that detect when a person leaves its luggage somewhere unattended. The camera then sends this information per SMS to security personnel. Another example is the automatic recognition of patient statuses that informs relevant people automatically in case of an emergency (Fujitsu 2018). The availability of AI/ML over SaaS platforms like IBM Watson increased while at the same time their costs decreased. These platforms support among other things predictive maintenance. Several use cases describe the analysis of IoT data to detect failures of equipment before they happen. The AI/ML software even includes the scheduling of the maintenance employees (Bonomi et al. 2012; Sun et al. 2016).

But how can we optimise the setup of the contract and the service delivery including the invoicing?

5.2.9 Blockchain

Definition

Blockchain is a distributed database that maintains a continuously growing list of ordered records, called "blocks. (Iansiti and Lakhani 2017).

Blockchain was first introduced by Satoshi Nakamoto in their 2008 paper "Bitcoin: A Peer-to-Peer Electronic Cash System". The words "block" and "chain" were used separately, but later popularised as a single word. At its most basic level, blockchain is literally just a chain of blocks, but not in the traditional sense of those words. When we say the words "block" and "chain" in this context, we are actually talking about digital information (the "block") stored in a public database (the "chain") (Investopedia 2019). Pwc in their article "Blockchain and smart contracts, 2017" says that the principle underlying blockchain is that all transactions made by all participants in the entire network are validated by mass collaboration and recorded in a continually reconciled database that is maintained across numerous computers. The transactions are put into groups called "blocks" (PwC 2017c). Transactions are added to a block until it is full and a new block has to be created. These blocks are linked together in an unforgeable way. This is achieved by closing a block with a "hash", thereby validating it. The next block is opened with this exact hash. If they do not fit, the chain has been corrupted. Because of the decentralised nature and the individual storage of the entire chain in separate places, a chain that was corrupted in such a manner can be easily spotted and excluded. This mechanism prevents the data to be subsequently altered. A "hash", a kind of digital fingerprint, is used to validate the blocks. This means that every member of the transaction can at any time, with absolute certainty and anonymity, verify the validity of a block, eliminating the need for a neutral middleman to vouch for the trustworthiness of the transactions.

At the moment use cases can be found mainly in the financial services, where smart contracts are used to verify money and asset transfers. The big advantage of the blockchain is that it stores data permanently and in a way that cannot be changed anymore. If we had to store data in the RE/FM industry in this way before, we had to use a notarial act, which was time and money consuming. With the help of blockchain this has become easier. We can easily document that a specific maintenance was done in time and that the parameters of essential equipment were in the proper operating area. We only have to carefully select the amount of data, as storage is still quite expensive. A much more unevaluated tool is smart contracts based on blockchain technology. In this case, the contract is "coded" on one of the specific smart contract platforms like Ethereum. These open software platforms are built on blockchain technology that enables developers to build and deploy decentralised applications. In addition, they provide basic or even advanced functionality to define and deploy smart contracts. What could this mean? Normally, to issue a bill costs around 20 to 30 Euro, so it is not possible or economically feasible to invoice rather small amounts of service charges. A smart contract helps. The contract is coded once, and whenever a customer asks for a specific service, it releases the service and charges it to the customer. An example is an e-trolley. When you have a contract with the specific provider, the system releases the trolley when presenting your credit card. The trolley as an IoT device sends information on the time used and distance driven. The smart contract then automatically adds this to the customer's invoice. Of course, the service company could program the smart contract platform by itself, but these costs would be much higher than using a platform like Ethereum. This can be used to charge small services like using a conference room in a cooperative workplace environment or a parking lot at the office. To sum up, this technology asks first to code the contract and its stipulations, which afterwards can be executed without interference of a human, thus reducing the cost of carrying out and billing the contractual services. But still, some services have to be carried out manually. Nevertheless, this is also changing. To carry out maintenance, especially in a hazardous area, we can apply, for example, robots.

5.2.10 Robotics

Definition

"The IFR's (International Federation of Robotics) use of the term "industrial robot" is based on the definition of the International Organisation for Standardisation: an "automatically controlled, reprogrammable multipurpose manipulator programmable in three or more axes." (ISO 8373 2012).

A robot is a reprogrammable, multifunctional manipulator, which is designed to move tools, parts, material or specialised devices through programmed motions to perform a variety of tasks (Stanford). It is the intelligent connection of perception into action. The term robot was first used in science fiction writer Karel Čapek's 1920s play "R.U.R.". Robot comes from the Slavic word robota and means "forced labourer" in Czech. Robots and drones find a wide variety of use cases, relieving workers from dangerous and strenuous manual labour and taking over repetitive and dull work. They are used as delivery service units, and to help labourers in factories and warehouses. They can be operated locally as well as remotely.

Robotics and drones are mainly used to carry out repetitive work. New versions are more flexible and can cooperate with the FS personnel. Examples for use cases are mowers and cleaning robots (Min Moon et al. 2015). Several of the cases describe a combination of robots and drones (Wang et al. 2010). This technology is mainly used, as mentioned before, for repetitive work or work in hazardous areas. Also, security tasks like going into a building and prove the solidity or to disarm a bomb are common use scenarios. But in several areas, humans still have to carry out the tasks. They can be supported during their work by augmented reality and be prepared to work by virtual reality.

5.2.11 Augmented/Virtual Reality

Definition

Augmented reality (AR) is a term for the live direct or indirect view of a physical, real-world environment whose elements are augmented by computer-generated sensory input. (Pintaric et al. 2005).

Virtual reality refers to immersive, interactive, multi-sensory, viewer-cantered, 3D computer generated environments. (Cruz-Neira 1993).

The term augmented reality was created by Thomas Caudell in 1990 (Lee 2012). This technology is used to "augment" or enhance the visual and auditory information a person gets about their environment by providing them with additional knowledge necessary to the completion of the current task. Computer-generated virtual imagery is overlaid live onto a direct or indirect real-world environment (Azuma 1997). The first virtual reality device was called "The Sword of Damocles". It was created in 1968 by Ivan Sutherland and Bob Sproull (Sutherland 1968, p. 757–764). Virtual reality refers to real-time interactive graphics where 3D models are combined with a display technology that allows users to be completely immersed in the model world and manipulate it directly. It relies on 3D stereoscopic head-tracker displays, hand and body tracking and binaural sound. An illusion is created of being part of this synthetic environment instead of observing it from an external point of view.

Applications for AR/VR can be found in training scenarios that allow students to be completely immersed in the situations they are preparing for. Maintenance workers who receive additional information about machine parts or may be even the latest data on what had happened before the breakage are also possible examples of use.

5.3 Affected Services

The results of the quantitative literature review regarding the affected services are shown in ◘ Fig. 5.2. The figure shows the occurrence rate of the affected services within all analysed cases. The emerging technologies affect the EN 15221-4 service "maintenance and operation". The usage of IoT (to deliver information of the status of equipment) and of AI/ML tools (to support, e.g. predictive maintenance) optimises "maintenance and operation". The whole way, how maintenance is carried out, is changed. IoT sensors help to reduce energy consumption as they provide an accurate data of the usage and therefore deliver information to carry out optimisation. "Logistics", "safety" and "security" and the "customer experience" can be enhanced by the use of big data, AI and ML. The use of these technologies for customers' experiences is gaining importance to create the desired "wow" effect. ML can be used to "predict" the demand or, even better, the desire of the customer and therefore to provide her or him personalised service experience.

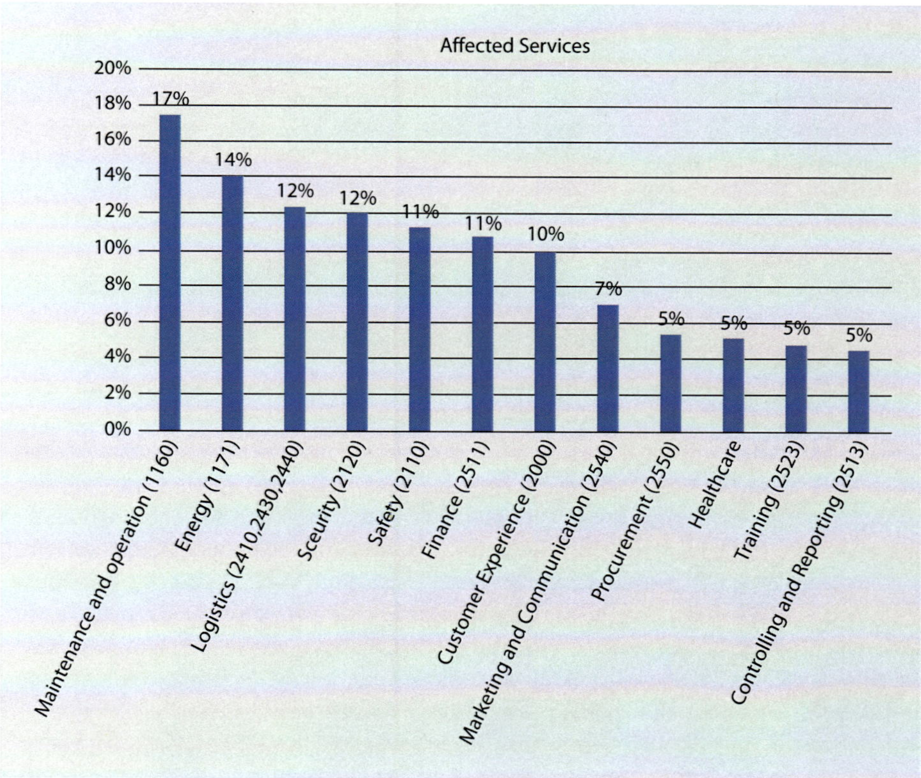

◘ **Fig. 5.2** Affected services according to the number of mentioning in publications as a percentage of the number of cases analysed (595) (authors own figure)

Jointly with blockchain, the tools mentioned above optimise "security", "finance" and "procurement". In the next subchapters, more use cases are described to show how the emerging technologies may influence the different Facility Services in detail.

5.4 Impact of Emerging Technologies on "Maintenance and Operation"

Definition

"Maintenance and operation" concerns buildings and their technical installations. This includes the help desk system, building management system, spare parts, oil and machinery and condition monitoring. It encompasses building operation, technical operation, technical maintenance and building maintenance" (EN15221-4 2018).

The service "maintenance and operation" is pointed out the most to be affected by smart building technologies (◘ Fig. 5.3). As shown, IoT is the most important technology affecting this service. IoT devices are used as providers of data about the current status of equipment and the building itself. This data is then delivered to big data and AI and further processed by ML to recognise patterns, mainly to support predictive maintenance and to derive actions based on these patterns (Krishnamurthy and Desouza 2014).

Example

KONE Elevators

KONE is a global leader in the elevator and escalator industry. It operates over a million transport units, moving a billion people on a daily basis. It is paramount to ensure that these building doors, elevators and escalators move safely and without glitches. Handling the ever-growing traffic demands of modern buildings and transport hubs is a challenge.

In collaboration with IBM's Watson IoT platform, KONE monitors the condition of elevators and escalators worldwide. IoT sensors gain continuous and detailed information on performance and usage, as well as wear. This information plus the information of operation (failure, repair and maintenance tasks carried out) is then automatically sent to a cloud to be remotely monitored and assessed. This data is used to optimise management and maintenance operations. By analysing the data of more than 1000 elevators over several years, ML was used to find patterns between the sensor data and potential breakdowns. Based on these patterns, algorithms were defined to predict failures and breakdowns. An algorithm may have several input streams like the velocity of the door and the noise in the cabin, which enables the system to predict specific failures like break of the light curtain before they happen. In most cases now, these predictions can be made one or even two days before they happen. As soon as the algorithm detects potential failures, ML tools reschedule the maintenance workers, so that they can set some maintenance tasks to prevent the failure to happen.

This process results in more detailed information about the escalators and elevators, fewer faults and less downtime, which in turn means less time spent waiting due to delays. Also, the teams only waiting to release people out of stuck elevators can be decreased, because these accidents are reduced to a minimum.

Facility Managers and building owners gain information and therefore control over their assets.

(KONE 2018).

The shift from reactive to predictive maintenance as observed in the KONE case study is a noticeable trend in the "maintenance and operations" service sector. Instead of practising crisis management due to sudden unforeseen failures in equipment, maintenance work, which can be scheduled and planned, can prevent these unforeseen failures. The ability to predict failures before they happen and to replace spare parts in time can save time, energy, resources and money.

Support work can be scheduled at less busy times, spare parts can be ordered in time, and unnecessary check-ups can be avoided. This last point is an additional advantage. Normally, preventive maintenance is used to prevent failures. Therefore, mainte-

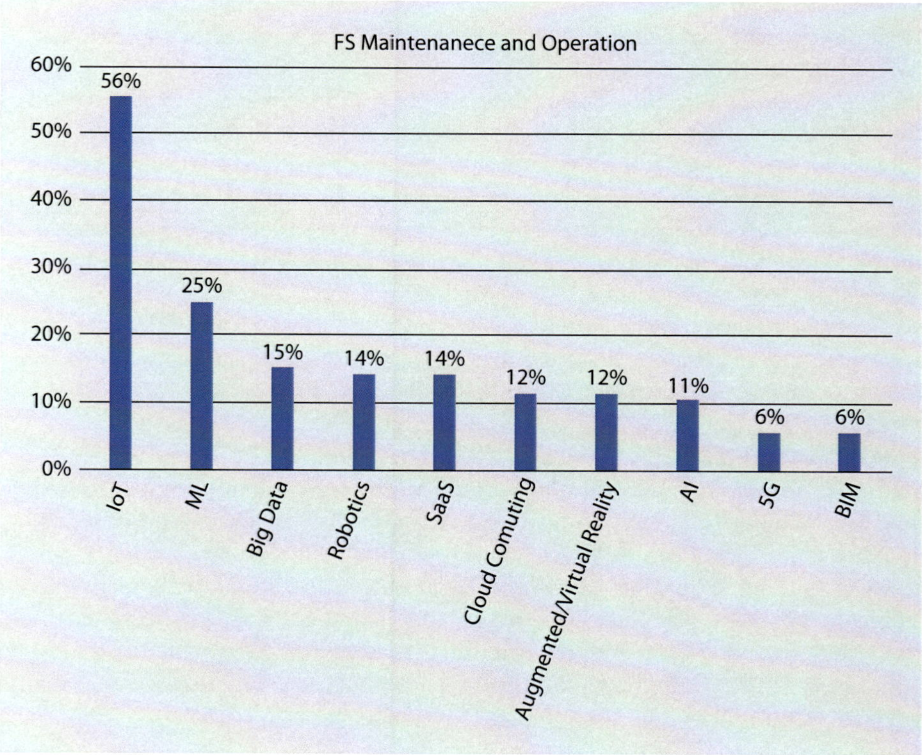

Fig. 5.3 Used technologies according to number of mentions in publication as a percentage of the number of cases in FS "maintenance and operation" (104) (authors own figure)

nance action plans are set up, meaning what tasks have to be carried out, how often and with which equipment. This data is based on experience, but sometimes the tasks or the intervals are too narrow to ensure proper operation. Predictive maintenance also helps to optimise these maintenance plans, as it delivers suggestions of necessary maintenance tasks and the time when they should be carried out. This data can be used to optimise the "traditional" preventive maintenance plans. The next examples show how this can be done.

Example

Trenitalia

Trenitalia is Italy's largest train operator. It runs more than 7000 trains per day, every day. In addition to moving passengers, it is also a large carrier of cargo, especially steel. It employs over 31,000 people and creates over € 5 billion in revenue annually. Punctuality is important to the customers as well as rail managers. Unforeseen downtime is harmful to the whole operation.

Usually, trains have fixed-schedule maintenance checks when a fault occurs or when certain distances have been travelled. By using IoT sensor data and ML, this "advance planning" approach is changed to a "conditional maintenance" concept. Temperature, pressure and other parameters are measured. This allows deducing how much used a certain component has been and whether they are damaged or not. Maintenance is then carried out before a failure occurs.

This helps to prevent breakdowns while trains are in operation as well as extended downtime due to surprising activities. Unplanned downtime and unnecessary activities are reduced. It is possible to plan maintenance operations in advance, thereby ensuring all necessary parts, tools and facilities and people will be available and on site when maintenance work is supposed to take place. All these steps ensure that the cost of operation stay low. In turn, the availability of trains and wagons increases. Sudden breakdowns of equipment are reduced.

Trenitalia uses ground diagnostics as well as on-board diagnostics to ensure smooth running of their operations. The goal is to perform only the required, but all necessary interventions at the right time, making sure that the right resources are available (Klyvø 2016).

Being able to plan and prepare maintenance work is crucial with regards to saving time and money. Predictive maintenance allows to plan ahead instead of reacting. Rather than repairing damaged machinery, parts that will soon cease to work can be replaced without damaging the whole apparatus. In addition to these resource-indulgent measures, planning ahead means that people are available, spare parts are ready, and space and tools are provided. This prevents losing time due to organising one or more of these resources. Downtimes can be shortened and unnecessary activity can be avoided.

This type of predictive maintenance, based on use data and machine status, helps to identify quality deviations, predict failure moments and secure availability. Predictive maintenance is heavily reliant on good data that can be monitored and properly analysed. This data is gathered by IoT devices and can be used not only to monitor machine parts.

These case studies are exemplary for the development of using IoT in combination with AI, ML, big data and cloud computing within Facility Management. Other technologies frequently used in "maintenance and operations" are augmented and virtual reality, which is used to train and instruct employees, for example. Drones and robotics take over dangerous and repetitive tasks like exchange of parts in hazardous areas or inspection of steep roofs.

Example

Cleaning

In Asia, a building façade maintenance robot has the ability to do cleaning work while moving along a horizontal and vertical rail. The new window cleaning tool system not only takes over the hazardous work from humans but also reduces water usage compared to manual cleaning by human labour and conventional automated building cleaning machines. Especially the water circulation system solves the problem of scattering and dripping used water by applying suction and recycle processes, thus preventing the contamination of workplace and surrounding areas. Although the water reduction by the proposed system was not big (about 20%), it certainly helps to increase cleaning an area with one loading of water from the robot by smart devices, which greatly affects the design of a compact and lightweight robot (Wang et al. 2010).

Another example are drones. Drones equipped with cameras can perform regular external inspections of commercial structures, like bridges or airplanes, with the images automatically analysed to detect any new cracks or changes on surfaces (Wellers et al. 2017; PwC 2017a).

This is why robots and drones are also mentioned in the area of "safety" and "security".

5.5 Impact of Emerging Technologies on "Energy"

Definition

"Energy" encompasses the energy supply to a built facility. This might include internal production of energy or procurement from external sources as well as the necessary infrastructure typical to a meter. The cost for producing and procuring energy as well as its operation, maintenance and infrastructure improvements are covered. It includes heating, cooling, electricity, gas, oil, wood and other energy sources. The internal distribution, as well as the consumption of energy with its related infrastructure, are not part of the FS energy (EN15221-4 2018).

"Energy", like "maintenance and operation", is dominated by IoT devices that collect data for further assessment. These data are analysed with the help of big data, ML and AI to find areas where efficiency can be increased or wastage can be reduced. Blockchain especially with its smart contracts enables the documentation but also new ways of cooperation of building owners, tenants and utility providers (◘ Fig. 5.4).

Let us start with a simple example, a building of my university.

5

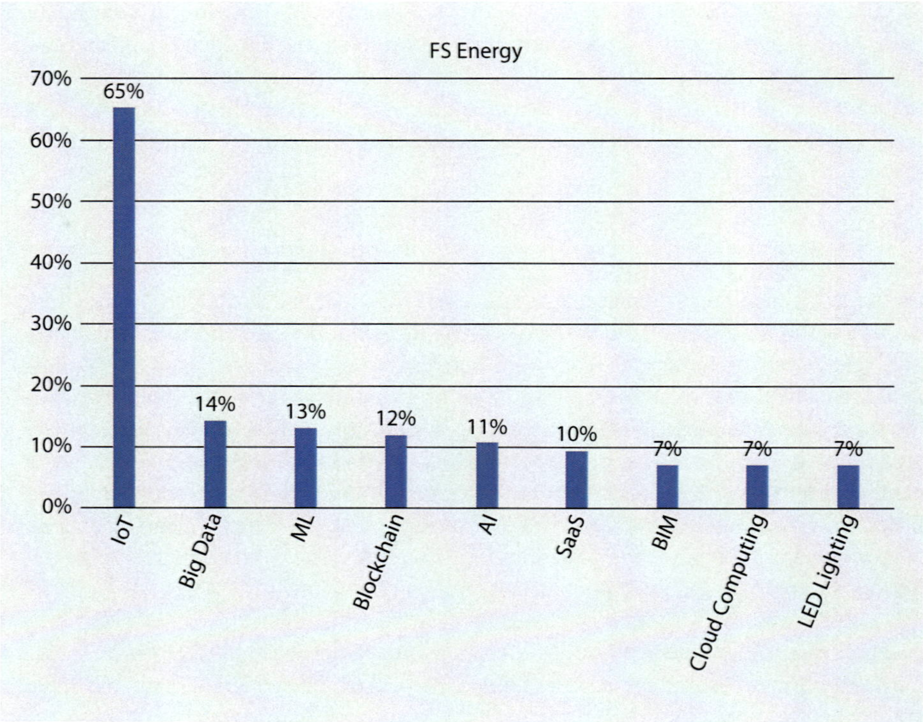

Fig. 5.4 Used technologies according to the number of mentions in publications as a percentage of the number of cases in FS "Energy" (84) (authors own figure)

Example

TU Wien

One of our buildings, hosting a big part of our IT-related departments, was under permanent optimisation by external specialists. They were asked in, did inspections and suggested optimisation. With a scientific cooperation, we changed the procedure. In the first step, the main energy-consuming equipment was defined. The chillers for cooling were identified. At this time, they were included in the building automation system only for failure handling. So we added IoT sensors to continually measure the energy consumption. The data was put to a big data system and an easy analytic tool to manually analyse the data implemented. Now it is easy to see the exact usage in different granularity, i.e. months, weeks and hours. After 3 months the first in-depth analysis was done. The energy consumption in January, February and March was the same. This goes in line with the temperature and the other weather parameters being the same over these 3 months. But what was astonishing was that during the full month of February, there were midterm holidays, so no students were in the building. As a consequence, according to the minor occupancy of the building, the sensors should have reduced the airflow, leading into lower energy consumption. But this did not happen. An external specialist would have had a hard time to find this out. Only based on detailed consumption and usage data, this would have been detectable. The cost of the whole installation was around the cost of one engagement of an energy specialist. These costs were easily covered by the optimisation of the occupancy control leading to lower energy costs.

In the next step, we will go more into other details like blind power usage.

In this case, we only used IoT and big data for their analytic capabilities but the analysis still was done by a human. As the gathered data grows and grows, this manual analysis is coming to reach its capability limits. ML can be used to gain more and easier insights.

Example

Google Data Centre

Google is the leading search engine on earth and as such uses huge amounts of data. This data has to be stored somewhere. This storage uses up large amounts of energy and produces heat. Reducing the amount of energy used for cooling these data centres has huge impacts. Google's servers are super-efficient and the company has heavily invested in green energy sources. Increasing efficiency with regards to computing power is an important area of Google's "energy" strategy.

By applying in-house DeepMind's machine learning to its own data centres, Google has reduced the amount of energy needed for cooling by up to 40%. A system of neural networks creates a more efficient and adaptive framework to better understand the dynamics of data centres and improve efficiency. Historical data is combined with real-time data from thousands of sensors collecting information on temperature, power, pump speed and so on. This data is used to train the neural network to predict the average future power usage effectiveness. This is done to ensure that the system will not go beyond operating constraints.

This technology can be used to improve power plant conversion efficiency, help office and manufacturing facilities to increase throughput and reduce energy and water usage (Evans and Gao 2016).

But ML can also be used in the design or refurbishment phase as a perfect support.

Example

Air-Conditioning

Machine learning techniques can be used to predict building A/C energy consumption to help with efficiently automating the air-conditioning process. One study focuses on an in-depth analysis of Stanford Y2E2 building dataset to model the effect of each building sensor measurement on the A/C system energy consumption. By training different data models using a variety of supervised learning methods, it was discovered that third-order polynomial support vector regression (SVR) model best predicts the building A/C system; however, all other trained models we studied generated acceptably low training error rates (smaller than 1.5%) and higher than 94% correlation with our labels. While linear regression is the simplest and least accurate model used in this study, it works well with a small training dataset and reaches the desirable accuracy faster than other models.

Working more efficiently is an effective way to influence energy consumption. But even an increase in efficiency will not necessarily lead to a decrease in energy consumption, since fossil fuels will be replaced with electric cars, multiplying our demand for clean, reliable, local and always available energy.

Example

GE Power

GE Power currently supplies 30% of the world's electricity and aims to build an "Internet of energy" in order to replace the traditional, one-way, linear model of energy delivery. The need for a robust and reliable energy network will increase as battery-powered cars take over our streets. Energy transmission and fast charging will be essential for this transition towards smart electric transportation. Using big data and machine learning, data gathered from IoT devices is used to herald this new development. Advanced analytics and ML already commonly applied to predictive maintenance and power optimisation can be used for critical infrastructure machinery. GE has a vision to create a "digital power plant", where profitability for customers and operation optimisation applied to power plants work together.

GE Power feeds data collected from sensors as well as machine data to its own asset performance management software. This enables monitoring of equipment produced by GE as well as third-party manufacturers, ensuring everything works as it should. Gathering and analysing data to create a more reliable energy network aims to reduce downtime, making the whole system more efficient (Marr 2017).

By ensuring that our electricity grids will be well equipped for a future where small-scale power plants like solar roofs, algae farms and windfarms will feed energy into the grid, our cities will be ready for a new green energy future. But for now, we still largely rely on fossil fuels. Finding untapped sources is therefore a major concern to fossil fuel corporations.

Example

Shell

Royal Dutch Shell is one of six oil and gas supermajors and the fifth largest company in the world measured by revenue. Drilling for oil and gas is not as lucrative as it used to be. It is therefore crucial to drill in locations where large amounts of fuels can be yielded. Shell achieves this by collecting and monitoring data that allows them to predict the likely size of gas and oil resources. This is achieved by observing low-frequency seismic waves below the surface of the earth. The waves are transformed based on the kind of sediment they transverse. Solid rock, gaseous materials and liquids all influence these waves and sensors can pick up the change. This enables to determine what kind of deposit can be found beneath the surface. This indicates the probable location of hydrocarbon deposits. A reading like this will involve millions of data points. The data is uploaded to an analytics system and compared to existing data from previous measurements. If the new data resembles previous findings from profit-yielding locations, a full-scale drilling operation will commence. The need for exploratory drilling is largely reduced (Marr 2016).

"Energy" is a versatile field. On the one hand, fossil fuel companies like Shell try to improve their yield and use emerging technologies to unlock new drilling locations. On the other hand, companies like GE firmly look into the future by developing solutions that will incorporate large industrial-size power plants with consumer-as-producer units into the smart grid.

We should not forget low-hanging fruits like the change of traditional lighting into LED lighting. In most cases, the payback period due to the energy reduction is quite long, and if the reduction of maintenance due to the longer lifetime of the bulbs is included, the picture changes dramatically. This proves again the intensive link between "maintenance and operation" and "energy". Another emerging technology playing an important role is the blockchain with its smart contracts. The smart grid and its complicated structure change the way of interoperation between partners like owners, tenants and utility providers. Owners putting photovoltaic plants on their roofs become utility providers. But in most countries, it is not easy for them to sell their energy to others. Some countries allow them to sell it to their tenants. In other countries, they can only use it to run "general equipment" like central heating and cooling devices. In most cases, they have to include classical utility providers as "handling agents". That asks for a large exchange of the already available IoT data about energy production and the usage of the different partners. Smart contracts and blockchain are a possible answer to this challenge.

5.6 Impact of Emerging Technologies on "Logistics"

Definition

"Logistics" concerns the transport and storage of information and goods, the transport of people and improvement of these processes (EN 15221-4 2018).

"Logistics" in this context includes the provision, distribution and storage of office supplies. It also contains moving furniture, ICT equipment and people. Mobility overall, meaning the transport of people and goods for organisational purpose, including fleet management, travel services and transport services, is covered as well (◘ Fig. 5.5).

IoT devices are once again widespread in this service area. The prevalence of IoT devices overall can be attributed to a sharp decline in price for these products over the last years. Gathering data and storing information have become relatively cheap over the last years. This has led to an increase of usage of IoT devices coupled with AI, big data, cloud computing and machine learning. Robotics and blockchain have emerged as pivotal technologies in the field of "logistics". Let us start with an easy example of automated guided vehicle (AGV) and how their usage can increase productivity at a hospital.

Example

Hospital Delivery

TUG robot can automate the delivery and transportation of the immense amount of materials including food, laundry and prescriptions that move through a hospital every day, freeing staff to focus on patient care and thus leading to better care and improved patient satisfaction scores. AGVs (automated guided vehicle) work 24 hours a day flexibly

5

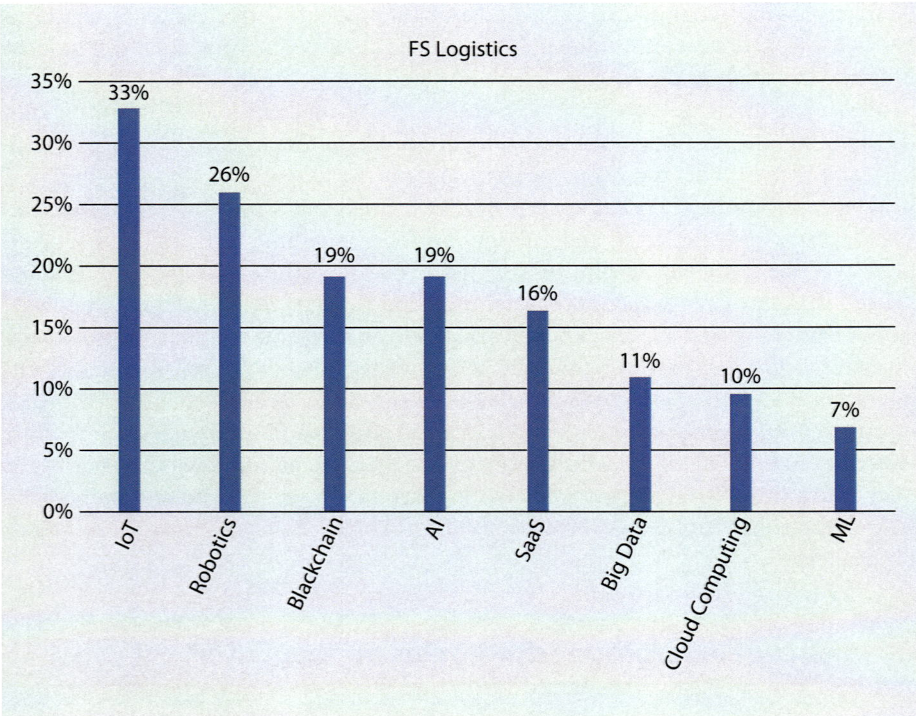

Fig. 5.5 Used technologies according to number of mentions in publication as a percentage of the number of cases in FS "logistics" (73) (authors own figure)

serving locations and departments as called upon. Robots resolve a multitude of manual delivery challenges such as saving time and labour cost and reducing hard work for humans. AGVs can be used to automate all material movement such as medicine, linen, laboratory, nutrition, waste and supplies (PwC, June 2017b).

Example

Transport for London (TfL)

In 2018, around 3.9 billion passenger journeys were conducted on Transport for London vehicles, including buses, trams, London Underground, DLR and London Overground. Charging fares is accordingly complex. Data is collected through sensors attached to traffic signals and vehicles as well as the ticketing system. London uses Oyster prepaid travel cards, first introduced in 2003 and greatly expanded in scope since. Passengers charge these cards in readily available charging stations. The cards are swiped when entering a bus or train. Transport for London collects huge amount of data about journeys taken. This anonymised data is used to produce maps, showing where and when people travel to. This allows for detailed analysis at the level of individual journeys. The main reasons for collecting and analysing data is to improve planning for services and to provide information to customers. For example, it is now possible to show that a large proportion of journeys taken involve more than one method of transportation, which was not possible when journeys were paid for individually in cash at each service. This allows TfL to understand how crowded certain buses or trains are at specific times and react accordingly. Big data analysis is also beneficial with regards to disruption response. When a blockage occurs, an alternative route is opened up and customers are informed via personalised message about the effects on their journey. This personalised approach is not only used in case of disturbances. When traveling a route frequently (i.e. commuters), information about service changes are included in updates (Marr 2015).

Monitoring not only the infrastructure but the people moving through it has been a huge success for TfL. Consumer satisfaction is at the core of this strategy. Making sure that the people using public transport can reliably and comfortably arrive at their destinations in time is a huge factor for customer acceptance and usage. Transporting goods instead of people comes with its own challenges.

Example

DHL

DHL supply chain is a subsidiary of Deutsche Post DHL Group and a leader in US contract logistics. Warehouses are highly complex environments, where locating, picking and distributing items happens under enormous time constraints and physical exertion by the staff. Supporting employees is a top priority for DHL's LocusBots. These work safely and collaboratively among warehouse staff, helping to locate, pick and transport items, eliminating the task of cart pushing. This pilot program will test various picking strategies within the warehouse. The robot's ability to communicate with the warehouse management system and the picker will also be assessed, as will its overall versatility and ability to navigate the warehouse. The LocusBot is expected to seamlessly integrate to the existing warehouse infrastructure. This solution is highly scalable and easy to deploy. It is expected to improve operational metrics and increase efficiency while relieving physical and mental stress from warehouse employees (DHL 2017).

With an expected increase in warehouse operations over the following years and shorter lead times demanded by customers, the need to speed up operations is a matter of fact. The same technology can be used for stocking up office supply, washroom devices, FM/FS warehouses, etc. But it also can support inventory management and picking, important tasks in the area of FM.

Optimising warehouse efficiency is an important factor in this process. But while warehouses operate on a relatively small scale, there are applications infinitely greater and more complex.

To give an example, keeping control over and increasing efficiency in ports is a major issue.

Example

Port of Antwerp

The seaport of Antwerp is part of a larger smart city initiative that aims to make Antwerp a European leader in IoT technology. It is Europe's second largest port after Rotterdam in the Netherlands. This project is conducted by a local start-up called T-Mining, collaborating with NxtPort, a digitalisation and smart port project at the port of Antwerp, launched in 2017. This big data platform contains all data from containers across the end-to-end logistics chain. The main focus of this project is to increase efficiency, decrease the reliance on paper, speed up operations and implement a digital supply chain. The Antwerp port project is mainly aimed at secure container release. This involves questions of security, efficiency and certainty. In ports, truck drivers who pick up containers have to identify themselves with an ID and a PIN code, generated for the specific container, which is a security risk. The blockchain solution eliminates this PIN code and replaces it with smart contracts. All data necessary is gathered in a database and digital rights are created by the blockchain, to ensure that only authorised personnel are able to access and pick up the container in question. This right is transferable between parties. This way it is clear at each moment who is in possession of what, who has the right to access and who has transferred this right. Everything is recorded within the blockchain. This creates a comprehensible, secure and unchangeable record of each transaction, saving time and therefore money in the process (I-Scoop 2017).

"Logistics" show a great opportunity for digitalisation processes. They often include repetitive tasks and are as a result easy to be optimised by the use of robots. Blockchain technology will make supply chains transparent and accountable. IoT and its auxiliary technologies will greatly improve efficiency.

5.7 Impact of Emerging Technologies on "Security"

Definition

"Security" deals with the protection of assets, property and people. It includes but is not limited to items like locks, card readers, cameras and emergency response plans (EN15221-4 2018).

Again, IoT is the most important technology in this service area. It is swiftly followed by blockchain, a relatively new technology with massive implication in this sector. As the Antwerp port case study has shown, the potential for blockchain as a major player in the security field is enormous, especially with regards to supply chain transparency (◘ Fig. 5.6).

Example

IBM Food Trust

The creation, transport and distribution of food is an essential industry, largely built on trust. Having an incorruptible ledger that guarantees that wherever the packaging says the food comes from is its actual source is a valuable commodity. IBM Food Trust creates this shared and secure record of transactions. It enables unprecedented visibility concerning the various steps of the food supply chain. This elevated level of transparency and accountability makes food smarter and most importantly safer for the consumer.

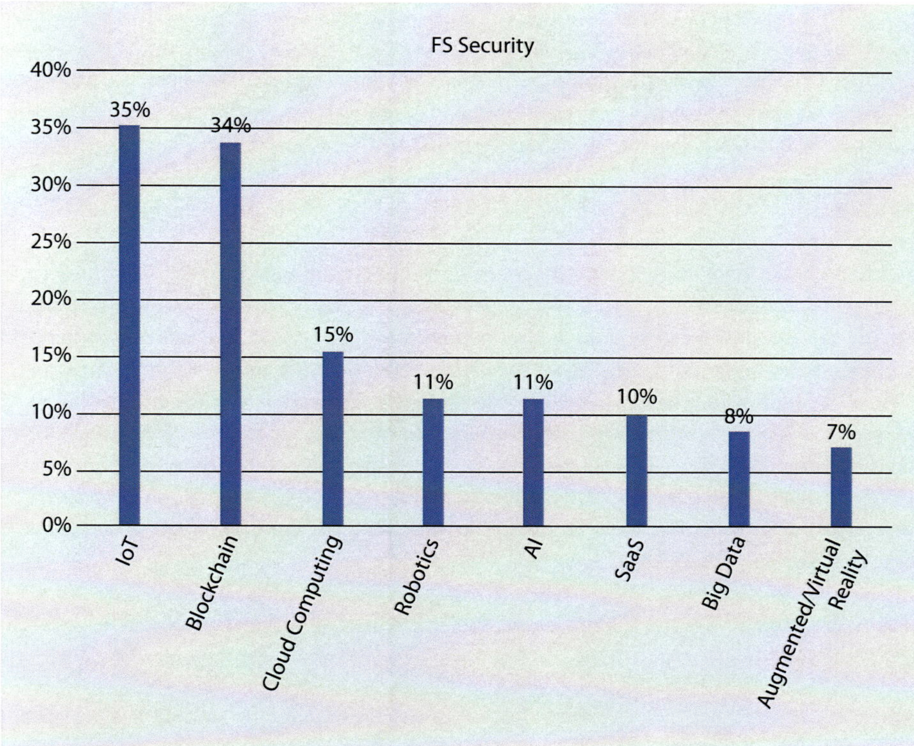

Fig. 5.6 Used technologies according to number of mentions in publications as a percentage of the number of cases in FS "security" (71) (authors own figure)

Blockchain technology is used to ensure that growers, processors, distributors and retailers are connected via a shared and permanent record. This is not only beneficial to the end consumer but it also reduces food loss and waste by up to $120 billion annually. Due to better supply and demand matching and to better waste hot spots' identification, massive savings, not just in monetary terms, can be reached. Food wastage is a huge burden to the economy as well as to the planet.

The blockchain enables better collaboration between individual supply chain players, increasing efficiency and reducing waste due to food spoilage. Everyone involved in the supply chain has access to information about real-time location and status of the produce. This data allows companies to localise the sourcing of ingredients, develop better supply and demand forecasting models and restructure contracts (IBM 2018).

This case study shows that using technological innovations can have immense, often unintended side effects. Improving communication between the parties involved saves time and energy. And because of the volatile nature of food products, massive amounts of resources that would otherwise have gone to waste can now be utilised. These benefits, in addition to the increase in certainty and food security for the consumer, represent a convincing argument for the implementation of this technology.

Security is not only a factor in highly demanding areas like air travel. Buildings and the properties around also have to be secured. Any entry point into a building is a possible security risk. With buildings largely constructed from glass, with multiple points of entry for various personnel (e.g. employees, visitors, delivery, etc.), the need to secure these properties from unwanted entries is immense.

Example

Knightscope

Knightscope is a start-up company, which has developed a mobile security robot known as the K5 that will drive around a factory, warehouse, parking lot or even a shopping mall. The robots are designed to detect anomalous behaviour, such as someone walking through a building at night, and report back to a remote security centre. K5 uses cameras, sensors, navigation equipment and electric motors – all packed into its dome-shaped body with a big rechargeable battery and a computer. The robots have a battery that could last about 24 hours on a single charge, though the K5 is supposed to monitor its battery life and wheel over to a charging pad when needed. If you are the one who needs help and a robot is nearby, you can press a button near the top of its head to summon someone remotely (Metz 2014).

Besides humans who want to gain access, the emerging technologies themselves provide new challenges.

Example

Anti-Drone Measures

Drones are becoming more and more powerful. In recent years, the possible altitude, range, endurance, air speed and precision of navigation have risen appreciably. In addition, they can transport increasingly more mass. At the same time, the number of incidents is on the rise: drones enter no-fly zones, e.g. at the airport or major events such as rock festivals or football matches. Yet drones can also be used for specific terrorist purposes. Consequently, German security authorities are alarmed, as no effective defence system has been devised to date. As a result, to defend against drones, Fraunhofer researchers and their partners rely on a variety of approaches and technologies. For detection and identification purposes, sensor technologies such as radio, acoustics, radar and/or infrared and electro-optics are employed. Under ideal circumstances, the sensors would serve to complement one another, but there is not yet any sensor that can detect everything. Each sensor has its strong and weak points. Visual optic sensors do not function at night or if there is rain and fog. In such a case, infrared or radar would be a better choice. If it is a question of the range of detection, then radar is superior to visual optic sensors and infrared sensors. Fraunhofer is developing a project that constitutes a complete system that covers the entire chain from detection to intervention. The system works with different types of sensors. Four high-resolution digital cameras, each equipped with 25 megapixel sensors, generate a 360-degree all-around view. When sensors detect a drone, the system compares the sensor data with the databank in real time. Ideally, the flying object will be immediately classified in a quick and reliable fashion. The software then displays information such as the maximum load and speed of the flying object. This information makes it possible to draw further conclusions about potential dangers and what defence measures to initiate.

But it is not only about physical access, it is also about the access to IT infrastructure and data.

Example

Saving Data

Remme has found a way to prevent hacking attacks and stop attackers from obtaining private information by using blockchain. The technology allows validating a certificate without the certification authority creating a trusted peer-to-peer (p2p) TLS connection. Certification authority is replaced by blockchain. Remme allows companies to issue and revoke their own self-signed certificates (Protocol by Remme, June 2017).

As can be seen, blockchain again is the emerging technology to solve some of the issues of access to IT systems.

"Security" is an important service. Like other services, the main technologies affecting it are IoT and its ensuing auxiliary technologies: AI, cloud computing, SaaS and big data. The prominence of blockchain, especially with regards to secure data storage and its trust function, is noticeable. Robotics, along with augmented and virtual reality, are also important technologies. Working together, they will make this service more efficient and secure.

5.8 Impact of Emerging Technologies on "Safety"

Definition

"Health, safety, security and environment" (HSSE) services protect people from external dangers and internal risks. It is concerned with the health and well-being of the people, especially with regards to their workplace. It ensures that a safe and sustainable environment is provided. Legal compliance and legal and organisational obligations are covered.

IoT affects the service "safety" to a high degree. Robotics, AI, big data, mobile apps and ML also have a disruptive impact on this service.

As mentioned, robotics, 5G and augmented reality are very important in this area. Multiple use cases show how they can take over dangerous tasks in inaccessible areas (◘ Fig. 5.7).

Example

Remote Devices

Being able to remotely access devices and heavy machinery depends on stable and reliant Internet access. This will make hazardous situations safer. 5G technology will allow machinery to be controlled from a distance. This will lower the risk for injury in dangerous environments. Work will also be completed more effectively. Industries like logging, mining, oil and manufacturing will benefit from that. Remote robots can also be used in less dangerous environments, like healthcare and remote surgery.

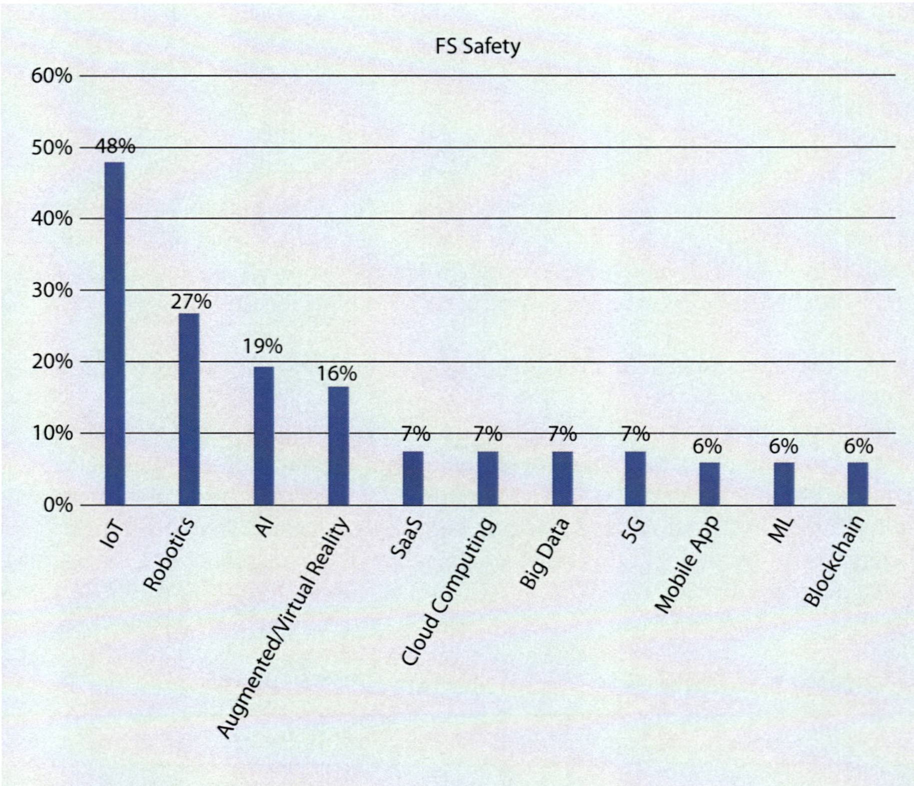

Fig. 5.7 Used technologies according to number of mentions in publications as a percentage of the number of cases in FS "safety" (67) (authors own figure)

5

This will also allow for real-time monitoring of plants and the conditions the work is being undertaken in. The benefits of remote device control, especially with regards to heavy machinery, are indisputable. The gain in safety for employees is immense, especially in industries with precarious work situations, like on offshore oil rigs. Instead of being subjected to these hazardous environments, workers can use the machinery from a safe distance without endangering themselves or others. Not only heavy machinery can be controlled remotely. Tasks that demand an extraordinarily high level of precision, stability and dexterity can also be taken over by remotely controlled devices. This of course is dependent on a reliable, fast, stable and affordable connection between control unit and machine (Ericsson 2017).

Another example are robots taking over specific hazardous tasks like cleaning of skyscraper windows.

Example

Cleaning

Four similar robotic cleaning systems are designed for a reversed cone-shaped glass facade at the top of the control tower at the Guangzhou Airport, in Guangzhou, China.

One system is composed of a robot moving along and cleaning the facade, and an automatic conveyer positioning, securing, supplying energy and water to, and recycling the dirty water from the robot. An on-board controller enables the system to work in a remote control mode or a fully automated mode under the supervision of an operator. The robot provides attaching, moving, cleaning and securing functions for cleaning the high-rise glass façade. In particular, the real-time control method of the vacuum in the cup is discussed to ensure high cleaning quality and security. The robotic cleaning system described is the first fully automated cleaning machine for the reversed inclining glass facade in China. It works effectively and reliably on the control tower of Guangzhou Airport (Wang et al. 2010).

By removing people from hazardous situations altogether, remote robotics in tandem with 5G Internet will revolutionise the way hard manual labour is performed. But sometimes, people cannot be completely removed from dangerous situations or environments. When natural disasters strike, health and safety of a massive number of people is at risk. Earthquakes are especially harmful in this regard.

Example

Earthquake Warning

Japan has 127 million inhabitants and is situated on the edge of the Pacific Ring of Fire. Earthquakes have devastated the country in the past, most notably in 2011, when the nuclear power plant in Fukushima was hit by a tsunami triggered by an earthquake off the coast. This disaster killed 16.000 people. Hakusan Corporation combines IoT technology with mobile apps to help protect the population of Japan. The government operates a seismological surveillance and early warning system. There are 1700 sensors across the country recording earthquake activity data, which is then analysed by the Japanese Meteorological Agency. Between 1.313 and 10.680 times per year, an earthquake hits the island. The system can help to reduce catastrophes by warning the population. However, these sensors only measure ground tremors, not the safety or stability of buildings. The iPhone's acceleration sensor can do exactly that. Hakusan developed an app called iJishin, which measures tremors while mounted to walls during earthquakes.

This data, in combination with big data analysis and IoT sensors, can help make predictions about possible damages on buildings inflicted by earthquakes. A collaboration with SAP Leonardo makes sure that data is collected and analysed at real-time speed, building a network for databased analytics with regards to earthquake damages. This can help first responders as well as official authorities to react accordingly, saving lives in the process (Brown 2018).

Not all "safety" applications are matters of life and death. Making workspaces safer is a worthwhile endeavour. Refurbishing existing buildings to make them safer, more sustainable, smarter and more welcoming is a challenge unto itself.

Example

Landbrauhaus Hofstetten

The privately owned brewery Hofstetten has been in business since 1449 and is therefore the oldest brewery in Austria. Over 700.000 litres of beer are produced annually. In 2015, the buildings underwent a massive renovation. In addition to a new lighting system based on energy-efficient LED lighting, the brewery is equipped with IoT sensors that measure temperature in the mash house, silos, cellar and all other areas of the beer plant. Furthermore, fire alarm systems with smoke detectors were installed in all areas. In case of smoke detection, an alarm chain is triggered and the fire brigade is autonomously notified ensuring the workplace is a safe environment.

The lighting design has a work and a tour guide mode, and at dusk, the outer lighting turns on automatically. Lighting switches have been replaced with presence sensors. Energy use is constantly monitored, ensuring that there is no overload.

Brewing beer produces steam, which is used in turn to heat the brewery. The outdoor ramps leading up to the brewery are heated with this energy and kept ice-free under all conditions, without an additional heating load. The cooling cellar where the beer is maturing for 5 weeks is kept at a constant temperature of 2,5 °C. The silos are also controlled by smart home technology, making sure that no overfilling takes place.

Windows and gates are equipped with sensors as well. Windows in the roof open and close automatically, depending on temperature. The main gate sends a message to the owner's phone if it is still open after 6 p.m. (Loxone Magazin 2018).

These case studies illustrate that old structures, entire countries and whole industries can be transformed and made safer because of digitalisation. Technology changes the way we are informed about disasters. It protects workers by taking dangerous tasks off their hands and lets their work be completed by remotely controlled machines instead. And it makes our workplaces safer by making sure the environment is well adjusted to our needs, freeing time for more productive tasks that was previously invested in making sure that all of the workplace's minutiae were taken care of. In addition, augmented and virtual reality can be used to train employees and support them in their daily work.

5.9 Conclusion

The chapter showed that smart building technologies are already widely used. IoT use cases are extensively spread. Due to a significant reduction of price and the availability of self-sufficient systems, their usage is widely spread. Moreover, big data, AI, ML and blockchain are important smart building technologies. Whereas many FM publications stress the importance of BIM, its impact according to the literature research is rather limited. Other technologies are mentioned much more frequently. The data gathered makes it possible to identify the effected services and the relationship between services and technologies. The services mostly affected are "maintenance and operation", "logistics", "energy", "safety" and "security".

In contrast to these results, most of the property management and facility service companies as well as the developers still use a lot of standard technology. Technologies like IoT, AI, ML and blockchain develop so rapidly, but start-ups or technology companies mainly use them. "Classical" companies are not yet taking up on these developments. They mainly lack best practice case studies that can directly be implemented in their companies.

However, one important issue has to be kept in mind. Digitalisation is not about technology or the more intensive use of emerging technology; it is about the customer and her or his demands.

Digitalisation is about:

- Customer orientation
- Human touch
- New service and product offerings with full customer/human touch orientation
- Single item production at the cost of mass production
- Wow effect
- Disruptive change
- New partnerships

Review Questions

1. Name and describe the four industrial revolutions.
2. Which emerging technologies are important for RE/FM/FS?
3. Which services are most effected?
4. Which emerging technologies change the service provision in the area of "maintenance and operation" and how?

References

Al-Fuqaha, A., Guizani, M., Mohammadi, M., Aledhari, M., & Ayyash, M. (2015). Internet of things: A survey on enabling technologies, protocols, and applications. IEEE Communication Surveys & Tutorials, Bd. 17, Nr. 4.

Anyoha, R. (2017). Can machines think? In *Harvard University Blog*, Special Edition about Artificial Intelligence. http://sitn.hms.harvard.edu/flash/2017/history-artificial-intelligence. Accessed 23 July, 2019.

Ashton, K. (2009). That 'Internet of Things' Thing. *RFID Journal*, 22 June 2009. https://www.rfidjournal.com/articles/view?4986

Azuma, R. T. (1997). A survey of augmented reality. *Pres-ence: Teleoperators and Virtual Environments 6.* 4 (August 1997), pp. 355–385. Cambridge, MA: The MIT Press.

BBC. (2019). *The history of machine learning*. https://www.bbc.com/timelines/zypd97h. Accessed 23 July, 2019.

Blieberger, J., Klasek, J., Redlein, A., & Schildt, G.-H. (1996). Informartik 3. Auflage., Springer Verlag: Vienna.

Bonomi, F., Milito, R., Zhu, J., & Addepalli, S. (2012). Fog computing and its role in the internet of things. *MCC Workshop Mobile Cloud Computing*. (pp. 13–16), August 17-17, Helsinki Finnland, ISBN: 978-1-4503-1519-7.

Brown, C. (2018). *Eine IoT-fähige App schützt Millionen von Menschen vor Erdbebengefahren*. In SAP Internet der Dinge. https://news.sap.com/germany/2018/02/iot-app-erdbebenschutz/?source=email-de-newscenter-newsletter-20180307&sap-outbound-id=526F6AD48661AB03FD50A9F1F54122A90DC90F7B. Accessed 23 July, 2019

Cambridge University Press. (2019). https://dictionary.cambridge.org/dictionary/english/sharing-economy. Accessed August 2019.

Christensson, P. (2012). App Definition. Von Tech Terms: https://techterms.com/definition/app

Cruz-Neira, C. (1993). Virtual reality overview. In *SIGGRAPH 93 Course Notes 21st International Conference on Computer Graphics and Interactive Techniques*, Orange County Convention Center, Orlando, FL.

DHL. (2017). *"DHL Supply Chain to use collaborative robots for innovative order fulfilment pilot" – Press Release*. http://www.dhl.com/en/press/releases/releases_2017/all/logistics/dhl_supply_chain_to_use_collaborative_robots_for_innovative_order_fulfillment_pilot.html

Dontha, R. (2017). *Who came up with Big Data? In Data Science Central*. https://www.datasciencecentral.com/profiles/blogs/who-came-up-with-the-name-big-data. Accessed 23 July, 2019.

Dörner, K., & Edelman, D. (2015, July). *What 'digital' really means*. https://www.mckinsey.com/industries/high-tech/our-insights/what-digital-really-means

EN 15221-4. (2018). *Taxonomy, classification and structures in facility management,* Austrian Standards.

Ericsson. (2017). *Critical control of remote devices*. https://www.ericsson.com/en/5g/use-cases/critical-control-of-remote-devices. Accessed 23 July, 2019.

Evans, R., & Gao, J. (2016). DeepMind AI reduces energy used for cooling Google data centers by 40 %. In *Google Sustainability Blog.* https://www.blog.google/outreach-initiatives/environment/deepmind-ai-reduces-energy-used-for/. Accessed 23 July, 2019.

Fox, A., Armbrust, M., Griffith, R., Joseph, A. D., Katz, R. H., Konwinski, A., Lee, G., Patterson, D. A., Rabkin, A., Stoica, I., & Zaharia, M. (2009). *Above the clouds: A berkeley view of cloud computing*. Department of Electrical Engineering and Computer Science, University of California, Berkeley, Rep. UCB/EECS, 2009, 28. Jg., Nr. 13.

Frey, C., & Osborne, M. (2013). The future of employment: How susceptible are jobs to computerisation?, University Oxford, Oxford, USA.

Fujitsu. (2018). *Develops Technology to Recognize Patient Status Using a Camera*. von http://www.fujitsu.com/global/about/resources/news/press-releases/2014/0513-02.html. Accessed 23 April, 2018.

Gartner IT Glossary. (2019). https://www.gartner.com/it-glossary/digitalization/; https://www.gartner.com/it-glossary/?s=chatbot. Accessed August 2019.

Herrenkohl, J., Magrans, M., Buisman, A., & Banerjee, A. (2017). *Digital trends in real estate, hospitality and construction. Building blocks for future growth*. EY Real Estate.

HPE. (2019) *What is cloud computing?* https://www.hpe.com/us/en/what-is/cloud-computing.html. Accessed 26 July, 2019.

Iansiti, M., & Lakhani, K. R. (2017). The Truth about Blockchain. *Harvard Business Review* (January – Feburary 2017).

IBM. (2018). *IBM Food Trust: Adding trust and transparency to our food*. https://www.ibm.com/blockchain/solutions/food-trust. Accessed 23 July, 2019.

IBM. (2019). *Cloud computing: A complete guide*. https://www.ibm.com/uk-en/cloud/learn/what-is-cloud-computing. Accessed 26 July, 2019.

Investopedia. (2019). *Blockchain explained*. https://www.investopedia.com/terms/b/blockchain.asp

I-Scoop. (2017). *Blockchain smart port case: efficient and secure container release in the port of Antwerp*. In I-Scoop. https://www.i-scoop.eu/blockchain-smart-port-project-case-container-release-port-antwerp/. Accessed 23 July, 2019.

ISO 8373. (2012). Robots and robotic devices — Vocabulary, Edition 2.

Jadeja, Y., & Modi, K. (2012). *Cloud computing – concepts, architecture and challenges*. https://doi.org/10.1109/ICCEET.2012.6203873.

Klyvø, T. (2016). *SAP predictive maintenance and service, SAP SE or an SAP affiliate company*. https://www.ddv.org/sites/default/files/sap_danmark.pdf.

KONE. (2018). *KONE revolutioniert die Anlagenwartung mit individualisierbaren Serviceverträgen und 24/7 Connected Services*. https://www.kone.at/news-und-referenzen/pressemitteilungen/kone-care-und-24-7-connected-services.aspx. Accessed 23 April, 2018.

Krishnamurthy, R., & Desouza, K. (2014). Big data analytics: The case of social security administration. *Information Polity*, p. 165–178.

Kubick, W. R. (2012). Big data, information and meaning. In: *Clinical Trial Insights* (pp. 26–28), Vol. 21, Issue: 2, Chicago, USA.

Laney, D. (2001). Meta Group (Gartner). *3D Data Management: Controlling Data Volume, Velocity, and Variety*. https://www.gartner.com/it-glossary/big-data/

Lee, K. (2012). Augmented reality in education and training. *TechTrends, 56*(2), S13–S21.

Lexology (2017). Artificial Intelligence (AI): What is it and how does it work?, Global, Ireland. Accessed August 2019.

Louridas, P., & Ebert, C. (2016). Machine learning. Published in: IEEE Software (Vol. 33, Issue: 5, Sept.-Oct. 2016).

Loxone Magazin. (2018). *Smarte Brauerei: Österreichs älteste Brauerei setzt auf Smart Home Technologie*. https://www.loxone.com/dede/smarte-brauerei/. Accessed 23 July, 2019.

Mäkilä, T., Järvi, A., Rönkkö, M., & Nissilä, J. (2010). How to define software-as-a-service – An empirical study of Finnish SaaS Providers. In P. Tyrväinen, S. Jansen, & M. A. Cusumano (Eds.), *Software Business. ICSOB 2010. Lecture Notes in Business Information Processing* (Vol. 51). Berlin, Heidelberg: Springer.

Marr, B. (2015). *How big data and the Internet of Things improve public transport In London*. In Forbes. https://www.forbes.com/sites/bernardmarr/2015/05/27/how-big-data-and-the-internet-of-things-improve-public-transport-in-london/#751e2b1a1be6. Accessed 23 July, 2019.

Marr, B. (2016). *Shell: Big data and big oil*. https://www.bernardmarr.com/default.asp?contentID=688. Accessed 23 July, 2019.

Marr, B. (2017). *GE power: Big data, machine learning and 'The Internet of Energy'*. https://www.bernardmarr.com/default.asp?contentID=1266. Accessed 23 July, 2019

Matt, C. (2009). Software as a Service, Z *Control Management, 53*, 151, Vol. 53, Issues: 3, Springer Verlag, https://doi.org/10.1007/s12176-009-0048-5.

Metz, R. (2014). *Rise oft he Robot Security Guards – Startup Knightscope is preparing to roll out human-size robot patrols*. https://www.technologyreview.com/s/532431/rise-of-the-robot-security-guards/

Moon, S. M., Shin, C. Y., Huh, J., Oh, K. W., & Hong, D. (2015). Window cleaning system with water circulation for building facade maintenance robot and Its efficiency analysis, International Journal of Precision Engineering and Manufacturing Green Technology, Volume 2, Issue 1, p. 65–72, Springer Verlag.

Moreno, M., Castaño, B., Barrero, D., & Hellín, A. (2014). Efficient services management in libraries using AI and wireless techniques. *Expert Systems with Applications, 41*, 7904–7913.

Nagl, W., Titelbach, G., & Valkova, K. (2017). *Digitalisierung der Arbeit: Substituierbarkeit von Berufen im Zuge der Automatisierung durch Industrie 4.0. Vienna: Institut für höhere Studien (IHS).*

Oxford University Press. (2017). Artificial intelligence. Oxford Reference.

Pintaric, T., Ledermann, F., Schmalstieg, D., & Wagner, D. (2005). "Towards Massively Multi-User Augmented Reality on Handheld Devices"; *Talk: 3rd International Conference on Pervasive Computing*, München, DE; 05-08-2005 – 05-13-2005; In: *Proceedings of the 3rd International Conference on Pervasive Computing*. https://www.ims.tuwien.ac.at/publications/tuw-139804

Protocol by Remme. (2017, June). *Keep your information safe with Blockchain technology*. https://medium.com/remme/keep-your-information-safe-with-blockchain-technology-87ed1e7636eb

PwC. (2017a). *Global Digital IQ Survey: 10th anniversary edition – A decade of digital keeping pace with transformation*. https://www.pwc.com/us/en/advisory-services/digital-iq/assets/pwc-digital-iq-report.pdf#515

PwC. (2017b, June). *What doctor? – Why AI ansd robotics will define New Health*. https://www.pwc.com/gx/en/industries/healthcare/publications/ai-robotics-new-health/ai-robotics-new-health.pdf

PwC. (2017c). Blockchain and smart contracts. Von PwC Germany: https://www.pwc.de/en/newsletter/it-security-news-en/blockchain-and-smart-contracts.html

Ray, S. (2018). *The History of AI*. In Towards Data Science. https://towardsdatascience.com/history-of-ai-484a86fc16ef. Accessed 23 July, 2019.

Russom, P. (2011). *Big data analytics*. In: TDWI Best Practices Report, pp. 1–40.

Schwab, K. (2016). *The fourth industrial revolution*. Portfolio Penguin, USA.

Stopajnik, E., & Redlein, A. (2017a). Current labour market situation and upcoming trends in the European Facility Service Industry. Reasearch group for Facility Management, TU Vienna, pp. 34–42.

Stopajnik, E., & Redlein, A. (2017b). The development of the outsourced facility service industry in Europe. *JFMA, 1*(1), 1–5.

Sun, Y., Song, H., Jara, A., & Bie, R. (2016). Internet of Things and big data analytics for smart and connected communities. *IEEE Access, 4*, 766–773.

Sutherland, I. E. (1968). A head-mounted three dimensional display. In *Fall Joint Computer Conference Proceedings*, pp. 757–764.

TechTerms. (n.d.). https://techterms.com/definition/app. Accessed August 2019.

Wang, W., Tang, B., Zhang, H., & Zong, G. (2010). Robotic cleaning system for glass facade of high-rise airport control tower. *Industrial Robot: An International Journal, 37*(5), 469–478.

Weiser, M., (1991). The computer for the twenty-first century, Scientific American Special Issue on Communications, Computers, and Networks.

Wellers, D., Elliott, T., & Noga, M. (2017). *8 Ways Machine Learning is improving companies work processes*. https://hbr.org/2017/05/8-ways-machine-learning-is-improving-companies-work-processes

Xu, L., He, W., & Li, S. (2014). Internet of Things in industries. A survey. *IEEE Transactions on Industrial Informatics, 10*, 2233–2243.

Workplace Management

Alexander Redlein, Claudia Höhenberger, and Pat Turnbull

A. Redlein (ed.), *Modern Facility and Workplace Management*,
Classroom Companion: Business, https://doi.org/10.1007/978-3-030-35314-8_6

Learning Objectives

After having finished this chapter, you will be able to answer the following questions:

- What is workplace management?
- What is workplace strategy?
- Why is it important to have a workplace strategy?
- What makes a good workplace?
- What are employees' needs regarding workplace and (surrounding) services?
- Who are the people responsible for workplace management?
- How can a workplace strategy be developed and applied?

6.1 Introduction

> *"It's not about the building, it's about the people. It is a place beyond the quiet, solo home office where you find energy, inspiration and collaboration".*
> Robin Bramman, Strategic Brand Consultant

Digitalisation has fundamentally altered the way we work. People are already working from the office, from home and from a wide variety of third-party locations without keeping to a strict 9/5, five-days-a-week schedule. The demand for flexibility will further increase as "digital natives" become an even bigger part of the workforce with Gen-Z entering the job market. The future of work will see a more flexible and more diverse workforce (Fraunhofer 2013). It is not only young people who disrupt the status quo. Mothers and fathers alike are interested in adaptable working hours, as are elderly people. As retirement age rises, more senior workers (with their valuable experience) remain a part of this shifting landscape. "Gap" months or years in the form of sabbaticals will also become more prevalent for people of all ages. In addition to age-related diversity, we will see an increasingly heterogenous workforce comprised of people from varying cultural, religious and socio-economic backgrounds, genders, able-bodied and disabled employees alike. In order to accommodate this diversified workforce, it is important for companies to provide values and an infrastructure that fully support their workers. This encompasses many factors, like accessible office design, a welcoming office culture, an engaging work environment and, of course, a digital framework that allows for flexibility with regards to when and where people work. In order to establish such supportive and experiential workplaces, it is important to create short-term interventions and a long-term, aligned business strategy.

Business strategy is important because it aligns all individual activities within a business entity toward a shared vision. It helps channel decisions about the organisation's focus, the investment of resources, what activities make sense and how to coordinate those activities across the entire organisation (Turnbull 2011).

Definition

Workplace strategy (WPS) is the alignment of the organisation's workplace with the business strategy in order to optimise the effectiveness of its people and achieve its strategic business goals. It takes into account different dimensions of a company, its physical and virtual work environments, culture, business processes, technologies and other resources.

So, not surprisingly, this is the starting point for the development of a workplace strategy – an appreciation for and understanding of the broader business and social context in which an organisation exists (CoreNet 2019).

Workplace strategy has become an important tool for business leaders who seek to attract and retain talent, optimise productivity, accelerate innovation and enhance brand image. This chapter provides an approach to understanding how to develop an effective workplace strategy, identify/engage key stakeholders and utilise relevant data to inform/enable successful strategy deployment.

Workplace strategy helps answer these questions:

- Is our workplace aligned with the business strategy, culture, values and brand?
- Is our workplace helping to optimise people's performance?
- Is our workplace, along with other assets, being used to drive desired business results?
- Is the strategy and infrastructure designed to quickly and easily evolve with the business?

This chapter so to say sums up all previous chapters, which mainly targeted on optimising RE/FM organisation and its IT support, benchmarking to identify best practice and digitalisation to disruptive optimise FS provision by new ways of human-centred services and products' provision. This chapter deals with the definition of the requirements and the provision of the work environment and its surrounding services to optimally support people, process and place of a company. It shows why it is important to steer this adaption process. It shows that designing offices with regards to employees' needs is a key factor in raising engagement, productivity and motivation in the workplace. This chapter explains how to develop and implement a workplace strategy that will enable companies to make their workplaces and service provision fit for the future. It helps to identify the people that should be involved in workplace management. A step-by-step implementation guide is provided to illustrate how a workplace management process positively impacts work environments.

6.2 Triple Bottom Line

People spend the majority of their day engaged in work-related activities. Creating an environment that is welcoming and invokes positive responses from its occupants does not materialise by happenstance. It is the result of a focused and thoroughly thought out process, involving many interested parties and carefully balancing sometimes conflicting interests against one another. Workplace management is fairly complex because it deals with technology and tools, people and culture and the workspace plus its surrounding services.

Technology allows for flexibility. But this flexibility can lead to culture degradation and a fragmented workforce, where co-workers hardly occupy the same space at the same time. Managing this highly individualised, de-centralised workforce is a challenge in itself.

By moving the focus of the workplace beyond just the function of transactional Real Estate, a successful workplace strategy will embrace people, planet and overall business objectives. Indeed, workplace strategy is a triple win to help achieve bottom line results:

6

- **People**: Employees are empowered with work environments that support private and collaborative learning as well as help create balance between work and life demands. This leads to increased engagement and retention.
- **Planet**: The natural environment wins as we deliver healthier and more sustainable places to work (with benefits that include reduced energy, improved water efficiency, reduced construction waste, better air quality, daylight harvesting, etc.). Effective work space evaluation and planning can lead to overall conservation of resources.
- **Profit**: Businesses reap the benefits of workplace strategy alignment to corporate goals, such as the ability to attract and retain talent, increase workforce productivity and reduce operating costs by optimising usable space and reducing unnecessary space in the workplace.

6.3 Importance of Workplace Management: Maslow's Hierarchy of Needs

As is evident by the list above, people are at the heart of workplace management. Employee needs must be taken into account in order to create workplaces that provide environments that foster productivity and therefore boost the bottom line.

It has been shown that an increase in productivity will do much more to increase profit than cutting office space could ever save (Lister 2019). Considering that their employees' social capital is a major factor for a company's success, organisations should strive to make their workers' motivation a core issue. Presenteeism, absenteeism, staff turnover and workers phoning it in are often symptoms of a larger problem: a disengaged workforce. And this problem is larger than many realise. According to Gallup (Nink and Robinson 2016), 24% of employees worldwide are actively disengaged and therefore less productive, less profitable and less loyal than highly engaged employees, which account for only 13% of employees worldwide.

A problem for knowledge work is that there is no clear metric with which to measure productivity. While quality weighed output per hour is applicable to some degree, it can never give the full picture and is often difficult to assess anyway. Metrics like absenteeism, turnover, health costs, output, performance and time worked are often used as key performance indicators (Bortoluzzi et al. 2018).

Example

Kate Lister (2019) has shown that presenteeism, where a person shows up to work without performing at their best, is more expensive than absenteeism and therefore a serious drain on a company's bottom line.

Qualitative metrics like self-assessed employee performance, perceived work ability, presenteeism and engagement can help to draw a clearer picture with regards to workplace productivity (Bortoluzzi et al. 2018).

Since human resources are our most valuable and expensive business asset, the question of how to motivate employees becomes central to any organisation's success.

6.3.1 People's Motivation to Work

What motivates a person to work? While deceptively simple, this question has engaged psychologists for a long time. In 1943, American psychologist Abraham Maslow crafted one of the most popular theories in this field, called *A Theory of Human Motivation*. In this essay he laid out five basic needs that every human craves to fulfil. These needs are physiological, safety, love, esteem and self-actualisation. While visualisations often use a pyramid to illustrate Maslow's idea of prepotency of needs (i.e. the next higher need takes over as prime motivator when a need is satisfied), he never conjures this specific image in the original essay (◘ Fig. 6.1).

The graphic clarity can lead to mis-readings of the scheme, where people think that one cannot "level up" to the next higher need until a need is satisfied, like in a computer game of motivation. Yet Maslow clearly states that multiple factors contribute to motivation simultaneously. As soon as a need is met completely, however, it no longer serves as a motivator (Maslow 1943).

Some experts have suggested that a two-level distinction is enough, with physiological needs ranked at the bottom separated from the higher-level needs on top (Lawler and Suttle 1972). Others have stressed that both higher- and lower-level needs are simultaneously unfulfilled with only the higher-order needs serving as motivators (Herzberg 1966). Herzberg conceived that job satisfaction stems from what a person does. Work will gratify needs such as competency, personal worth, status, achievement and self-realisation. Job dissatisfaction stems from work-related factors such as technical problems, interpersonal relationships on the job, salary, company policies and working conditions. An improvement in the workplace environment therefore, while not leading to job satisfaction, will lessen dissatisfaction in the job.

6.3.2 Maslow's Basic Needs Applied to the Work Environment

Psychologist Mario Conforti (1972) proposed to use Maslow's hierarchy of needs in the workplace to provide employees with greater personal satisfaction, which in turn can result in greater job motivation. He suggests that employees are most productive when their physiological, safety and social ("love") needs are relatively satisfied and when

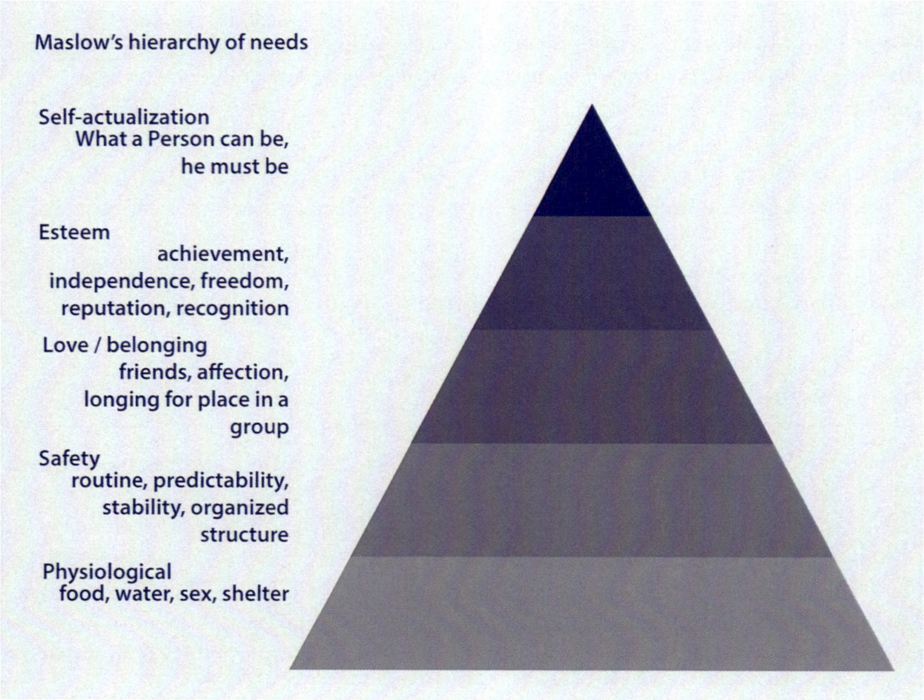

Fig. 6.1 Maslow's hierarchy of needs visualized as a pyramid. (Based on McDermid 1960)

6

esteem and self-actualisation serve as primary motivators. Certain conditions must exist as a prerequisite to basic-need satisfaction, among them justice, fairness, honesty, orderliness and the freedom to speak, act, investigate, express and defend oneself. These prerequisites depend on the employees' relationship to the company and his supervisors. Feelings of achievement and pride are vital for employee job satisfaction, as is mutual respect between the worker and the organisation.

Legendary management consultor Peter Drucker has stressed time and again that workers are more than physical assets and should therefore be treated accordingly. He proposed as early as 1942 (*The Future of the Industrial Man*) that employee's social and psychological needs should be met (Drucker 1942). Cary L. Cooper (2013) suggests that Drucker was the precursor of the movement for well-being at work.

Workplace consultant Kate Lister also applies Maslow's hierarchy of needs to the workplace (2014). Her primary concern is the well-being of the workforce, which she defines as:

Definition

"Employee Well-Being includes employee wellness, but also addresses the psychological well-being of the individual worker, addressing considerations such as worker engagement, choice and control, work-life balance, etc." (Lister 2014, S. 2).

From this short excerpt it is evident that her approach to foster motivation in the workforce is a holistic one, touching subjects such as physical, social and emotional state of the worker, how absenteeism and presenteeism affect productivity, the cost of well-being programs for employers and their direct and indirect return of investment and the role workplace strategy plays. The cost of poor well-being, for the worker as well as the employer, is considerable.

Example
The will to implement and improve well-being programs is not the same around the world. Whereas in Europe and Canada an increased engagement, followed by reduction of absenteeism and a boost in productivity, is key, in the United States the main driver is a reduction in healthcare costs, followed by an increase in productivity and the reduction of absenteeism (Buck Consultants a Xerox company 2012).

The unholy trinity of absenteeism, presenteeism and low engagement is costing businesses dearly. Presenteeism is especially dragging for a business, since the employee is present but does not work to his or her full capacity, be it due to mental or physical ailments.

Example
While someone suffering from depression stays at home for 7 days a year, that same employee will lose on average 36 days to presenteeism, when they officially spend time at the office, but are not as productive as they could be (Lister 2018). But with the introduction of a culture of well-being in the workplace, this situation can be remedied. Research shows that engaged, happy and healthy employees produce more while costing less. With just a 10% increase in well-being, a noticeable effect can be observed: People perform better and do so on more days per month. At the same time, unscheduled absences due to illness and accidents curtail and presenteeism is also reduced by 24% (Lister 2014).

Lister (2014) uses Maslow's hierarchy of needs as a framework for the worker's basic and advanced needs in the workplace. Physiological and safety needs are pooled as "wellness", whereas belonging, esteem and self-actualisation are put together as "well-being".

Lister, Herzberg, Conforti, Maslow, Drucker and others stress that the prevalence of a satisfactory work environment is necessary before meaningful work can be realised. Which raises the question – what is a satisfactory workplace?

6.3.2.1 Meeting the Needs

While the importance of hierarchy in Maslow's theory can be (and indeed is) debated, the categories mentioned provide a good base to assort human needs (■ Fig. 6.2).

6.3.2.2 Physiological

Chief among the physiological needs is health. Workplaces can help to fulfil this need by providing healthy food, a proper space to consume them in and enough time to do so. In addition to nutrition, the office layout can be arranged to encourage walking, by for example centralising printing stations. Fitness programs complement in-work health

Fig. 6.2 Maslow's hierarchy of needs in the workplace. (Based on Lister 2014)

6

initiatives. Outside views and natural daylight along with sufficient artificial lighting inside are important (Lister 2014).

The topic most complained about by office workers is temperature (IFMA 2009). For offices, 20–22 °C is the suggested ideal temperature. Perception of temperature depends on many factors like level of activity, amount of clothing worn, air humidity, temperature of surfaces and speed of air (Redlein et al. 2014).

Being able to control one's environment and adjust it to one's need are effective tools to assuage workers. In addition to temperature, other environmental factors like air quality and humidity are highly important.

Whereas in the German-speaking countries only in case of air-conditioning, some legal requirements concerning temperature and humidity exist, in Scandinavia and Asia, the following diagram is used to determine the array within which a person feels comfortable with regards to humidity and temperature. Comfort and therefore wellness for inhabitants of spaces is enabled in this range (Fig. 6.3).

In addition, reduction of CO_2 levels will improve productivity (Redlein et al. 2014). Biophilic design can help employees to feel connected with nature, making the workspace more comfortable in the process. This also has side effects concerning air quality, relative humidity and CO_2 levels (Sanchez et al. 2017).

The ability to work uninterrupted is supremely effective when it comes to improving productivity. Recovering from an interruption takes an average of 23 minutes (Mark et al. 2008). As a result, noise awareness is key, especially in open office arrangements. Reducing unwanted distractions by introducing noise reduction measurements but also email, phone and meeting guidelines can also potentially help to create timeslots where concentrated and uninterrupted work is possible. However, not all interruptions are counterproductive. If the context for the interruption is the same as for the task at hand, interruptions can have beneficial results (Mark et al. 2008). As a consequence, people working in similar fields should be seated near one another.

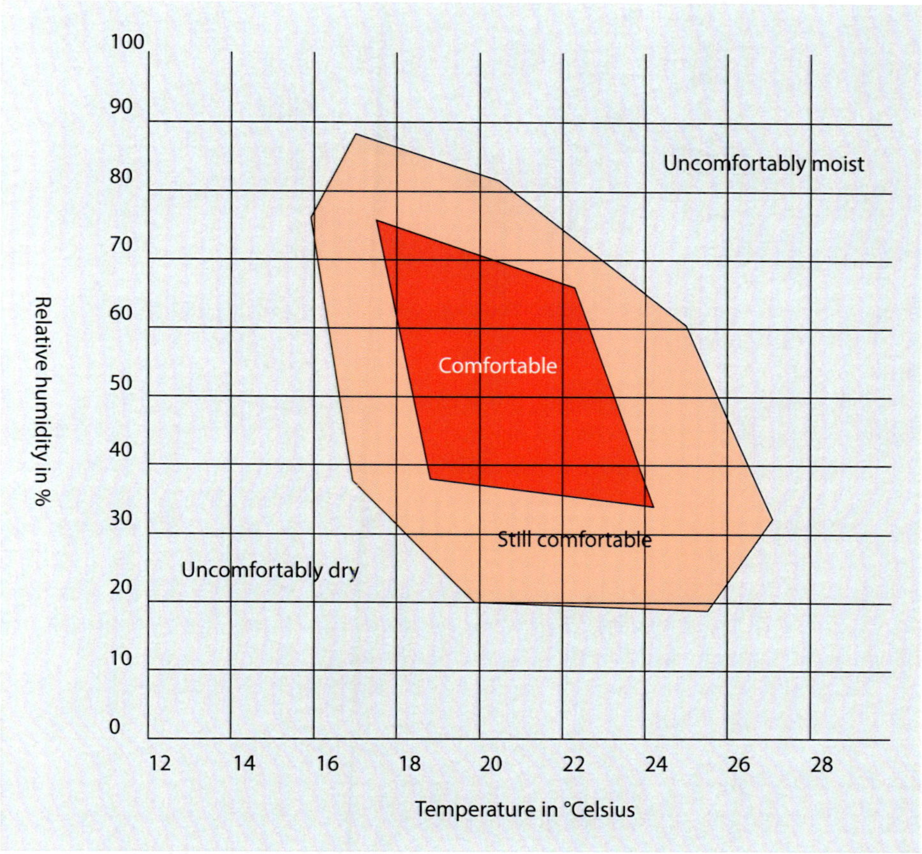

Fig. 6.3 Comfort in practical use. (Based on Leusden and Freymark 1951)

Facility Services supporting this goal are among others "workplace", "plants and flowers", "HSSE", "people occupational health", "catering and vending", "office supplies, stationary", "maintenance and operation", and many more.

6.3.2.3 Safety

Stability and predictability are the leading characteristics of safety. Employees need to feel that the workplace is a stable environment with certain rituals and routines (Guenzi 2013). Equitable and fair treatment of all people working in the organisation helps to underscore this principle.

Realistic work schedules that are challenging without overpowering employees and clear instructions encourage a motivated environment where failures are seen as opportunities to learn and grow. Programs designed to help build resilience can improve performance, since it gives employees the ability to recover from personal as well as professional setbacks and increases their ability to deal with stress (Williams et al. 2018). Employees' mental health in general should be part of a thorough wellness program.

Fig. 6.4 Examples of workspaces supporting communication and belonging. (Copyrights © deloitte/feelimage)

Digitalisation has many benefits, but it can also lead to over-expenditure by often highly motivated employees who feel like they have to be "on" 24/7 (Marsh 2017). While this commitment can be positive temporarily, in the long run it often leads to burnt-out people who will need a long time to recover. Strict boundaries concerning after-work should be put in place to protect self-exploitation. Privacy in the real as well as the virtual world is essential as well.

Furniture and work tools should be ergonomic to ensure that only the mind but also the body is well taken care of. Downtime areas for withdrawal and task-based work areas are good additions to the office layout (Lister 2014).

This need is cared for by Facility Services like "hospitality", "workplace safety", "security", "furniture" and so on.

6.3.2.4 Belonging

The third tier of workplace needs to deal with the urge of employees to feel connected with each other as well as the company (Lister 2014). Clear and open communication is paramount in this category. It drives everything from team dynamics to office culture. Self-managed work with regards to when and where employees labour on their tasks demands open and honest communication from all participants. Remote workers can often feel left out which is why it is important to make them feel part of the team (Fig. 6.4).

Community spaces help to foster an informal atmosphere where people can connect with each other. Short distances to minimise walking distance, visual access and convenience foster communication, as do open spaces (Lister 2014). Coincidental meetings in informal areas support the formation of strong ties between co-workers.

Office gossip, while often seen unfavourably and disruptive by managers, also aids to establish strong bonds between employees, gives an opportunity to vent anger before resentment can build up, reinforces the social rules and norms of the workplace and helps to spread useful information (Moss Kanter 2010; Grosser et al. 2010). Discouraging gossip or banning it altogether often has adverse effects and increases negative gossip.

Facility Services in support of belonging are "space management", "artworks", "hospitality", "meeting rooms and events" and many more.

6.3.2.5 Esteem

Autonomous and independent work is carried out in task-based work zones that are designed to engage the senses and offer a variety of experiences (Oseland 2009). Mutual trust, respect and transparency are required between employee and company and are a prerequisite for a culture of openness.

Remote and independent work and self-managed worktime can only function when supervisors treat employees fairly and with respect. Managers guiding this complex milieu need to be considerate and helpful, give advice when necessary and support when needed (Mawson 2017). Employee involvement in decisions, especially with regard to their well-being or workload, is desirable.

Achievements should receive praise (Berinato 2010). Recognition and the chance to "show off" constructively is beneficial to employee well-being. An atmosphere where everybody feels comfortable to contribute is preferable to one where employees feel out of control. Scarcity leads to resentment and as a worst case to blame culture (Edmondson 1999).

Managers need to show that employees are valued. Constructive criticism, praise and recognition should be delivered when appropriate. This also helps to make progress visible and gives employees a benchmark to see how far they have come and what is still ahead.

While primarily a question of management style and office culture, this need is also serviced. "ICT" provides the necessary infrastructure to make remote and flexible work possible, especially with regards to "connectivity and telecommunication". "Training" and general "HR" also ensure that employees feel respected and valued.

6.3.2.6 Self-Actualisation

It is personally fulfilling and empowering to work for an organisation where not only the work is meaningful, but that also supports the individual employee to reach their personal goals.

Being able to work fully independent and in control with regards to when, where, how and to some extent even what is done is liberating and empowering. This not only involves remote work done from third-party locations but also includes the freedom to choose an ideal work setting within the organisation's premises. Abolishing hierarchy and entitlement-based provisioning is an important step towards the democratisation of the work environment, where workers have a say in the direction an organisation should take in the future (ISS 2011).

A corporate consciousness that takes active responsibility for a company's social and environmental effects is important. Work that has an outcome beyond earning money is the perfect goal, especially for many young employees (Agarwal and Karerat 2019). Operating for a company that shares a person's values and takes measures to implement valuable actions injects a sense of purpose and aspiration to mundane tasks. Even if a company is not involved in the world-saving business, it can still engage in CSR (corporate social responsibility) schemes and make a profit while serving people and the planet to create a sustainable future for the employee, the company and the planet (Turnbull et al. 2016).

"Space management" and "Real Estate optimisation" are among the services needed to optimally manage offices that cater to an increasingly distributed workforce. "Sustainability" goals can help a company to fulfil its CRE goals.

6.4 Workplace Management: Implementation Guideline

As is apparent, in order to satisfy these diverse employee needs, a collaboration of Facility Management, human resources, Corporate Real Estate, finance, marketing, IT, business unit leaders, employee advocates and the C-suite is necessary to create a workplace that is effective, representative of the organisation and its culture, and supports employee satisfaction, health and well-being. To coordinate the demands of these stakeholders and to ensure that the transformation of the workplace will be lasting and adaptable to changing business needs, a solid strategy has to be put into place.

Every organisation has its own unique challenges and opportunities concerning its workplace strategy, but each also has the opportunity to utilise workplace as an effective tool that encourages people to behave in ways that, when aligned with an organisation's goal, will assist in achieving the desired business results (◘ Fig. 6.5).

6.4.1 Methodology to Define Workplace Strategy

Defining a company's optimal workplace strategy requires several steps:
1. Define goals and targets
2. Identify core, extended and partner teams
3. Define and categorise processes to determine infrastructure and service requirements including capacity planning
4. Create status reports

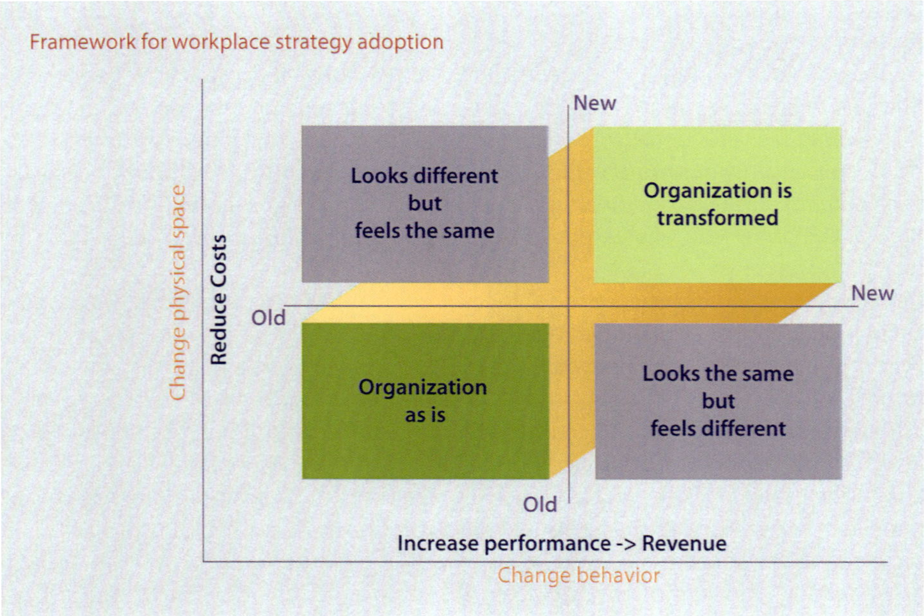

◘ **Fig. 6.5** Framework for workplace strategy adoption. (Redlein 2019a)

5. Evaluate Real Estate and preliminary space designs
6. Coordinate/guide architects, planners and specialists
7. Manage change processes and marketing activities

6.4.2 Define the Goals and Targets

> *"The first step toward creating an improved future is developing the ability to envision it". Anonymous*

Getting executive and senior management understanding and endorsement of workplace strategy goals is critical to the success of your program. Dialogue at this level also helps ensure that the Real Estate and Facility Management strategy aligns with the organisation's strategic plan. Alignment provides a more fertile environment for executive and senior management buy-in and involvement. Getting executive and senior management approval and engagement is shown to be a critical first step on the path to success. From there, the organisation's strategic planning team can coordinate with the workplace planning team to optimise results (Turnbull 2011).

Definition

Sometimes referred to as a strategic facility plan, strategic workplace plan or Real Estate and facility life cycle management plan, workplace strategy refers to aligning an organisation's work patterns with its environment to enable peak performance and reduce costs. Regardless of name, workplace strategy (indeed, workplace management) should be part of, and integrated into, a company's business strategy to support the overall goals of the business entity (Heery 2009).

To begin, the goals of the project or initiative have to be defined and aligned with the overall business goals. Key strategic business goals often include, but are not limited to, the following:
- Attract and retain talent
- Create a culture shift
- Increase productivity
- Support creativity, innovation and team-oriented work
- Reduce cost
- Reducing the environmental impact of facilities and the workforce

In most projects, a combination of goals is defined. Goal definition and alignment should be done together with decision-makers (executive management). The achievement of the goal should be quantifiable, such as "increase employee satisfaction rating to 90 %" or "15 percent cost reduction target". Measurement supports the evaluation of the success of the project when it is finished and gives clues as to where improvement might be needed.

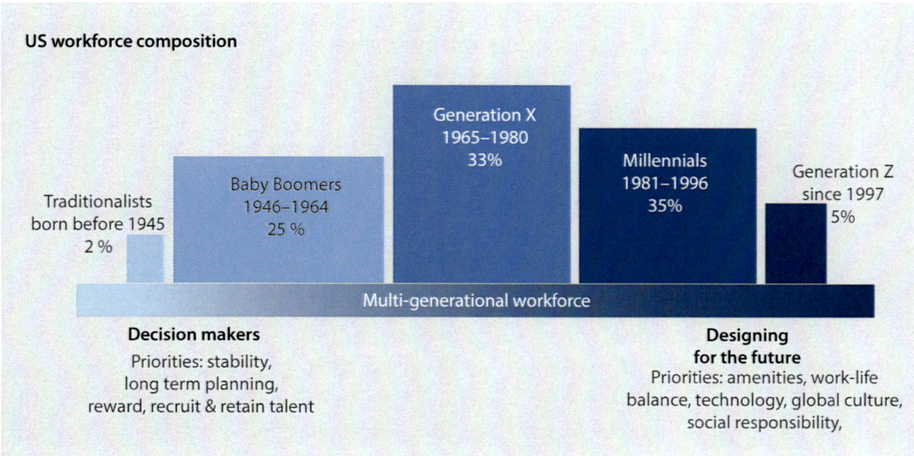

6

Fig. 6.6 Changes in workforce composition at Panduit. (Redlein 2019b)

Example

An excellent example of goal alignment is found in the Panduit case study (Fig. 6.6). The challenge was to define and develop executive management understanding of Real Estate and Facility Management's ability to contribute to overall corporate goals relating to their global vision, innovation, collaboration and sustainability plans. Success hinged on executive leadership support, employee engagement, functional area collaboration, innovative design and intelligent technology integration. Panduit successfully delivered its new 5-story, 280.000 sf, 800-employee capacity, LEED-gold-certified headquarters building. Through the strategic alignment of RE/FM initiatives with C-suite goals, they were able to develop a shared vision with full stakeholder engagement. Through the application of intelligent, well-planned unified physical infrastructure and open-source technology platforms, the work environment was future-proofed for technological advancements (see full case study in Appendix).

6.4.3 Defining the Team

> *"Talent wins games, but teamwork and intelligence win championships".* Michael Jordon

The next step is to define the workplace management team. As described by Turnbull (2011), this team consists of stakeholders who represent the employees and management who will be using the new office environment and solutions. There is not one person who defines or implements workplace strategy. Rather, it is a selection of stakeholders who contribute to the entire strategic planning and implementation process. There might be a project manager overseeing an aspect of the workplace strategy project

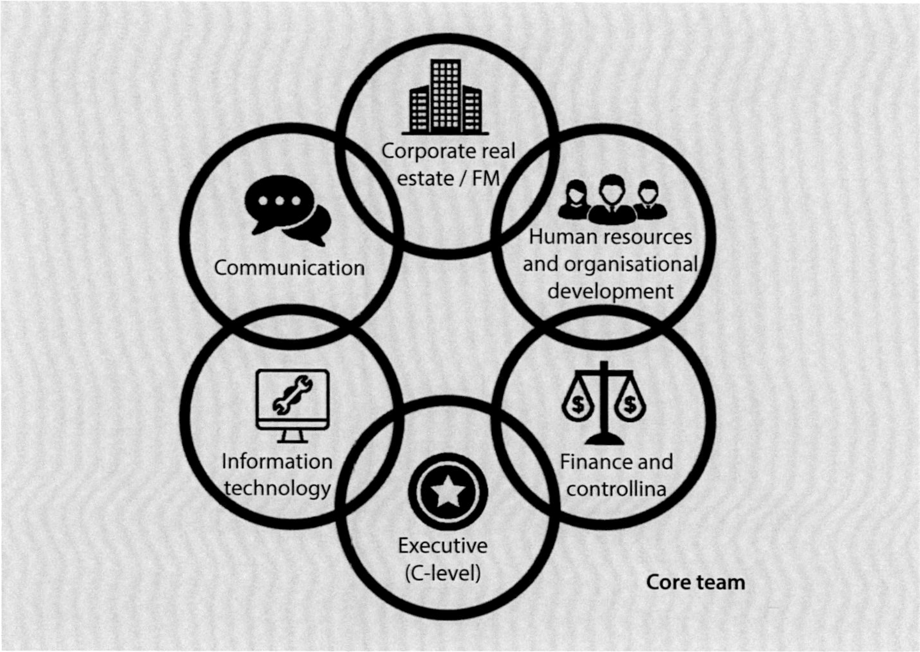

Fig. 6.7 Core team of stakeholders. (Redlein 2019c)

but facility managers and workplace strategists can also take the lead (depending on experience and skill set) in order to drive change in the workplace. The process consists of focused teamwork up front, exceptional communication and people skills and ongoing strategy reviews as well as post-change evaluations.

Executive leadership support and "buy-in" is critical to success and stakeholder engagement is especially important for ultimate acceptance of the project. Thought should be given to who is part of the planning teams, who should only be consulted, etc. The specific time for extended stakeholder engagement varies in the process. The senior leadership and workplace planning team should seek input and ideas from other stakeholders such as business unit leaders, operations personnel, sales and marketing, customer service, plant management, engineering, etc. Broad stakeholder engagement, especially business unit leaders, helps provide perspectives and information about planned developments, competitive threats and performance projections in the organisation. IT department involvement is critical in our digital age and new environments will be greatly enhanced with the help of the information and communication technology (ICT) departments. It is becoming more and more common to collect data from every workplace, device and telecommunication tool (such as VOIP technology) through a variety of integrated building sensors. Activities are coordinated, implemented and measured to inform workplace effectiveness. Sustainability goals can also have an important impact on innovative workplaces (Figs. 6.7 and 6.8).

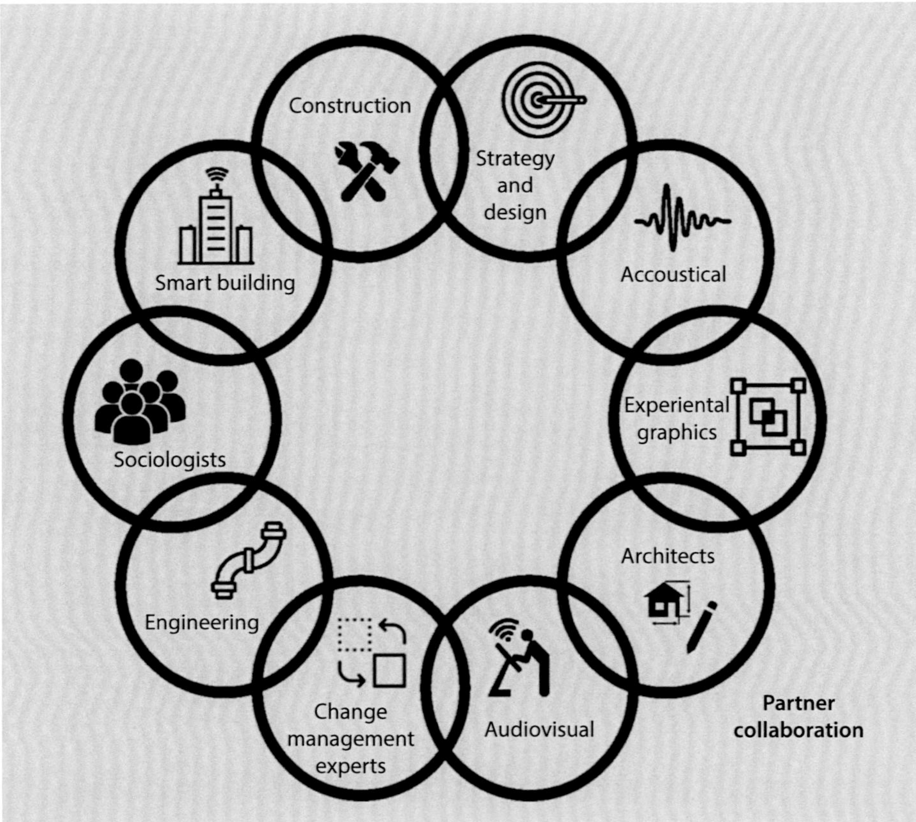

Fig. 6.8 Potential partners for workplace management projects. (Redlein 2019c)

It is the responsibility of the team leader, the person who is charged with developing the strategy (such as the workplace strategist), to understand the organisation's requirements and recommend a workplace solution that will address current and future needs as well as budget constraints. While workplace strategy often provides a response to either running out of space or having too much space, workplace management is much more than that. Workplace management provides a platform to introduce organisational change and impact broad enterprise goals such as productivity, innovation and/or operational efficiencies.

Table 6.1 represents the majority of stakeholders involved with workplace strategy design in terms of sources of information that may or may not be available to the workplace strategist when formulating their plan. The matrix was designed as an easy visual aid, a checklist for appropriating stakeholder engagement and where they are involved in supplying data to the workplace strategy planning team. These resources include the C-suite (CEO, CFO, CMO, CTO), the business unit leaders, support organisations (sales, sustainability, customer service, etc.) as well as the Facility Management and

Table 6.1 Workplace strategy matrix (Turnbull 2011)

Required workplace strategy information

Departmental sources:	C-Suite	Business units (BUs)	Finance	Marketing/ sales	HR	IT	Sustainability officer	RE	FM	Workplace strategist
Organization analysis: corporate and business unit strategies										
Corporate strategy	•		•							
Business model (keep the same or change?)	•	•	•				•			
Branding/image (keep the same or change?)	•			•			•			
Cultural environment	•			•	•					
Financial strategy	•		•							
Business/market environment	•	•		•						
Marketing/sales strategy	•	•		•						
Organization analysis: corporate and business unit strategies										
Business unit strategy	•	•	•							
Existing conditions (employees by location, type of space...)		•			•	•			•	
Demand/revenue growth[5]	•	•	•	•	•					
Need for collaboration with Other BUs	•	•								
Historical growth/ reduction		•	•		•					
Strategy maps, scorecards, metrics	•	•	•	•	•	•	•	•	•	•
Leadership interviews	•	•						•	•	•
Business continuity & risk management policies		•	•		•	•			•	
ERP data and analysis (ROA, NPV, etc.)			•							
Organization analysis: HR strategy										
Headcount for BUs & contract workers (existing)					•					
Employee costs			•		•	•			•	
Historical trending			•		•					
Labor market opportunities					•					
Labor contract issues by site		•	•		•					
Workforce planning	•	•			•					
Technology: IT strategy										
Corporate IT strategy	•	•				•				
Data center / cloud / outsourcing strategy						•				
Mobility strategy					•	•		•	•	•
Smart building strategy						•	•	•	•	•
Financial strategy										
Corporate financial strategy (reduce costs, improve productivity)	•		•							
Relocation & improvement costs		•	•		•	•		•	•	•

Table 6.1 (continued)

	Departmental sources:	C-Suite	Business units (BUs)	Finance	Marketing/ sales	HR	IT	Sustainability officer	RE	FM	Workplace strategist
Required workplace strategy information	***Financial strategy***										
	Annual and NPV costs			•							
	ROI analysis	•	•						•		•
	Capital planning						•		•	•	•
	Gov's/legal regulations/issues		•	•					•		
	Space analysis: real estate & FM										
	Goals and objectives								•	•	•
	Challenges and opportunities								•	•	•
	Occupancy strategy								•	•	•
	Site analyses	•	•	•	•	•	•	•	•	•	•
	Total cost of occupancy of entire portfolio (by building)								•	•	•
	Space utilization study								•	•	•
	Lease abstract data & projections (FAS/IAS)			•					•		
	Charge-back Policies		•	•					•	•	
	Technology (IWMS/ CAFM & GIS including analytics)		•						•	•	•
	Technology (CAD & BIM)									•	
	Workplace standards & guidelines									•	•
	Sustainability strategy & policies							•		•	
	Performance metrics & benchmarks			•		•	•	•	•	•	•
	RE market data & analysis			•					•		
	Building condition assessments								•	•	
	Scenario plans ("what if")	•	•	•	•	•	•	•	•	•	•
	Adjacency analysis (+/– travel time, distance: people, places, things)		•			•	•	•	•	•	•
	Stack plans									•	•
	Block plans									•	•
	Project management										•
	Building condition assessments								•	•	
	Scenario plans ("what if")	•	•	•	•	•	•	•	•	•	•
	Adjacency analysis (+/– travel time, distance: people, places, things)		•			•	•	•	•	•	•
	Stack plans									•	•
	Block plans									•	•
	Project management										•

corporate Real Estate groups (◘ Table 6.1: *Dimensions of Workplace Strategy, Work on the Move: Driving strategy and change in workplaces (Turnbull* 2011).

Below, Turnbull (2011) describes the C-suite and other leader roles that are critical in strategy development:

- **By C-suite**, we mean the executive management team otherwise known as chief executive officer, chief operating officer, chief financial officer, etc. It is important to understand the corporation's strategic direction and plans, including quarterly updates/events that might alter the direction of that plan during the course of a year.
- **Finance**: While CRE often reports directly to or is in a dotted line reporting structure to finance, it is important that the workplace strategist understands the financial direction of the company, as well as understands the best strategy for a leased and/or owned portfolio and how newly proposed changes to Real Estate accounting rules (FASB/IASB4) change that strategy.
- **Human resources**: HR is the source of data necessary to understand workforce planning. HR can help with headcount (both employees and contractors), total cost of ownership (cost per employee), historical trends, labour market statistics, workplace planning, on–/off-boarding analyses and any other information related to the workforce and the provisioning of the workplace.
- **Information technology**: Technology and changes to existing IT infrastructures make it increasingly important for the workplace strategist to understand the capabilities, strategies and plans relating to this functional area. What already exists and what opportunities are available for new technologies that could enhance operational efficiency – such as "bring your own device" (BYOD) or "bring your own technology" (BYOT). Sensors and security, as well as cloud computing versus data centres versus outsourcing models. Will new technologies be integrated or stand-alone solutions? These and many more questions should be addressed by the IT department.
- **Real Estate and Facility Management**: Obviously, much of the information for designing and implementing a workplace strategy will come from the Facility Management and corporate Real Estate Departments. A critical list of data/information is listed below in ◘ Table 6.1, "Workplace Strategy Matrix".
- **Business unit leaders**: These leaders are essential for gaining an understanding of overall organisational structure, how business units tie to the overall business strategy and how each unit responds to corporate initiatives. Important data from these stakeholders include future headcount, location analysis, revenue growth, work initiatives, change in workplace requirements (such as more laboratories or less office space for a particular unit), historical trends, strategy mapping and performance monitoring and measurement. This information may come from embedded workplace strategists, Facility Management, Corporate Real Estate planning or interviews with key members of the leadership team.

- **Marketing and sales**: It is important for the workplace strategist to understand sales and marketing strategies for increasing revenue, for communicating most effectively with existing and potential customers, and for understanding their relationships with each of the business units. Information on branding and image, overall corporate culture, and sales, marketing and business development strategies are important to understanding the organisation's corporate direction.

6

◘ Table 6.1, below, provides a matrix of resources for important organisational information used in workplace strategy development. It includes the majority of stakeholders involved with workplace strategy design and the type of information they contribute to plan formulation. The matrix was designed as an easy visual aid, a checklist, to appropriate stakeholder engagement and where they are involved in supplying data to the workplace strategy planning team. Resources include the C-suite (CEO, CFO, CMO, CTO), the business unit leaders, support organisations (sales, sustainability, customer service, etc.) as well as the Facility Management and corporate Real Estate groups (Turnbull 2011).

6.4.4 Define and Categorise Processes to Determine Infrastructure Requirements Including Capacity Planning

> *"You cannot solve a problem from the same consciousness that created it. You must learn to see the world anew".* Albert Einstein

Analysis of the current state (where an organisation is) coupled with scenario planning of the future view (goals and assumptions about where the organisation wants to be) is a critical step to the successful development and implementation of a forward-looking workplace strategy. The analysis around capacity planning is fairly detailed and can involve the use of a variety of tools/questioning techniques to help inform decision-making and strategy development. Let us examine what makes a plan successful, what the trade-offs are in different workplace environments, where sustainability fits and, lastly, how to deal with increasing degrees of uncertainty in today's world.

Fundamentally, we want to understand activity – what people do, how they do it and who they do it with. Analysis of work processes helps define activity:

- Routine vs. complex
  - Creative vs. procedural
  - Focused vs. relaxed
  - Noisy vs. quiet
  - Space-demanding vs. compact
- Individual vs. team; project
- In-house vs. outside
- Contact with customers: intensive, frequent, rare, none

Table 6.2 Overview of the "workspace" of office buildings (table compiled by authors)

Activity	Space and amenities
Concentrated: nonroutine, noninteractive and singular	Cube in open office, private enclosed office, touchdown space (for mobile workers), phone booth, library
Collaborative work	Conference/team room with videoconferencing, white-boards and/or tabels, group workstations for co-working
Socialization	
Rest/relaxation	Home like environments (den, kitchen tabel, backyard porch) Hotel-like (lobby) Park (nature trails, lake)
Eat	Restaurants, cafes, gardens (fresh vegetables)
Play	Basketball court, biking, skate boarding
Sustainability	Energy efficient systems, natural light
Work-life balance	Childcare, dry cleaner, wellness clinic, fitness center

Information gathered begins to define what kinds of spaces exist versus what is needed (Table 6.2):

Example

Workspaces are shaped by work processes. Every action needs to be considered and spatialised when possible. As an example: The higher the rate of interaction with customers and internal interaction, the more the need for special meeting areas arises. If there is a lot of telephone conversation, noise reduction measures have to be taken. The analysis also takes into account the intensity of internal communication. This data is used for the allocation of the departments and the teams within each department. Teams with a high demand for communication should be located nearby.

The needs of the individual employees must also be considered. Temperature control, CO_2 levels, adequate lighting and amount of natural light, biophilic design, personal health and well-being, ergonomics, engaging design, designated areas like private/concentrative space, nourishment, meetings (formal as well as informal), specialised work zones for teams and individual focused work, task-based work areas, and creative work areas are all useful ingredients for an appealing, effective workspace.

It has been shown that office layout has clear impacts on the perceived productivity of employees. Enclosed office spaces are beneficial due to their level of privacy and limited distractions. Open office plans on the other hand are more productive due to their easy access to informal meeting spaces. While enclosed shared offices can be perceived as overcrowded and prone to interruptions, they lower the threshold for communication and knowledge transfer is enhanced. This shows that it is important to match office environment to work processes.

Example

Some examples of this principle are presented here:

Routine work processes and team orientation are best supported by team environments. Examples are shown in the following figures. Individual complex work requires areas that support employee concentration and focus, like think tanks. Examples of areas for concentrated, focused working are shown in the following figures. And social areas for team building are shown in the following figures.

Collaborative work area. (► Rawpixel.com from Pexels)

Shared workspace area. (Marc Müller from Pexels)

Focused work area. (Pexels)

Community work area. (Nguyen Nguyen from Pexels)

Based on this analysis, the requirements for the infrastructure, including capacity planning, can be identified.

6.4.4.1 Current State

"The Big Bold Shift Study" (Hood and North 2011) confirms that all credible workplace initiatives have to start with data. Management ranks are not swayed by opinions, but even the most entrenched views are more likely to be won over with high-quality data. Typically, in a workplace strategy context, this involves three interconnected sources:

- Utilisation studies (to find out who is where and how often)
- Observation studies (to report independently on how space is being used)
- Surveys (to gauge employee reaction to space and understand workplace expectations that currently prevail and may need to be changed)

A summary of these three interconnected data collection sources (Hood and North 2011) is provided below:

6.4.4.2 Utilisation Studies

Utilisation studies are a good way of understanding the current situation of space usage. These studies can take several forms and provide different values in the workplace strategy process, as detailed below:

- **Log-in data**: Useful, but requires system development to convert this data into planning advice (i.e. locating port locations, possible privacy issues).
- **Badge entry data**: Only works when there is rigid discipline around use of a badge swipe for entry and exit of a building. This supplies little information on where the employee is actually residing or what he or she is doing. Possible privacy issues to be considered.
- **Active badges**: From a facility standpoint, this is the ideal solution because it allows an individual's every movement to be tracked; however, this would be considered very invasive by many.
- **"Desk checks"**: Usually accomplished by an individual walking around with a plan and a clipboard and noting the presence of individuals. Some consulting organisations have become quite sophisticated with this approach and use GPS technology to automate the data gathering and apply it directly to floor plans. Regrettably, these are limited by the amount of times that an individual can be expected to pass through a space taking readings.
- **Sensing technologies**: Sensors are located at work settings and record the presence of individuals. Readings can be taken every few minutes and build up rich volumes of use data over a period of time. These solutions tend to be more expensive but create the best data. Privacy concerns can be addressed by allocating results for clusters of work settings rather than individual settings so as to depersonalise the data.
- **Reservation systems**: Only record bookable space and are therefore limited in scope. Reservation systems can also be abused and do not always convey an accurate picture of actual occupancy in spite of utilisation checks.

- **Measurement** of car park use, water and food consumption: Though creative and noninvasive, they do not typically provide sufficient data to merit management credibility and are not recommended. They may be correlated with more detailed studies to provide snapshot readings of utilisation without the need for the more significant deployment of measurement resources.

When performing utilisation studies, other additional considerations include:
- **Timing**: The more data over the longest period of time will obviously lead to the best results, but at a very minimum 2 weeks of study with at least two readings, one midmorning and one mid-afternoon, are required.
- **Privacy of data**: Recording when and how people use the office space is an important issue and companies vary in terms of the monitoring and observation that is permitted. Some companies will not release badge entry data beyond the security function, believing it to be an invasion of privacy. Others articulate a greater freedom to monitor and record individual employee activity. In some cases, this is not even a company decision. In Europe, for example, new privacy laws forbid companies from installing monitoring devices to measure employee activity or share employee data. Such parameters will require that you make implementation decisions that work for the culture of your company: respect any legal or social mandates in effect and develop the approach that will meet your company's anticipated needs for data legitimacy.

As a word of caution, differences between employee accounts of presence and actual occupancy of space can vary greatly. Therefore, it is recommended that objective third-party utilisation studies should be undertaken. The reasons for variances range from an honest overestimation as to how much time one spends at one's desk to deliberate agendas to influence the result of a study by misrepresenting information toward what one might expect to be the way the data is used. There are a few possible reasons for this:
1. The survey subject just simply does not recount his business movements with any kind of authentic accuracy.
2. The person interviewed suspects an ulterior motive to the question and is anxious to establish the most lengthy presence in the office with a goal of maintaining support for a dedicated space allocation.

6.4.4.3 Observation Studies

The point of observation studies is to use objective third parties to observe what is going on in a way that self-reporting cannot achieve (Hood and Bowen 2011).
- Who are the observers?
- What are they observing? Typically, they are looking to see how things are being used and what things work and what do not. They can observe barriers to worker effectiveness and possibly offer the best answer to the question: How do I know if my workplace is more, or less, productive?

The following are examples of the kinds of questions for which one might want an observer to answer:

- Are virtual communication tools being used at this site?
  - Audio/teleconferencing?
  - Net meeting/virtual classroom?
  - Videoconferencing?
  - WebEx?
  - Streaming media?
  - Instant messenger?

- Are employees sufficiently well-trained in these tools?
  - Does the application open quickly?
  - Can they open the application?
  - Is everyone present familiar with its operation?
  - Does use of tools seem basic, medium or advanced?

- How is the workplace working?
  - What activities are not part of the intended use scenario?
  - Are there items being stored incorrectly?
  - Is the atmosphere positive or negative, and what seems to make it so?
  - What is the general level of engagement between employees?
  - Is there equipment that is not working properly?
  - What is the appearance of the space?

- How are office protocols for allocation and use of space being observed?
  - First come, first served?
  - Respect for others? Noise?
  - Reservation systems used properly?
  - Holding disruptive meetings in the open?
  - Pagers and mobile phones on vibrate mode?

The outcome of these studies, of which the above questions are only a small example, will enable you to talk in a very informed fashion about the overall level of existing workplace effectiveness.

6.4.4.4 Employee Workplace Surveys and Workshops

There is almost universal agreement that surveying employees is a good idea. It brings forward an idea of what is on peoples' minds and identifies areas of concern and need for focus. Employees often have excellent ideas that can bring about process efficiencies. As a matter of practice, however, the authors find that the timing of when employees are surveyed varies greatly. In some cases, the survey comes early in the concept stage of strategy development. In other cases, employee surveys have come late in the process and used as more of a change management tool. It is wise to heed Hood's caution, however, that "sometimes employee comments are informed by their expectations, which may or may not be correctly set".

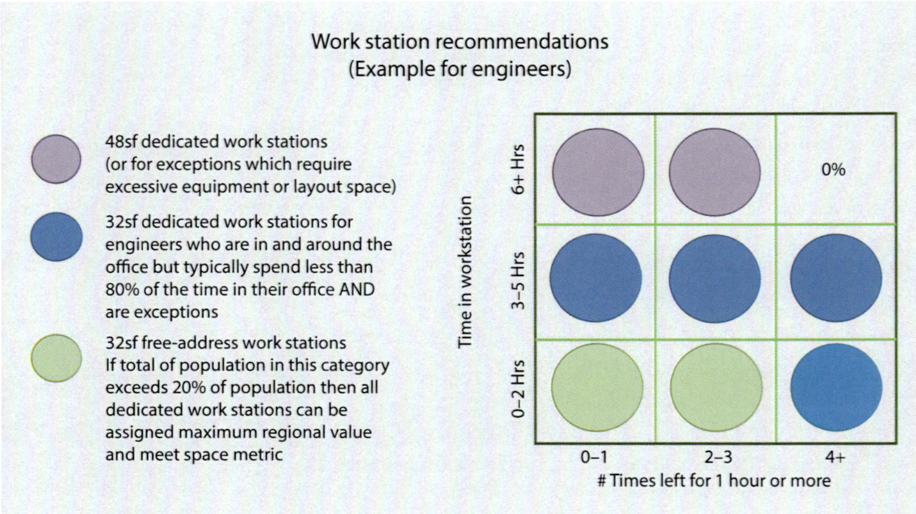

6

Fig. 6.9 Determining who gets what kind of space; (Work on the Move: Driving strategy and change in workplace (Hood and Bowen 2011))

As long as the expectations are managed and the underlying business logic of the transformation is well articulated and understood, an employee population can internalise changing conditions and learn to live with it. The bottom line is that satisfaction and needs surveys are very helpful but have to be considered carefully.

Hood (Hood and Bowen 2011) advocates that the best results flow when the three sources of data – utilisation, observation and employee survey data – are used together. "Each offers to the other the value of validation that either confirms, or casts doubt, on the need to respond. When used together, the three tools create valuable program design direction".

These tools help to determine who gets what kind of space, how much space and why (Fig. 6.9).

6.4.5 Status Report

> *"In highly successful change efforts, people find ways to help others see the problemsin ways that influence emotions, not just thought".* Dan Cohen

The results of the prior steps, especially the "as-is" and the "should-be" process analysis, and the derived requirements for infrastructure and services are stated in a status report, which is the basis for the further steps. The report also includes an estimation of the space needed for each of the office types and a rough space design (which team should be located where). This data provides the framework for evaluations as to whether a building is capable of supporting the requirements and is efficient. It is also the basis for the interior design and office furniture planning (Fig. 6.10).

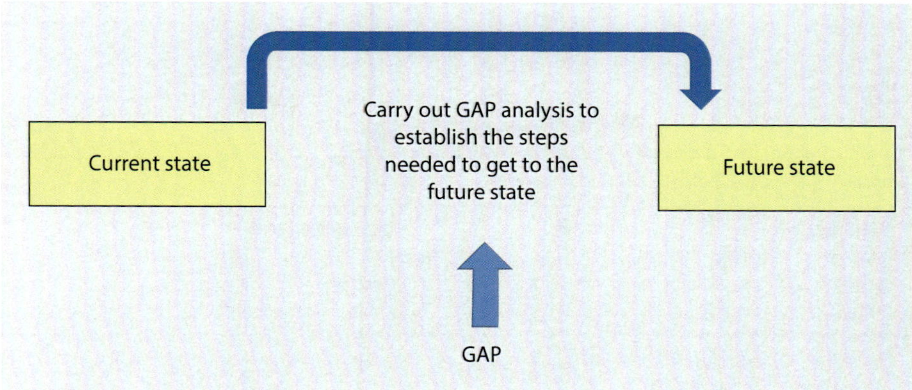

Fig. 6.10 Gap analysis. (Based on ► Leancor.com)

That said, the core of the matter is always about changing the behaviour of people, and behaviour change happens in highly successful situations mostly by speaking to people's feelings (Kotter and Cohen 2012).

Many templates and tools exist but a very simple way to track steps to a future state is a customised Word document or Excel spreadsheet to track progress on multifaceted projects. An organised structure for capturing data is critical (Fig. 6.11).

On a larger scale, companies also use tried and true evaluation and status report models such as the AEEA or the balanced scorecard model (Fig. 6.12).

In his book, *"Thinking for a Living: How to Get Better Performance and Results from Knowledge Workers"*, Thomas Davenport (2005) states that although most jobs require a base of knowledge, knowledge workers "have high degrees of expertise, education or experience, and the primary purpose of their jobs involves the creation, distribution or application of knowledge" (Vickers 2019). It is estimated that anywhere from 28% to 45% of the US workforce is now made up of knowledge workers (McKellar 2005).

Amazon describes the book as follows: "Based on extensive research involving over 100 companies and more than 600 knowledge workers, *"Davenport"* provides rich insights into how knowledge workers think, how they accomplish tasks, and what motivates them to excel. Davenport presents a parallel framework for matching specific types of workers with the management strategies that yield the greatest performance.

Knowledge workers create the innovations and strategies that keep their firms competitive and the economy healthy. Yet, companies continue to manage this new breed of employee with techniques designed for the Industrial Age. As this critical sector of the workforce continues to increase in size and importance, that is a mistake that could cost companies their future. Thomas Davenport argues that knowledge workers are vastly different from other types of workers in their motivations, attitudes, and need for autonomy – and, so, they require different management techniques to improve their performance and productivity. "*Thinking for a Living*" reveals how to maximize the brain power that fuels organisational success." (Amazon 2019).

6

WORKPLACE Evolutionaries
a Community of IFMA

WE ACTION AGENDA

Update: April 26, 2019

Action Agenda:

Location:	Monthly / Ongoing	**Wfnsd asodfn aljod**
Date:	April 26, 2019	5sdfas I
Time:	Ongoing	Asdfa asdf
		sdfsadf

Attendees: asdfasfd Leadership Team
Distribution: Asdf asdfjasdfa;

Prepared by: P Turnbull — Chicago, June 28, 2019

Decision Responsibility/History

Date	Action item	Owner(s)	Deadline	Status
4/1/19	Aas s asidf oasdofj			
	• Askdjflks asoei alsf;lsdjkf;l asaosj o;weitjaj;lahj	asd	April 1	Complete
	• sdfasdfsdahadfjdfjadjf			
4/22	• asdfasdfasdf	asdf	April 23	Complete
4/24		asdf/asdfasdf	April 25	Complete
3/21/19	Assdfja asdlfkj;la lgjsdgj			
3/23	• sdf sldfj;skdjf asdlkfj;lsdfj asdlfkj	asdf	April 17	Complete
4/17	• a asdf asodfnwi saohoan,mxcv ;oi	asdfasdgh	April 25	Complete
4/17	• sadfnasldkjf ;sldkfj;alskdjf elj	asdsdfas	April 24	Complete
4/25	• **sldkf asdkgas gpaosdgjal;**	**asdgasdg**	**May 1**	**In Process**
4/29	• **sd a asdfj;lsdkjf aaskjdfladlasdkjfl;asdkjf;alskdjf;lasdkjf**	**Aadfa/asdf**	**April 29**	**In Process**
	• **Askd ajg alskdaos**	**All**	**May 5**	**Open**
	• **Ssdfjak ai asdfosid ;sadjfk**	**Asdf/adf**	**May 10**	**Open**

Fig. 6.11 We action agenda. (Turnbull 2019)

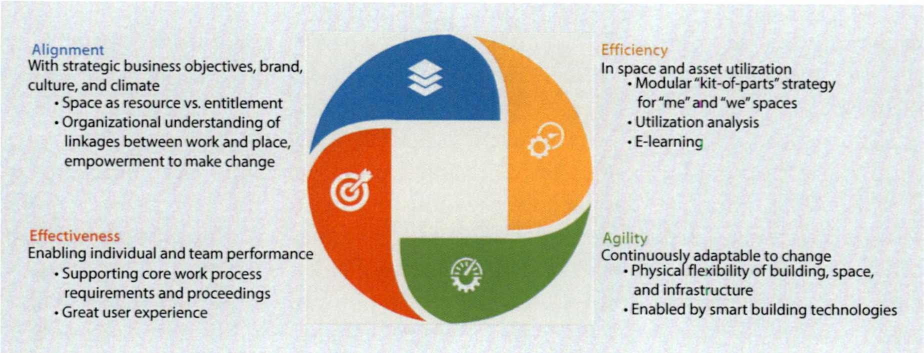

Fig. 6.12 Workplace goals: the AEEA model. (Based on CoreNet Global Learning 2017) (Redlein 2019d)

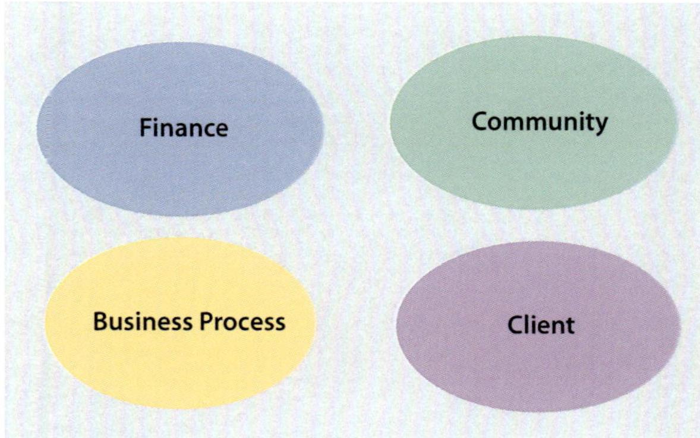

■ **Fig. 6.13** Workplace goals: the balanced scorecard. (Redlein 2019e)

In some ways, digitalisation can make us less productive (Mandel et al. 2005). Evidence suggests that knowledge workers have become burdened with lots of low-value, internal/external communications and they need help managing social networks more efficiently (Vickers 2019). The desire to boost employee productivity led to the creation of tools such as the "dashboard" which (basically) is a "productivity enhancement" tool. One such dashboard is a matrix-style process model known as the balanced scorecard which helps track knowledge worker performance against top line strategy/ bottom line results which, in turn, can be measured and communicated (■ Fig. 6.13). The balanced scorecard is but one of these models to help identify performance objectives or outcomes and their observable drivers. Norton and Kaplan (1992) apply the balanced scorecard to workplace goals:

- Financial perspective: measured by return on investment or economic value added
- Customer perspective: measured by customer's satisfaction and retention, by market penetration and account share
- Internal processes perspective: measured by quality improvements, decreased response time, decreased cost or rate of new product introduction

These models also provide a process for measuring continuous improvement. The process is continuous and should be a series of strategy reviews throughout the year. By spreading strategy reviews throughout the year, workplace strategy can focus on and resolve one issue at a time, as well as adapt to changing conditions (Mankins and Steele 2006).

In any case, understanding what is important to measure is of critical importance. Only "measure what matters" to your specific business and be proactive in your thinking about how you will be able to sustain measurement requirements (■ Fig. 6.14).

6.4.6 Real Estate Evaluation and Initial Space Design

At this stage, many corporations choose to enlist the assistance of an architect, who can evaluate the portfolio along a number of critical dimensions (■ Fig. 6.15).

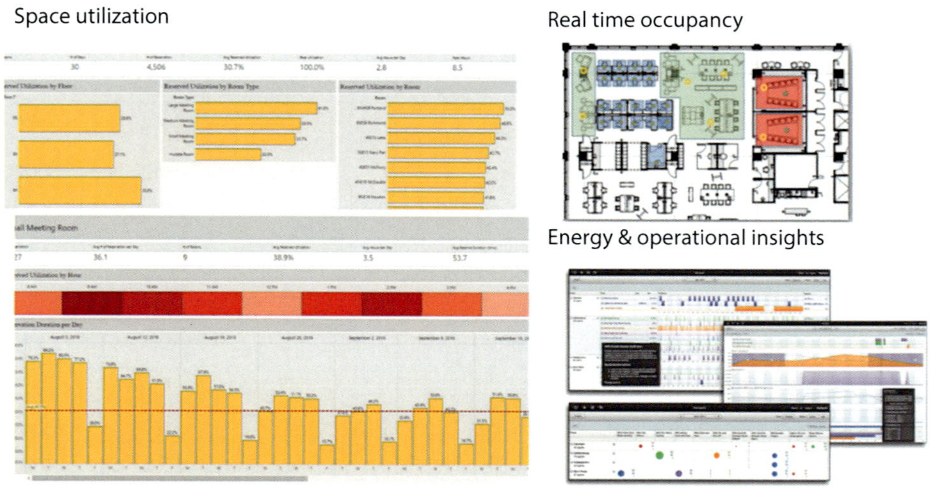

Fig. 6.14 FM/RE measurement dashboard. (Phillips S. 2019)

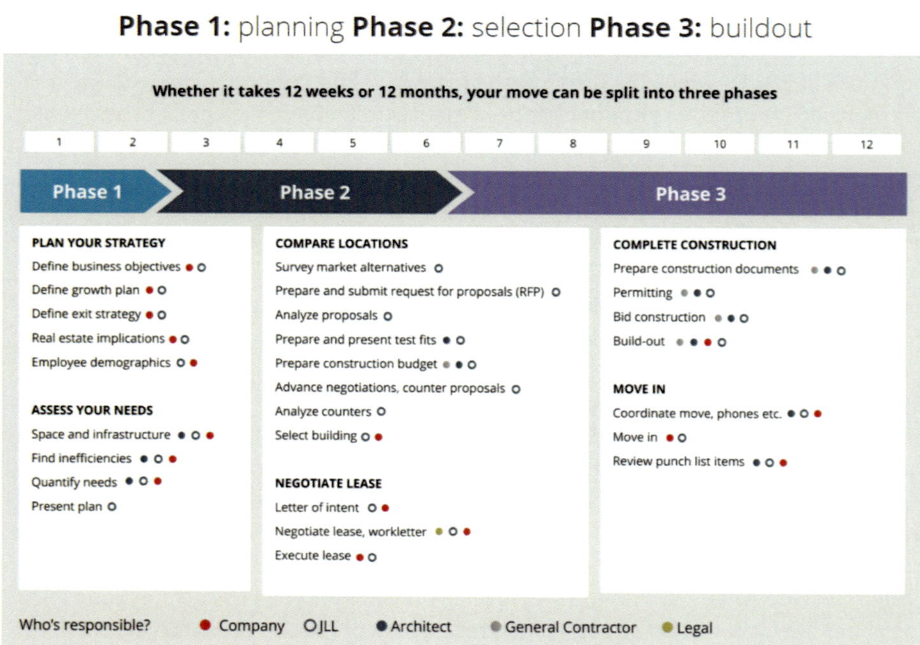

Fig. 6.15 JLL guide of finding office space relocating company (2019)

As a rule, definition and alignment of workplace strategy goals and objectives should take place before the evaluation of Real Estate options, as the decision about size and type of building, new construction or renovation could potentially change based on the result of the defined goals. The early formulation of a workplace strategy team, prior to hiring a Real Estate broker, architect or designer, can also save a significant amount of time and money, since the company only has to travel down the path one time once it has considered the alternatives early in the process.

Since Real Estate is typically the second-largest expenditure in a company's budget (with the exception of companies with high technology requirements, where it is the third largest), any decision made with respect to a Real Estate requirement will greatly impact the corporate operations. This significant financial impact coupled with the immobility of a facility and the large costs associated with a reconfiguration or relocation creates a necessity to plan early in order to secure the best options with the most leverage. Moreover, a Real Estate decision can affect every facet of your business: productivity, revenue, well-being, sustainability and future success.

At this stage, there is a translation of the programming data into scenario space plan(s). This is a fundamental element of the Real Estate and design planning process. Programming defines what will go into the space, general size or occupancy and scenario. Space planning defines how those environments will fit into various Real Estate options. This all happens in the "predesign" phase (◘ Fig. 6.16).

Angie Lee (Lee 2005), vice president, Global Sector Leader–Office Workplace with Stantec offers an elegant, high-level outline of the workplace predesign activities:

1. Project Initiation	* Workplace strategy assessment tool * Portfolio opportunity assessment * Benchmarking * Functional group assessments (HR, IT) * Communications and change management strategy * Sponsors Workshop * Leadership interviews
2. Assessment and Business case	** Space utilization study* ** Observation study* ** Work style survey and segmentation* ** Scenario options, Financial modelling and business case presentation*
3. Solution design	* Employee/manager focus group * Solution design workshop and blitz teams (real estate, IT, HR) * Workplace design guidelines
4. Implement and Support change	* Implementation support plan * Change management campaign * Performance management
5. Continuous improvement	* Workplace program management * Workplace playbook (operations guide) * Impact assessment (on space planning and real estate processes)

◘ **Fig. 6.16** Real Estate analysis within workplace strategy development process. (Developed by Patricia Roberts and team, Jones Lang LaSalle). Duerk D. (1993). Architectural Programming: Information Management for Design. (Based on Wiley)

6.4.7 Predesign

6.4.7.1 Project Kick-Off/Visioning Session

- Meet with executive management team responsible for setting and communicating the company's vision and mission.
- Determine and discuss current and future business and operational issues that may impact the work process such as churn, flexibility, organisational structure, etc.
- Determine and discuss cultural issues such as workplace behaviour: the process to receive clients, customers or vendors, amenities for employees, security issues, etc.
- Discuss the use of technology and its impact on the workplace.
- Discuss the relationship between image/brand and the workplace and how this correlates with the vision and mission of the company.

6.4.7.2 Workplace Standard Evaluation and/or Development

- Review current standards.
- Confirm workstation and private office requirements.
- Review internal work processes and technology requirements.
- Provide opinions on workplace standards to support work processes as requested.
- Review existing furniture inventory and the potential reuse in the renovated facility.
- Identify supplemental or new furniture products to be incorporated into or replace current furniture where applicable.

6.4.7.3 Programming

Lee explains that programming is a term architects like to use for what goes into a building. The client takes the data they have gathered from the workplace strategy exercise and writes a program or gets help from an architect who performs predesign architectural services. The program is a list of all the spaces to go into the building and their general size and occupancy. The requirements can be taken out of the status report.

6.4.7.4 Facility Assessment

- Review current office facilities for ADA compliance (Americans with Disabilities Act).
- Provide building code analysis in existing office facilities.
- Review existing mechanical, electrical, plumbing and fire protection systems.
- Conduct physical field surveys.
- Develop CAD plans based on field surveys for planning purposes.

6.4.7.5 Space Plan(s)

Likewise, space planning organises the space, furniture and functions to work together and most effectively accommodate the needs of the employees and visitors. It starts with an in-depth analysis of how the space is to be used. The designer then draws up a plan that defines the zones of the space and the activities that will take place in these individual zones. The space plan also defines the circulation patterns that show how people will move through the space. In the initial planning, stages are "dumb" (i.e. the symbols are generic and do not contain any data). Since ubiquitous design symbols are used, these plans are sometimes called "block" plans, which are used for the "test fits" and help visualise what can fit into the space and various layout scenarios. Eventually, the selected space and plan are developed into a full space plan with specific symbols and details of all the furniture, equipment and hardware included.

What is both important and helpful is to see the layout for a space with several test fits. Building owners often already have a mock-up of the space that they can quickly modify to give you a sense of what is possible. Outside vendors often provide a more detailed, high-level test fit in the hope of securing your business.

Based on the approved program and workplace standard report and using electronic documents generated via the facility assessment process, the design firm then prepares for the client's approval:

- Space plan(s) indicating system furniture outline, locations of full height partitions and doors, departmental adjacencies and circulation patterns
- Final plan to be incorporated into a "master space plan"

6.4.7.6 Project Scope Development

- Select general contractor via negotiated bid process.
- Develop overall budget and timeline based on master space plan.
- Identify phasing scenarios and mark swing space.
- Confirm annual budget against cash flow diagram.

6.4.8 Coordination and Guidance of Architects and Planners

> *"Design and Change are two sides of the same coin. Goals must align in order to achieve success. Workplace Strategy is a change process strategy that shapes behaviors and so is good design".*
> Introduction to Workplace Strategy, CoreNet (2019)

In the next step, architects, planners and specialists need to be hired to convert the status report into a detailed space and furniture plan that, on one hand, fulfils the defined requirements of the status report and, on the other hand, fulfils all legal requirements like code and industrial safety regulations.

Design coordination is a broad term describing the integration of designs prepared by different members of the project team to create a single, unified set of information that can be constructed without clashes between components. Effective design coordination can help to reduce costs, delays and disruption that can be caused by problems on site and the need for remedial or abortive works and redesign (Fig. 6.17).

6

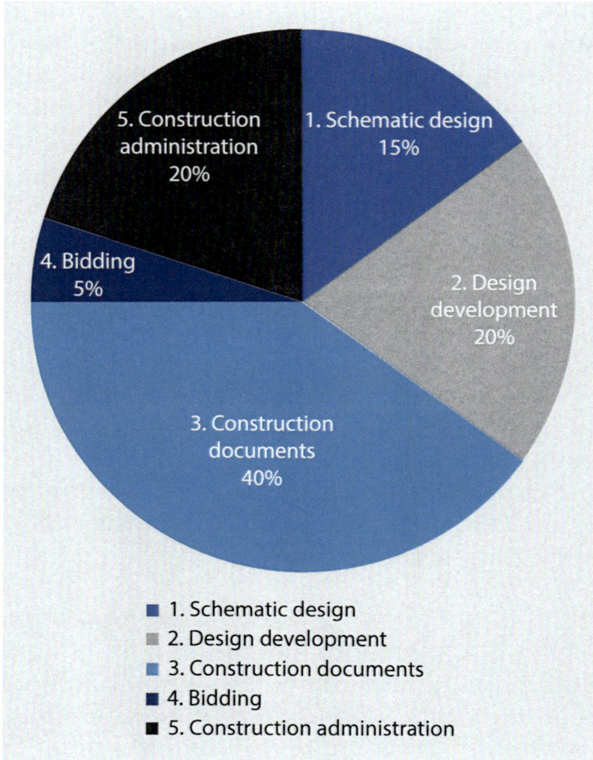

Fig. 6.17 Design phases incl. fee/cost splitting. (Rogers 2018)

1. *Schematic design*	**15% of architectural fees**
2. *Design development*	**20% of architectural fees**
3. *Construction documents*	**40% of architectural fees**
4. *Bidding*	**5% of architectural fees**
5. *Construction administration*	**20% of architectural fees**

Definition

In its broadest sense, design coordination can simply mean ensuring that designers understand what they are responsible for and in particular who is responsible for the interfaces and junctions between different design packages. In a more specific sense, design coordination can refer to the actual process of ensuring that design solutions can be integrated, in particular, mechanical, electrical and plumbing (MEP) designs, which as they permeate through the entire building are frequently the source of coordination problems (▶ https://www.designingbuildings.co.uk/wiki/Design_coordination).

Below, Lee (2005) offers a very well-organised view of what happens in the design and implementation process.

6.4.8.1 Schematic Design (SD)

Schematic design is the first phase of actually designing the project. Think of it as the preliminary drawing phase. It will typically account for about 15% of the architect's work and fees on the entire project. During this phase, the architect and the client discuss the project and any requirements provided by the client. The architect does precedent research and any analysis of the property including zoning and building code issues that may affect the specific development. Individual space planning is done at this time where the client provides the architect with a list of what spaces are going into the building. Programming is a part of schematic design. The architect establishes the size, location and relationships between all the spaces.

Upon approval of the space plan, the architect/designer proceeds with design conceptualisation. This will be generated based on the visioning session and the direction articulated during the programming phase:

- Confirm base plans within CAD tools.
- Confirm and finalise space plan.
- Verify existing conditions and related drawing accuracy and make any adjustments necessary.
- Verify applicable building codes and ADA requirements.
- Develop preliminary colours and material palettes for general feedback and selection
- Establish preliminary budget and schedule.
- Evaluate existing furniture (if applicable) and/or provide suggestions, along with furniture dealer, for new.

6.4.8.2 Design Development (DD)

Design development accounts for approximately 20% of the architect's work and fees. In design development, the architect and client work together to select materials including interior finishes and products such as windows, doors, fixtures, appliances and materials. The architect revises the initial drawings based on the client's comments from the schematic design phase, capturing more specifics and details with these freshly revised sketches. Preliminary engineering will start on the structure as well as plumbing, electrical, HVA systems, energy analysis and any other project-specific systems. At the end of design development, a good deal of product selection and system design should be progressing.

Upon approval of the design concept and general direction, we will further the development of design to include three-dimensional volumetric studies:

- Finalise colours and material palette and distribution.
- Select furniture systems, case goods and seating.
- Provide outline furniture specifications and location plan(s).
- Review millwork design details.

- Develop and finalise lighting design including ceiling materials and placement of general, task and ambient lighting fixtures.
- Coordinate specification and pricing process with furniture dealer.
- Refine budget and schedule.
- Review design drawings with engineering partner to be identified.

6.4.8.3 Construction Documentation (CD)

6 The construction document phase is the largest of all the phases for the architect and will be about 40% of the architect's work and fees, of course that may vary a little from project to project. In the construction document phase the architect and engineers will finalise all the technical drawing and engineering including detailing. HVA systems, plumbing, electrical, gas, energy calculations and all products and materials are selected and/or scheduled. The architect produces multiple drawing sets, including a filing set for approval from the building department and a separate set of construction drawings for the general contractor.

Upon client approval of the design documents, construction documents will be prepared for the purpose of bidding, permit acquisition and construction:

- Team coordination.
- Confirm telecom/data system requirements.
- Review budget and schedule with all team members.
- Document preparation:
  - Demolition plan(s)
  - Construction plan(s)
  - Voice/data/electrical outlet location plan(s)
  - Reflected ceiling plan(s)
  - Finish plan(s) and schedule(s)
  - Details, sections and elevations
- Prepare required specifications for interior architectural construction
- Coordinate engineering and interior architectural documents.
- Conduct internal quality assurance process.
- Furniture:
  - Review furniture plans and specifications as prepared by the furniture dealer.
  - Coordinate furniture procurement process with the furniture dealer.
  - Upon completion of the furniture strategy, coordinate with the furniture dealer to determine a phasing strategy for new and reconfigured furniture based upon the construction phasing scenario.

6.4.8.4 Bidding and Negotiations (BD)

Bidding is where the owner prepares to select the contractor for the job and sign contracts to proceed with construction. This phase will typically take up 5% of the architect's time and fees. Multiple contractors submit bids on the job or the client can directly hire a contractor without getting competitive bids. The architect's role here will be to assist the client, answer contractors' questions and provide any additional documentation if requested by or needed by the contractor.

Having an architect on your side during the bidding phase of construction is of great advantage to you: aiding in the development of a list of qualified contractors for your bid list as well as submitting bid packages to bidders, reviewing submitted bids, providing analysis and helping to compare the cost figures that you receive from your bidders. This phase will ensure the contractors you are considering for your construction project are reading the blueprints correctly and are providing an accurate bid (apples to apples) for your project.

Designer/architects will issue drawings and specifications for final pricing of both construction and furniture and will participate in the bid process:

- Issue construction drawings for subcontractor bidding.
- Issue or coordinate final furniture specifications for dealer's use.
- Assist in review and analysis of proposals.
- Provide stamped drawings for permit application.

6.4.8.5 Construction Administration (CA)

The construction administration phase of this process is the last phase and accounts for about 20% of the architect's time and fees on a project. Even though this phase is the longest scheduled phase, it is not the majority of the architect's work. On most projects architects do *not* supervise construction. They periodically visit the job site to see progress and ensure the contractor is following the plans per the architectural design intent. If requested, however, architects can review contractor's monthly invoices to confirm work completion, answer questions and provide additional information relative to issues that arise.

After bids have been reviewed and contracts awarded, they will provide periodic observation of the progress of the project to review construction with regard to budget, schedule and design intent:

- Field observation of construction progress.
- Review shop drawings and submittals.
- Attend construction team meetings on a weekly basis (assume a ---- week construction duration with one (1) meeting per week).
- Evaluate applications for payment, process change proposals and issue certificates for payment.

6.4.8.6 Move-In and Follow-Up

In this phase either the tenant or the architect/designer has to assure the following:

- Inspect completed work with the final punch list prepared by the general contractor to ensure quality and completeness.
- Secure operating manuals and as-built drawings from the general contractor.
- Distribute post occupancy questionnaires 3 months after move-in and summarise responses as they relate to facility operations and performance of the new facility.

In the DACH region the design phases are similarly defined under the HOAI (Honorarordnung für Architekten und Ingenieure (2013); Germany) regulation and the HIA (Honorar Information Architektur, Austria (Arch+Ing 2010)), which is a nonbinding guidance.

To coordinate and guide architects and designers, the use of contracts and service-level agreements as well as design-specific tools such as BIM is encouraged.

The emerging use of building information modelling (BIM) and its use in Facility Management is a catalyst for a continuous two-way communication between the design consultants and the workplace strategic planning team. BIM involves creating and managing digital information for the design, construction and operation of built assets. BIM can help ensure that collaborative practices are adopted and standard methods and procedures used and that designers are contractually obligated to provide specific information at specific stages of a project.

The use of BIM as a process to create an environment to help coordinate and guide the internal planning and/or design consultants is encouraged.

6.4.9 Change Management Processes and Marketing Activities

> *"It is not the strongest of the species that survives, nor the most intelligent ... It is the one that is the most adaptable to change".* Charles Darwin

As in most cases, changes in the organisation go together with changes in the workplace and vice versa. It is important to manage the change process. Only an optimal change management program can ensure that the whole project is successful.

A strategic planning process must account for the real and perceived challenges to the changes proposed to the people of an organisation. People prefer the familiar to the comfortable and prefer the comfortable to the better. Fear of change usually means fear of loss of control. Staff who are told their jobs are changing, or the business process they are part of is being redesigned, are usually afraid they will not have the knowledge or skill to succeed in the new conditions. They fear not being able to perform well, or they resent the extra effort they assume it will take to learn the new procedures.

Let us be very clear: Very few people universally resist change. What they do resist – and resent – is being changed, with no control over where, when or how that change is imposed on them (Ware 2011).

Ware goes on to say that people do not universally demand stability; what most of us want is predictability, or at least a reasonable level of personal control over whatever changes we are experiencing. And when organisational staff believe that they are contributing to positive change (meaning they see benefits in it for themselves), they will not only get on board; they will usually be chafing at the bit to help make things better.

Leading organisational change is at the heart of what workplace professionals do, whether they realise it or not. There are three core principles for creating constructive organisational change:

1. Developing a clear and compelling vision of the future
2. Building a case for change that appeals to both logic and emotion
3. Shaping a widely participative process for moving forward (Ware 2011) (◘ Fig. 6.18)

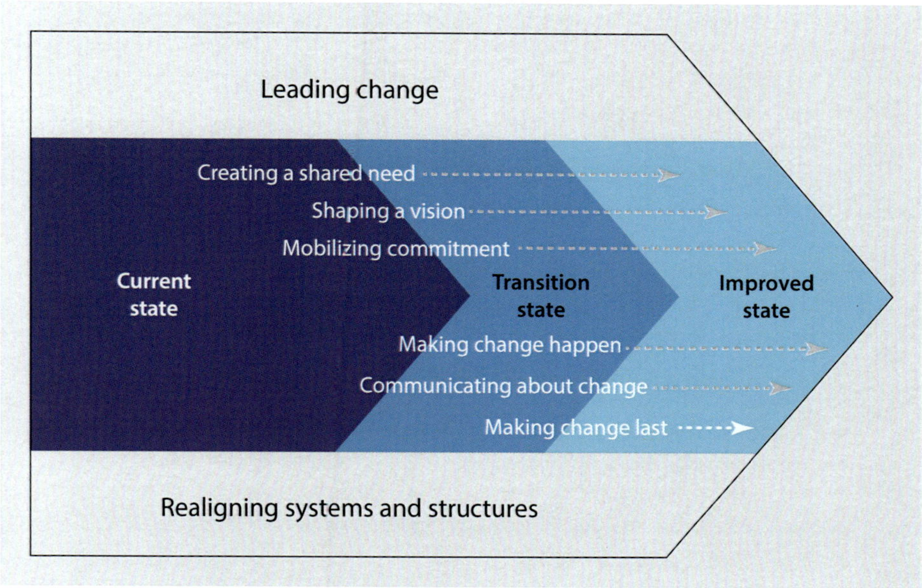

Fig. 6.18 A framework for change. (Robertson 2000)

Jim Ware (2011) beautifully summarises Kotter's eight steps (the sequence is critically important) as follows:

$$\mathbf{C} = \mathbf{D} \times \mathbf{V} \times \mathbf{P}$$

$$\text{Change} = \text{dissatisfaction} \times \text{vision} \times \text{process}$$

1. Create a sense of urgency.
   The more people who understand why the change is needed and share a desire to make it happen, the more likely the change program will succeed. Contributing catalysts that drive change include economic conditions, changes in client requirements, mergers or acquisitions, technology innovations or simply the decision to remain at the forefront of your field.
2. Pull together the guiding team. Recruit the small, core group of leaders, stakeholders and influencers who you need to help you design and implement the change.
3. Develop the change vision and strategy.
   Work with the core team to build the case for change; incorporate their perspectives, which will create the clear sense of your goals and help persuade others. Leaders must undertake a thorough analysis of the risks and opportunities associated with the proposed change. When it is determined that benefits for change outweigh risks, a strategy is developed for implementation. Without proper planning, organisational change initiatives will undoubtedly fail. In this step of the model, the foundation for execution is established. Critical elements of the plan must include:

- Planning for the impact of the change on individuals who will be most affected
- Planning for the impact of the change on the systems within the organisation that will be most affected
- A step-by-step plan for integrating the change into the organisation
- A review plan to measure the success of the proposed change

4. Communicate for understanding and buy-in.

   Develop an explicit communication strategy and do not simply rely on a barrage of press releases and speeches. Plan events that give others a chance not only to hear about the whys and wherefores of the change, but to ask questions and make suggestions. Regardless of how the change occurs, a leader's most pivotal role in this step is to maintain open lines of communication among team members.
   - Define individual responsibilities.
   - Announce and launch the change.
   - Adhere to timetables.
   - Promote the anticipated benefits of the change.
   - Stay focused and positive.
5. Empower others to act.

   The more you can spread the "gospel" and give others the means to do things in furtherance of the change, the more the change will gain momentum.
6. Produce short-term wins.

   As the old saying goes, "nothing succeeds like success". Short-term wins prove the new concept, create winners and lead to even wider acceptance of the new future.
7. Do not let up.

   Review the direction, adapt and adjust. If things are going well and you have a number of short-term wins to point to, it becomes all too easy to slack off, to assume that it will be all downhill from here on. Nothing could be further from the truth; be persistent, and stay focused on the end state, because there is a major tendency for individuals and organisations to slip back into their old habits when the pressure for change drops off.

8. Make it stick by creating a new culture.

   If you have gotten this far, the new processes, new workplaces and new procedures will have become the "new normal". While old habits die hard, new ones can in fact take their place. Find ways to "legitimise" new habits by recognising individuals who exemplify the new culture and by incorporating new performance measures in compensation.

   Methods to support the change include:
   - Open project meetings with clear goals and decisions.
   - Integration of employees and management.
   - Information provisions for employees.
   - Piloting of the new concepts with feedback possibilities.
   - Analysis of employee satisfaction.

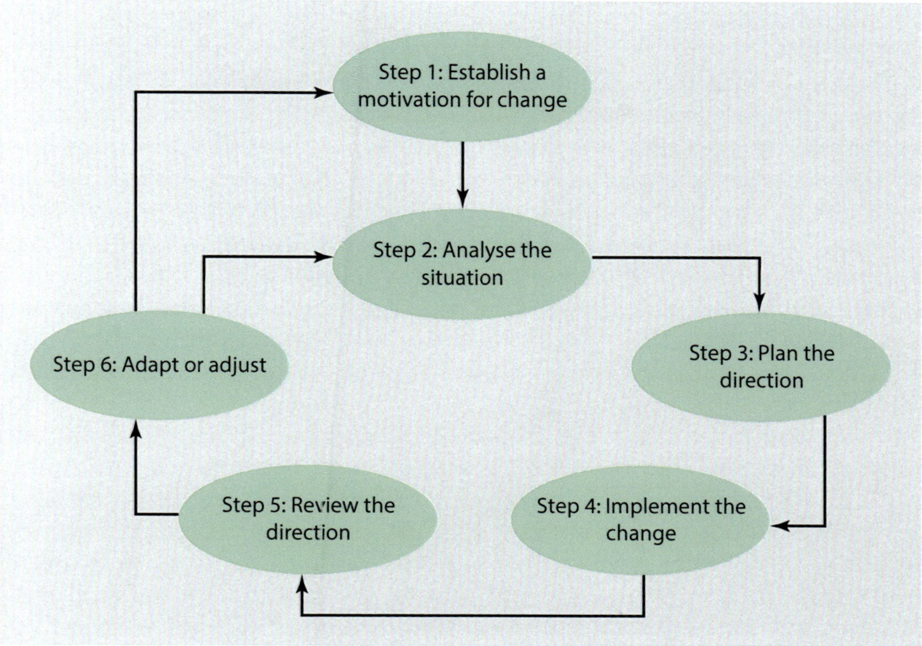

Fig. 6.19 Change management step by step. (Based on 2017 Dale Carnegie & Associates, Inc. All rights reserved. change_management_101217_ebook)

At the risk of sounding redundant, change is enabled by tools like those described here for one simple reason. Formal diagnostic tools transform conversations about change from purely emotional arguments about what the "facts" are into objective, informed considerations of possible future states. These kinds of tools bring data into the equation, but just as importantly they pull many more people (and their perspectives) into the conversation. Only when this is done can the realisation of the optimisation of space and infrastructure planning be done successfully (Fig. 6.19).

A successful change of the workplace is inevitably linked to good workplace management. In order to enhance brand image, profitability and most importantly productivity, having a strategy in place and a dedicated team to implement it is unavoidable.

A workplace is more than just a space where work is done. It can be evocative of an organisation's brand, its values and its image. It can be coordinated with the business strategy and help to drive coveted business results. It can evolve with the business, shrink and grow as needed. A workplace can be a comfortable environment for the people working there and help them to work at the best of their abilities.

In order to be all these things, key players have to be brought to the table to define what the organisation is, what it wants to be and how all this can be expressed in the workplace.

6.5 Conclusion

Digitalisation and an increase in diversity with regards to gender, age, levels of ability and cultures have altered the way we work and our workplaces are changing accordingly. Flexibility concerning when, where and how work is done will also increase. Workplace management is the tool with which to steer this adaption process. It allows companies to align their workplaces with their business strategy, their culture, values and brand. Workplace management helps to optimise people's performance by providing them with spaces and surrounding services that are designed with their needs in mind. This is a key factor in raising engagement, productivity and motivation in the workplace. Workplace management also allows companies to best utilise their assets to drive desired business results. And it helps to make sure that the strategy and infrastructure can evolve with the business.

This chapter explains how to develop and implement a workplace strategy that will enable companies to make their workplaces fit for the future. It helps to identify the people that should be involved in workplace management. A step-by-step implementation guide is provided to illustrate how a workplace management process positively impacts work environments. It defines the "final" product, the work environment including the services necessary to add value to the core business and enables it. Therefore, it comprises the chapters beforehand, which described single views and put them now together in the broad picture.

? Review Questions

1. What is workplace strategy (WPS)?
2. What is the triple bottom line?
3. What are the main drivers for human motivation according to Maslow?
4. Which are the basic human needs according to Maslow?
5. How can these needs be translated and applied to the workplace?
6. What are the main steps to define and implement a workplace strategy?
7. Who are the key players concerning workplace change management and how can they be identified?
8. What are work processes? How do they shape the workspace?
9. What is space programming?
10. What are the main design phases?
11. How does the process continue once the office has been adapted and workers have moved in?
12. What are the eight steps to foster change in the workplace?

References

Agarwal, R., & Karerat, S. (2019). Work place wellness. *Facility Management Journal, 29*, 52–55.

Amazon. (2019). Thinking for a Living: How to Get Better Performances And Results from Knowledge Workers: How to Get Better Performance and Results from Knowledge Workers. https://www.amazon.de/Thinking-Living-Performances-Knowledge-Performance/dp/1591394236.

Berinato, S. (2010). Success gets into your head – and changes it. *Harvard Business Review, 88*(1–2), 28.

Bortoluzzi, B., Carey, D., McArthur, J., & Menassa, C. (2018). Measurements of workplace productivity in the office context: A systematic review and current industry insights. *Journal of Corporate Real Estate, 20*(4), 281–301.

Buck Consultants a Xerox company. (2012). Working Well: A Global Survey of Health Promotion and Workplace Wellness Strategies. San Francisco, CA: Buck Consultants, LLC.

Conforti, M. (1972). Practical applications of Maslow's theory of human motivation in industry. *Occupational Health Nursing, 20*(12), 10–13.

Cooper, C. (2013). Peter Drucker and the wellbeing agenda. *Strategic Direction, 29*(<b>ISSN: </b>02580543), 22.

CoreNet (2019). Introduction to Workplace Strategy. Virtual Online Course. Atlanta, GA: CoreNet Global.

Davenport, T. (2005). *Thinking for a living: How to get better performance and results from knowledge workers*. Boston: Harvard Business Press.

Drucker, P. (1942). The Future of the Industrial Man. New York, NY: Routledge.

Duerk, D. (1993). Architectural Programming: Information Management for Design. 8. John Wiley & Sons.

Edmondson, A. (1999). Psychological safety and learning behavior in work teams. *Administrative Science Quarterly, 44*(2), 350–383.

Fraunhofer, I. A. O. (2013). *Arbeit der Zukunft. Wie wir sie verändern, wie sie uns verändert*. Stuttgart: IAO.

Grosser, T., Lopez-Kidwell, V., & Labianca, G. (2010). A social network analysis of positive and negative gossip in organizational life. *Group & Organization Management, 35*(2), 177–212.

Guenzi, P. (2013). How Ritual Delivers Performance. Von Harvard Business Review: https://hbr.org/2013/02/how-ritual-delivers-performanc.

Heery, G. (2009). Strategic Real Estate & Facilities Planning. Los Angelas, CA: Brookwood Group.

Herzberg, F. (1966). Work and the nature of man. Cleveland. *World, 290*, 339–341.

Hood, C. & North, K. (2011). Big Bold Shift Study. CoreNet Workplace Community Webinar, Atlanta GA. https://www.scribd.com/document/105388744/2012-the-Big-Bold-Shift-Paper-Final.

Arch+Ing. (2010). Honorar Information Architektur. Vienna, Austria: Bundeskammer für Architekten und Ingenieurkonsulenten.

Honorarordnung für Architekten und Ingenieure. (2013). Berlin, Germany: Bundesministeriums der Justiz und für Verbraucherschutz sowie des Bundesamts für Justiz.

Hood, C., & Bowen, M. (2011). Implementing a mobile workplace strategy. In C. Hood & M. Bowen (Eds.), *Work on the move: Driving strategy and changes in the workplace*. Houston: IFMA Foundation.

IFMA. (2009). Temperature Wars. Savings vs. Comfort. Houston, TX: IFMA Foundation.

ISS. (2011). Vision 2020. Copenhagen Institute for Futures Studies, Copenhagen, Denmark.

Kaplan, R., & Norton, D. (1992). The Balanced Scorecard—Measures That Drive Performance. Harvard Business Review, 79.

Kotter, J., & Cohen, D. (2012). *The heart of change*. Boston: Harvard Business Review Press.

Lawler, E., & Suttle, J. (1972). A causal correlational test of the need hierarchy concept. *Organizational Behavior & Human Performance, 7*(2), 265–287.

Lee, A. (2005). Proposal Scope Template. AREA Design LTd, https://www.linkedin.com/in/angie-lee-faia-iida-leed-02282210/

Leusden, P., & Freymark, G. (1951). Darstellung der Raumbehaglichkeit für den einfachen praktischen Gebrauch. *Der Gesundheitsingenieur, 72*(16), 271–273.

Lister, K. (2014). What's good for people? In *Moving from wellness to well-being*. New York: Knoll.

Lister, K. (2018). The Dollars and Sense of Well-Being. Workdesign Magazine. Arlington, VA: Workspace Design Magazine.

Lister, K. (2019). Show me the money – The bottom line on workplace change. *Facility Management Journal, 29*, 38–42.

Mandel, M., Hamm, S., Matlack, C., Farrell, C., & Palmer, A. (2005). The Real Reason You're Working So Hard... and what you can do about it. BusinesWeek.

Mankins, M., & Steele, R. (2006). Stop making plans; start making decisions. *Harvard Business Review, 84*(1), 76–84, 133.

Mark, G., Gudith, D., & Klocke, U. (2008). The Cost of Interrupted Work: More Speed and Stress. Human Factors in Computing Systems. Florence, Italy: *Proceedings of the SIGCHI Conference on Human Factors in Computing Systems*.

Marsh, M. (2017). *Melissa Marsh: The key ingredients of an ideal workplace" in ISS Service Futures*. Von ISS: https://www.servicefutures.com/melissa-marsh-the-key-ingredients-of-an-ideal-workplace. abgerufen.

Maslow, A. (1943). A theory of human motivation. *Psychological Review, 50*(4), 370–396.

Mawson, A. (2017). 6 Factors to Leverage Knowledge Worker Productivity. FMJ IFMA, S. 44–46.

McKellar, H. (2005). The knowledge (worker) economy. *KM World, 14*(9), 2.

Moss Kanter, R. (2010). Column: Powerlessness Corrupts. Harvard Business Review, S. 36.

Nink, M., & Robinson, J. (2016). The Damage Inflicted by Poor Managers. Von Gallup Business Journal: https://news.gallup.com/businessjournal/200108/damage-inflicted-poor-managers.aspx?g_source=EMPLOYEE_ENGAGEMENT&g_medium=topic&g_campaign=tiles.

Oseland, N. (2009). The impact of psychological needs on office design. *Journal of Corporate Real Estate, 11*(4), 244–254.

Redlein, A., Humhal, C., Zobl, M., Seibert-Giller, V., & Marković, O. (2014). *Endbericht zur Studie: Optimierte Unterrichtsräume in Kärntner Pflichtschulen.*

Redlein, A. (2019a). Adapted from Suzanne Verity, Instructor-led training (ILT) for CoreNet Global 2017, https://cantilever-instruction.com/portfolio-items/ilt-for-real-estate-professionals/.

6

Redlein, A. (2019b). Based on data from Pew Research Center, April 2018, https://www.pewresearch.org/fact-tank/2018/04/11/millennials-largest-generation-us-labor-force/.

Redlein, A. (2019c). Adapted from Turnbull 2009.

Redlein, A. (2019d). Adapted from CoreNet Global Learning 2017.

Redlein, A. (2019e). Adapted from Kaplan, R., & Norton, D. (1992). The Balanced Scorecard—Measures That Drive Performance. Harvard Business Review, 79.

Robertson, K. (2000). A framework for change. then 1999, 2003, 2004: CoreNet Global. Adapted from Change Association Process (CAP) materials developed by GE Management Development Institute, Colorville, New York.

Rogers, E. (2018). Phases of Architectural Design. Von Wagstaff & Rogers Architects: http://www.wagstaffrogersarch.com/blog/phases-architectural-design.

Sanchez, J., Vega Sanchez, S., Ikaga, T., Ichihara, M., & Harimoto, K. (2017). The impact of greenery and daylight on productivity and well-being at the workplace: an experimental case study. Journal für Facility Management(15), 20–32.

Turnbull, P. (2011). Workplace Strategy: What it is and why it is important. In P. Turnbull (Ed.), *Work on the move: Driving strategy and changes in the workplace*. Houston: IFMA Foundation.

Turnbull, P., Redlein, A., & Schloss, L. (2016). Corporate social responsibility. In P. Turnbull, A. Redlein, S. Lisanne, D. Coles Levine, & N. Sanquist (Eds.), *Work on the Move 2: How social, leadership and technology innovations are transforming the workplace in the digital economy* (pp. 111–131). Houston: IFMA Foundation.

Vickers, M. (2019). *Struggling to manage knowledge workers | AMA*. Von AMA Articles: https://www.amanet.org/articles/struggling-to-manage-knowledge-workers/. abgerufen.

Ware, J. (2011). Change management as a core competency for facilities managers. In J. Ware (Ed.), *Work on the move*. Houston: IFMA Foundation.

Williams, A., Parks, A., & Whillans, A. (2018). Improving resilience among employees high in depression, anxiety and workplace distress. *International Journal of Management Research, 9*(1–2), 4–22.

Supplementary Information

A. Redlein (ed.), *Modern Facility and Workplace Management*,
Classroom Companion: Business, https://doi.org/10.1007/978-3-030-35314-8

Appendix

A Case Study: Panduit (*Work on the Move: Driving strategy and change in workplaces (IFMA Foundation, 2011)*)

Panduit Corporation

United States

Panduit is a global manufacturer of physical infrastructure solutions that support power, communications, computing, control, and security systems. The company has a global coverage of more than 4,000 employees with support in over 120 countries. Founded in 1955, Panduit is headquartered in Tinley Park, Illinois.

The Challenge

Panduit Corporation opened its five-story, 280,000 square foot world headquarters in a suburb of Chicago in 2010, providing a state-of-the-art intelligent building to better serve its customers, partners, and employees.

The building represents a dramatic leap forward in integrated, sustainable building design because it is built on the principle of a "Unified Physical Infrastructure," which combines ultimate visibility and control for all building systems: communications, computing, power, security, and HVAC.

The challenge was to define and drive the C-suite's understanding of RE/FM's ability to contribute to overall corporate goals relating to the following:

- Global vision
  - Providing world-class facilities for every Panduit employee
  - Rewarding long-time employees and attract/retain talent
  - Creating healthy places to work
- Innovation
  - Helping deliver cohesive, branded message about Panduit's ability to contribute to high-performance building design
  - Demonstrating a unified physical infrastructure for control and the interoperability of all building systems
  - Creating open protocols and flexible infrastructure platform for future technological advancements
- Collaboration
  - Providing an environment that encourages communication, personal growth, and teamwork
  - Developing an integrated and cross-functional project delivery model for teams to utilize to produce on-time, on-budget, quality results
- Sustainability
  - Creating an environmentally sustainable and healthy place to work
  - Designing facilities to reduce their environmental impact
  - Providing quantifiable energy and operational cost savings
  - Achieving LEED Gold certification

Success hinged on executive leadership, employee engagement, functional area collaboration, innovative design, and intelligent technology integration. An innovative financial model called the "EBS Model" (essential, business, and strategic) was developed to help evaluate options through a consistent set of filters for efficient decision-making and consensus building. After passing the EBS test, products were then trialed and rated in a newly constructed mock-up area by Panduit employees. Multiple feedback surveys were undertaken to ensure best-in-class solutions were being implemented.

The Solution

This Panduit case study exemplifies the following:

- Alignment of RE/FM initiatives with C-Suite objectives to deliver enhanced business results
- Innovative practices surrounding the real estate delivery process, the design of flexible, integrated and sustainable work space, and the intelligent application of technology to enable the delivery of a sustainable, healthy and productive work environment
- The effectiveness of a unified physical infrastructure to provide real-time analytics, enabling better building management at a lower cost while increasing service levels
- Power of using RE/FM to support talent retention, productivity enhancement, cost reduction, brand development, education and training, sustainable design, and a healthy work environment
- World-class implementation using integrated project delivery and strategic partnerships to deliver best-in-class results:
  - Cisco Connected Real Estate (CRE)
  - Panduit Connected Building Solutions (CBS)
  - Panduit Data Center Solutions (DCS)
  - Gensler Architecture & Interiors
  - AEI (Affiliated Engineers Inc) for M&E
  - Haworth Architectural Products, furniture systems, seating, storage, and case goods
  - Kayhan International, master furniture consultation, and delivery/service
  - Lutron, Tridium, Liebert

Impact to Business Strategy

Panduit successfully delivered its new five-story, 280,000 square foot, 800-employee capacity, LEED Gold certified headquarters building in April 2010. The company met its financial objectives and future-proofed its investment with an adaptable, state-of-the-art building design. The building includes office, conference, and training space with open office concepts and the integration of the latest technologies to drive productivity, safety, reliability, and sustainability.

Through the strategic alignment of RE/FM initiatives with C-Suite objectives, we were able to develop a shared vision with full stakeholder engagement. Through the application of an intelligent, well-planned unified physical infrastructure and open-source technology platforms, the work environment has been future-proofed for technological advancements.

New ways of working were tested and employed, including private, collaborative, social, mobile, and virtual space. These new workplace strategies helped increase employee satisfaction, attraction and retention of talent, and employee productivity and reduced the facilities/workforce environmental impact.

Furniture was one of the most important elements of our long-term sustainability plan. Creating the right footprint/kit of parts (Haworth's "Integrated Palette"), and selecting adaptable products

(Haworth's raised access floor and moveable wall systems), supported our desire for a completely modular, flexible building interior and contributed mightily to our vision of a sustainable workplace.

Throughout the course of the project, the building was developed to become an effective business tool to support core business strategies and marketing initiatives, such as using the building as an educational tool to:

1. Help customers during "visioning" process
2. Provide case study example for the project "execution" phase (supports vision)
3. Demonstrate that if vision and execution are in alignment, then the delivery of sustainable design and a productive work environment can be ensured

Results

People

People impact:

- Increased staff productivity up to 30 percent
- Increased employee satisfaction and retention (surveys showed greater than 50 percent improvement)
- Increased customer service levels through the use of the unified physical infrastructure through which real-time analytics enabled better building management at a lower cost
- Enhanced the Panduit brand by providing a building that serves as a training center and case study for visioning, executing, and continuous improvement
- Improved employees' attitudes by creating a healthy, contemporary, connected place to work that has employees excited about coming to work
- Increased global communication and collaboration through effective use of technology to communicate and bring employees together
- Health and safety and business continuity were also positively impacted

Planet

Operating gains:

- Achieved LEED Gold certification
  - Sustainable site (9 out of 14 points)
  - Water efficiency (4 out of 5 points)
  - Energy and atmosphere (7 out of 17 points)
  - Materials and resources (7 out of 13 points)
  - Indoor environmental quality (13 out of 15 points)
  - Innovation and design process (5 out of 5 points)
- 23 percent below ASHRAE 90.1 2004 base design
- 30 percent increase in outside air over ASHRAE 62.1, 2004
- Reduced energy consumption (electricity average cost/SF US$1.01)
- Reduced energy consumption (gas average cost/SF US$0.02)

Profit

ROI of five years for all building systems and efficiency gains:

- Reduced cabling costs by greater than 10 percent
- Reduced outlets by 25 percent
- Reduced IT space by 67 percent
- Increased staff productivity up to 30 percent
- Reduced reconfiguration costs up to 20 percent

Project Team

FM Project Manager	Darrin Norbut, Associate AIA, LEED Green Associate, Director Real Estate & Facilities, Panduit Corporation Kevin Hoffmeyer, MBA, LEED Green Associate, Sr. Manager Facilities, Panduit Corporation
Architect/Interior Designer	Cary Johnson, Gensler, Chicago
Contractor	Power Construction
Furniture Manufacturer(s)	Haworth
Furniture Dealer(s)	Kayhan International
Furniture Installer(s)	ISI
Consultant(s)	AEI Affiliated Engineers Incorporated
Location of Project	Tinley Park, Illinois